1,000+ Little Things
Happy Successful People
Do Differently

Inspiration for the Rest of Us

Marc & Angel Chernoff
www.marcandangel.com

DEDICATION

*To our fans, friends and family
who inspire us every day.*

3 Ways We Failed Our Way to Happiness

I. Rejected from Seven Universities

When I was 18, I wanted to be a computer scientist. So I applied to seven U.S. universities known for computer science. MIT, Cal Berkley, Georgia Tech, etc. But I got rejected by all of them.

Soon thereafter, a high school guidance counselor told me to apply to The University of Central Florida in Orlando, which had a rapidly growing computer science and engineering program. Out of desperation, I did. And I got accepted and received a scholarship.

And when I settled on Orlando, the move changed my life.

I met Angel there – my wife and the love of my life. And I met a professor, Dr. Eaglan, who convinced me to switch from the school of computer science to the school of computer engineering, with a strong focus in web design and technical writing – two skills I use today to run the blog you are reading now (a website that makes me happy and financially supports my family).

If I hadn't been rejected by those seven computer science schools, neither of these priceless encounters would have taken place.

II. Your Writing is Not Good Enough

While in school, I began to enjoy my technical writing classes so much that I decided to take a few creative writing electives too. I absolutely fell in love with writing inspiring stories and expressing myself in prose.

So I applied for a part-time editorial position at the school newspaper. I sent them five articles I had written along with my application. Two days later I received an email which cordially explained that my writing was not good enough.

That afternoon, I went home with a bruised ego and told Angel what had happened. She hugged me and said, "Regardless of what anyone says, if writing makes you happy, you should keep writing. Because that's what happy writers do. They write."

And after a bit more discussion, she added, "I like writing too. We should start our own little writing club and write together." A few minutes later, Angel and I turned on my computer and registered the domain name marcandangel.com, and our blogging days began.

In other words, if my five articles hadn't been rejected by the school newspaper, the article you're reading right now would never have been written.

III. *Fired for Doing the Right Thing*

After college Angel used her business degree to land a head store manager position at a major retailer. She was in her twenties and she was running a $40,000,000 store all by herself. Although some of the regional executives thought she was too young, she was doing far too well for them to do anything about it.

Until one day in 2009, when one of her floor managers got a DUI on a Friday evening and went to jail. He didn't have enough money to post a $600 bail, so he called Angel to let her know that he would not be able to make it to work the next day. Angel decided to lend him the $600 he needed. The regional executives found out about this and fired Angel the next morning without a valid explanation.

Suddenly Angel had a lot of free time on her hands. While she looked around for another job, she spent her afternoons marketing our blog. She learned all about social media marketing, and opened accounts for us on Facebook, Twitter, and other social networking sites – the primary source of traffic to our blog today.

We didn't know it then, but the traffic was going to grow exponentially over the next three years, and by January 2012 our blog would be making enough money to completely replace Angel's lost salary, allowing her to work on it full time and get paid for being happily passionate.

If Angel hadn't been fired, none of this would have happened.

Failures Along the Road to Happiness

As our friend Steve Jobs once said, "You can't connect the dots looking forward; you can only connect them looking backwards. So you have to trust that the dots will somehow connect in your future. You have to trust in something – your gut, destiny, life, karma, whatever. This approach has never let me down, and it has made all the difference in my life."

The truth is, it happens just like that. What seems like the end of the road may just be a cul de sac. It feels like rejection. It feels like failure. But it isn't.

You simply ran out of road on that route. Time to back up, turn around, and look for a new route to get where you want to go. And as long as you keep smiling and moving forward, the road ahead is going to be far better than you can imagine. Because eventually, through all its twists and turns, it leads to happiness.

So if you're currently struggling, hang in there. Remember, sometimes the best thing that can possibly happen to you in the long run is not getting exactly what you want right now.

That's precisely what this book is about: staying true to your path, rising to you full potential, and finding joy in the struggles of life.

'1000+ Little Things Happy, Successful People Do Differently' is a series of our best articles, stories, quotes, and thought provoking questions on *Happiness, Adversity, Relationships, Self Love, Passion, Productivity, Success, Simplicity, Finance,* and *Inspiration.*

Although you can, don't feel pressured to read this book sequentially from beginning to end. Choose a topic/part that you're struggling with and skip directly to it. Digest a few pages at a time, mull over the ideas that move you, and gradually turn them into positive habits in your life.

TABLE OF CONTENTS

Part One
Happiness

Wake up every morning
with the idea that something
wonderful is possible today.

HOW TO **LOVE**

More People Like Him

You'd like Jaydee a lot. Most people do. He's the kind of guy who listens when you talk, who smiles often, and who says things that make the people around him smile. He's intelligent, but in a way that makes others feel comfortable. It's the way he expresses himself in simple terms that you can understand – almost like he's articulating the thoughts you already have in your head, but haven't yet found the right words to say aloud.

It doesn't matter who you are either. Jaydee always has a way of relating to you. Because, in a way, he's been there with you all along. He can think like you, so he understands you. So many of us have limitations in our perceptions. We understand the soldiers but not the politics governing the war. We understand the people who go to the movies but not the ones who attend NASCAR races. But somehow Jaydee gets all of us. It's his gift.

If he hasn't actually been to the NASCAR race you're talking about, he'll be honest about it – but he'll make you feel as if he was right there with you. And once you

return home after spending a night with Jaydee, you'll catch yourself smiling and thinking that there needs to be more people like him in the world. Because if there were, there would be far less to worry about.

Jaydee passed away today. I don't really want to discuss the details, because honestly they aren't relevant. It could have been a car accident. It could have been old age. We are often far too concerned with how people died, rather than how they lived. And I want you to know how he lived. He told stories – lots of stories that contained subtle insights and wisdom about our lives and the world around us. And today, I want to share with you the last story he told me before he died:

His Last Story

One Sunday morning when I was a little boy my father surprised me and took me to the fishing docks. But instead of fishing, like all the other little boys and girls were doing with their fathers, we sat down on the end of one of the docks and watched all the other children fish. For hours, we sat there and watched until we left without ever casting a single fishing line into the water.

I was simultaneously sad and angry. On the drive home I told my father that I'd never forgive him for being so cruel to me. He looked at me, smiled and said, "I love you, Jaydee." When I didn't respond, he asked, "Did you notice how happy all the other little boys and girls were? Did you see their smiles? Could you feel the happiness in their hearts?" After a moment of silence I quickly snapped, "I don't really care! I just want to go fishing like everyone else!" My father sighed and kept driving.

We went back to the fishing docks dozens of Sunday mornings throughout my childhood. And each time we saw hundreds of other little boys and girls jumping and laughing and celebrating as they reeled in fish. But we still never cast a single fishing line into the water. We just sat there on the end of that same dock and watched. And my father never explained why. But he didn't need to. Because years later, as I entered adulthood, I suddenly realized that those mornings we spent sitting on that dock was where I learned how to love.

5 *Character* TRAITS that Make You *Happy*

Character is not the only component of happiness. There are also: approaches to thinking, (Shakespeare's 'Hamlet" tells us that "Nothing is good or bad as thinking makes it so."), learned skills in concentration, fundamental beliefs, personal values and specific actions that detract from or add to contentment and well-being. But character is still the essential component.

Why Character Matters

Who we are makes a difference. The way we treat others matters. The decency or indecency that fills our hearts and minds matters. Our values as expressions of what we believe and how we live our lives really does make a difference to our happiness. The traits we've developed over time is of no little consequence to how we feel about who we are.

When we look in the mirror, it's often our character (or lack thereof) that speaks the loudest.

But not all character traits are created equal, at least not insofar as happiness is concerned. Following, then, are those traits I'm convinced will have the greatest impact on your happiness.

1 *Courage*

Courage is resistance to fear, mastery of fear, not absence of fear.
-Mark Twain

Fear is the great thief of happiness. It is parent to surrender. It sneaks in closed doors and robs us of resolve and the commitment and ability to endure to the end.

Courage, on the other hand, is fear's great nemesis. It challenges fear, pushes it back, and keeps it in check by taking steps toward its objection. Courage thereby shatters the shackles of fear, sending it into the insignificant margins of obscurity.

Courage allows us to challenge our comfort zones, approach people and situations, embrace life and accept the pain that's inevitable in all of life's changes and challenges. Without courage, happiness is a little more than an illusion, a temporary mirage, a puff of smoke that dissipates into thin air at its first challenge.

2 *Patience*

Patience is waiting. Not passively waiting. That is laziness. But to keep going when the going is hard and slow – that is patience.

How happy are impatient people? This is a rhetorical question, of course. The answer is obviously "not very." At least not for very long. Impatience is another major bully to happiness. It pushes happiness out of the neighborhood almost as soon as it shows up.

But learning to accept and allow, to go with the flow and relax a bit is critical to living a happy life. Impatience is often the irritation we feel at the loss of control. But life bubbles and gurgles in ever-changing streams and flows of unpredictable activity. It simply is not 100% controllable. And the more we try to control and manipulate the outcome of life and the events that boil up around us with any kind of precision, the more frustrated we'll be at the effort.

So breathe. Relax. Take it in. Be patient. Learn to accept the uncertain and buddy up to the unpredictable. Let life happen, at least a little. You'll find it that much more beautiful and happy when you do.

3 *Gratitude*

Gratitude changes the pangs of memory into a tranquil joy.

-D. Bonhoeffer

To be grateful is to notice the good amidst the bad, the color against the backdrop of gray, the lovely even as it's surrounded by the ugly. It's to count your blessings and recognize how beautiful life is even when life isn't quite going as planned.

Learning to be grateful requires the desire to see what's sometimes hard to locate for those who are not accustomed to seeing it. It requires retraining your mind to think about the silver linings in life. But for gratitude to affect happiness in the deepest way, requires it to permeate your soul, encompassing attitude and thought, and becoming the general way you perceive life.

Gratitude doesn't ignore the difficulty of challenges. But it focuses on benefits and opportunities of challenges. The Chinese characters for the word "crisis" literally mean "danger" and "opportunity". All challenges and crises are opportunities.

When we're grateful, our problems don't disappear, they simply occupy less space in our hearts, minds and lives. The reason is that grateful people are focused on that for which they are grateful. By definition, that means the difficult, disappointing and painful commands less of our attention.

As a matter of fact, I don't believe there is a single more important character trait to your happiness than developing the persistent, even automatic grateful response to life.

4 *Love*

Darkness cannot drive out darkness;
only light can do that.
Hate cannot drive out hate;
only love can do that.

-Martin Luther King Jr

Love conquers all, as they say. And while perhaps not always technically true (I don't think any person's love of murder would make this act of violence any less evil, for instance), love certainly goes a long way to being nearly true. To recognize the centrality of love to living a happy life, just imagine a life lived without it. Imagine a hateful, loveless life of happiness (I know. That's the point. It's not possible).

The more love that beats in your heart, the happier and more buoyant your heart will be. The more you love life, the more life will love you back.

Love overlooks weakness and closes its eyes to idiosyncrasies. It accepts, seeks, and empowers what's best in others. This is the road to travel.

5 *Forgiveness*

To forgive is the highest, most beautiful
form of love. In return, you will receive
untold peace and happiness.

-Robert Muller

There's not much more conducive to happiness than the ability to forgive quickly, spontaneously and freely.

People who hold on to pain, who nurse their wounds, who call out the troops to seek vengeance for the wrongs done to them, may win battles here and there. But the war against unhappiness will largely be lost before it's even started.

Refusal to forgive with exaggerated and lingering resentments lead to a self-imposed imprisonment.

It's the very bars that keep others imprisoned in our hearts that keeps happiness far away, at a distance, peering in at best. It's time we free ourselves by letting old pain dissipate into the darkness, so new opportunities can take us to greater heights of joy.

So, have you forgiven your parents for their weaknesses as parents? Have you forgiven the playground bully or abusive ex-spouse, or your neglectful children or inconsiderate neighbor or insensitive church leader?

If you haven't, you're picking at the open wounds that can only irritate, infect and fester. Such open wounds often turn cancerous, metastasizing, entering the blood stream of other relationships, infecting them with its mortal disease as well.

Instead, open your heart to forgiveness. Then your heart will finally be open enough to catch its share of happiness as well.

Afterthoughts

So much ink has been spent on the power of positive thinking and optimism and finding your passion to live a happy life. I write about such things myself. But not enough ink has dried on enough pages to draw enough connections (perhaps with the growing exception of gratitude) between character and our personal happiness. I hope this oversight is soon corrected. And I hope this post helps close that gap a bit.

So where does that leave us? We are left with the knowledge of what traits to develop, but also of the distance we have to travel to develop them.

The beauty of life is that we can change. We can learn and grow and mature and expand, acquiring traits we don't yet have or haven't yet fully developed. All it takes is a little humility, the desire to start and a little determination to see it through. You might want to start by adding those character traits to your list too.

10 ~~HABITS~~ You Must ~~QUIT~~ to Be *Happy*

When you quit doing the wrong things, you make more room for the things that make you happy. So starting today...

1 Quit procrastinating on your goals

Some people dream of success while others wake up and work hard at it. Action and change are often resisted when they're needed most. Get a hold of yourself and have discipline. Putting something off instantly makes it harder and scarier. What we don't start today won't be finished by tomorrow. And there's nothing more stressful than the perpetual lingering of an unfinished task.

The secret to getting ahead is simply getting started. Starting, all by itself, is usually sufficient to build enough momentum to keep the ball rolling. So forget about the finish line and just concentrate on taking your first step. Say to yourself, "I choose to start this task with a small, imperfect step." All those small steps will add up and you'll actually get to see changes fairly quickly.

2 Quit blaming others and making excuses

Stop blaming others for what you have or don't have, or for what you feel or don't feel. When you blame others for what you're going through, you deny responsibility and perpetuate the problem. Stop giving your power away and start taking responsibility for your life. Blaming is just another sorry excuse, and making excuses is the first step towards failure; you and only you are responsible for your life choices and decisions.

3 Quit trying to avoid change

If nothing ever changed there would be no sunrise the next morning. Most of us are comfortable where we are even though the whole universe is constantly changing around us. Learning to accept this is vital to our happiness and general success. Because only when we change, do we grow, and begin to see a world we never knew was possible.

And don't forget, however good or bad a situation is now, it will change. That's the one thing you can count on. So embrace it, and realize that change happens for a reason. It won't always be easy or obvious at first, but in the end it will be worth it.

4 Quit trying to control the uncontrollable

If you try to control everything, and then worry about the things you can't control, you are setting yourself up for a lifetime of frustration and misery.

Some forces are out of your control, but you can control how you react to things. Everyone's life has positive and negative aspects – whether you're happy or not depends greatly on which aspects you focus on. The best thing you can do is to let go of what you can't control, and invest your energy in the things you can – like your attitude.

5 Quit talking down to yourself

Nothing will bring you down quicker than berating yourself. The mind is a superb instrument if used right, but when used incorrectly, it becomes very destructive. Be aware of your mental self-talk. We all talk silently to ourselves in our heads, but we aren't always conscious of what we're saying or how it's affecting us.

As Henry Ford once stated, "Whether you think you can, or you think you can't, you're right." One of the major causes of why we fail is due to self-doubt and negative self-talk. The way to overcome negative thoughts and destructive emotions is to develop opposing, positive emotions that are stronger and more powerful. Listen to your self-talk and replace negative thoughts with positive ones, over time you will change the trajectory of your life.

6 Quit Criticizing Others

The negativity you bleed out toward others will gradually cripple your own happiness. When you truly feel comfortable with your own imperfections, you won't feel threatened or offended by the imperfections you see in other people.

So stop worrying about the flaws you see in everyone else, and focus on yourself. Let the constant growth and improvement in your own life keep you so busy that you have no time left to criticize others.

7 Quit running from your problems and fears

Trust me, if everyone threw their problems in a pile for you to see, you would grab yours back. Tackle your problems and fears swiftly, don't run away from them. The best solution is to face them head on no matter how powerful they may seem.

Fears, in particularly, stop you from taking chances and making decisions. They keep you confined to just the small space where you feel completely comfortable. But your life's story is simply the culmination of many small, unique experiences, many of which require you to stretch your comfort zone. Letting your fears and worries control you is not 'living,' it's merely existing.

Bottom line: Either you own your problems and fears, or they will ultimately own you.

8   *Quit living in another place and time*

Some people spend their entire lives trying to live in another time and place. They lament about what has been, what they could have done, or what might become. However, the past is gone, and the future doesn't exist. No matter how much time we spend thinking and lamenting about either, it doesn't change anything.

One of life's sharpest paradoxes is that our brightest future hinges on our ability to pay attention to what we're doing right now, today.

We need to live more in the moment. Living in the moment requires active, open, intentional awareness on the present. Don't

fantasize about being on vacation while at work, and don't worry about the work piling up on your desk when you're on vacation. Live for now. Notice the beauty unfolding around you.

9   *Quit trying to be someone you're not*

One of the greatest challenges in life is being yourself in a world that's trying to make you like everyone else. Someone will always be prettier, someone will always be smarter, someone will always be younger, but they will never be you. Don't change so people will like you. Be yourself and the right people will love you, and you'll love yourself more too.

10   *Quit being ungrateful*

Not all the puzzle pieces of life will seem to fit together at first, but in time you'll realize they do, perfectly. So thank the things that didn't work out, because they just made room for the things that will. And thank the ones who walked away from you, because they just made room for the ones who won't.

No matter how good or bad you have it, wake up each day thankful for your life. Someone somewhere else is desperately fighting for theirs. Instead of thinking about what you're missing, try thinking about what you have that everyone else is missing.

10 Mistakes UNHAPPY People Make

A person does not have to be behind bars to be a prisoner. People can be prisoners of their own concepts, choices and ideas. So tell the negativity committee that meets inside your head to sit down and shut up.

When you dream, you better dream big; when you think, you better think big; and when you love, you better love truthfully. Happiness is a choice. There are no excuses for not trying to make the very best out of your life. There are no excuses for living in a way that consistently makes you unhappy.

Here are ten happiness mistakes to avoid:

1 Thinking you have already missed your chance

Your life, with all its ups and downs, has molded you for the greater good. Your life has been exactly what it needed to be. Don't think you've lost time. It took each and every situation you have encountered to bring you to the current moment. And every moment of your life, including this

one right now, is a fresh start. You just have to learn three little words that can release you from your past regrets and guide you forward to a positive new beginning. These words are: "From now on..."

2 Using failed relationships as an excuse

Life doesn't always introduce you to the people you WANT to meet. Sometimes life puts you in touch with the people you NEED to meet – to help you, to hurt you, to leave you, to love you, and to gradually strengthen you into the person you were meant to become.

3 Changing who you are to satisfy others

No matter how loud their opinions are, others cannot choose who you are. The question should not be, "Why don't they like

> *Life isn't about waiting for the storm to pass,*
> *it's about learning to dance in the rain.*

me when I'm being me?" It should be, "Why am I wasting my time worrying what they think of me?" If you are not hurting anyone with your actions, keep moving forward with your life. Be happy. Be yourself. If others don't like it, then let them be. Life isn't about pleasing everybody.

4 Putting up with negative people and negative thinking

It's time to walk away from all the drama and the people who create it. Surround yourself with those who make you smile. Love the people who treat you right, and pray for the ones who don't. Forget the negative and focus on the positive. Life is too short to be anything but happy. Making mistakes and falling down is a part of life, but getting back up and moving on is what LIVING is all about.

5 Focusing all of your attention on another time and place.

This day will never happen again. Enjoy it. Cherish your time. It's often hard to tell the true value of a moment until it becomes a memory. Someday you may discover that

the small things were really the big things. So learn to appreciate what you have before time forces you appreciate what you once had.

6 Overlooking what you have to focus on what you don't have.

Most people end up cheating on others and themselves because they pay more attention to what they're missing, rather than what they have. Instead of thinking about what you're missing, think about what you have that everyone else is missing.

7 Dwelling on the things you can't change.

If you hadn't fallen down, you would never have learned how to get back on your feet. If you hadn't been forced to let go and move on, you'd never have learned that you have the strength to stand on your own. If you hadn't lost hope, you would never have found your faith. The best often comes after the worst happens. You can either move on, or you can dwell on the things you can't change. Either way life does move on with or without you. So learn from the past and then get the heck out of there. You will always grow stronger from the pain if you don't let it destroy you.

8 Constantly sacrificing your own happiness for everyone else.

Never let your own happiness wither away as you try to bring sunshine to others. Life is not about making others happy. Life is about being honest and sharing your happiness with them.

9 Losing track of your own goals and ideals.

Knowing who you are is one thing, but truly believing and living as yourself is another. With all the social conditioning in our society we sometimes forget to stay true to ourselves. Don't lose yourself out there. In this crazy world that's trying to make you like everyone else, stay true to your awesome self.

10 Dealing with the stress of deceiving others.

If you say you're going to do something, DO IT! If you say you're going to be somewhere, BE THERE! If you say you feel something, MEAN IT! If you can't, won't, and don't, then DON'T LIE. It's always better to tell people the truth up front. Live in such a way that if someone decided to attack your character, no one would believe it. Live so

that when the people around you think of fairness, caring and integrity, they think of you.

And remember, life will never be perfect, no matter how hard you try. Even if you pour your heart and soul into it, you will never achieve a state of absolute perfection. There will always be moments of uncertainty; there will always be days where nothing goes right. But as time rolls on you will learn that even the most imperfect situations can be made better with a little love and laughter.

9 HABITS of *Super* **POSITIVE** + People

Life is full of positive experiences. Notice them. Notice the sun warming your skin, the small child learning to walk, and the smiling faces around you. Smell the rain, and feel the wind. Live your life to the fullest potential by reveling in the beauty of these experiences, and letting them inspire you to be the most positive version of YOU.

What would happen if you approached each day intentionally, with a positive attitude? What would happen if you embraced life's challenges with a smile on your face? What would happen if you surrounded yourself with people who made you better? What would happen if you paused long enough to appreciate it all?

Living a positive life is all about creating positive habits to help you focus on what truly matters. This is the secret of super positive people. Here are nine simple ideas to help you follow in their footsteps.

1 *Wake up every morning with the idea that something wonderful is possible today.*

Smiling is a healing energy. Always find a reason to smile. It may not add years to your life but will surely add life to your years. A consistent positive attitude is the cheapest 'fountain of youth.' You've got to dance like there's nobody watching, love like you'll never be hurt, sing like there's nobody listening, and live like it's heaven on Earth.

2 *Celebrate your existence.*

Your mind is the window through which you see the world. The way to make this the happiest day ever is to think, feel, walk, talk, give, and serve like you are the most fortunate person in the whole world. Open minded, open hearted, and open handed.

Nothing more is needed. All is well... and so it is.

3 *Appreciate life's perfect moments.*

Your life isn't perfect, but it does have perfect moments. Don't let the little things get you down. You've got plenty of reasons to look up at the sky and say, "Thank you, I will do my best to make this a great day." So slow down and pause for a moment to stand in awe of the fact that you are alive, and that you have the ability to rediscover life as the miracle it has always been.

4 *Embrace life's challenges.*

Uncharted territory in your life is not good or bad, it just is. Yes, it may rattle your foundation, and you may be tempted to pullback, say you can't do it, or bail completely. But these are exactly the conditions that set you up for massive amounts of personal growth. Each experience through which you pass operates ultimately for your own good. This is the correct attitude to adopt, and you must be able to see it in this light.

5 *Become addicted to constant and never-ending self improvement.*

It doesn't have to be January 1st to give yourself a chance to make the most out of your life. Every day is a new day to learn, grow, develop your strengths, heal yourself from past regrets, and move forward. Every day gives you a chance to reinvent yourself, to fine-tune who you are, and build on the lessons you have learned. It is never too late to change things that are not working in your life and switch gears. Using today wisely will always help you create a more positive tomorrow.

6 *Live and breathe the truth.*

It's the most positive, stress-free way to live, because the truth always reveals itself eventually anyway. So don't aim to be impressive, aim to be true. Those who are true are truly impressive. Being true means having integrity; and integrity is doing the right thing even when you know nobody is watching.

7 *Fill your own bucket.*

Choose to be happy for no reason at all. If you are happy for a reason, you could be in trouble, because that reason can get taken away from you. So smile right now because you can right now, and make it a point to fill your own bucket of happiness so high that the rest of the world can't poke enough holes to drain it dry.

8 *Help the people around you smile.*

Today, give someone one of your smiles. It might be the only sunshine they see all day. Sometimes just a single genuine smile or compliment can lift a person's spirits to new heights. At the right time, a kind word from a stranger, or unexpected encouragement from a friend, can make all the difference in the world. Kindness is free, but it's priceless. And as you know, what goes around comes around.

9 *Spend time with positive people.*

Life's way too awesome to waste time with people who don't treat you right. So surround yourself with people who make you happy and make you smile. People who help you up when you're down. People who would never take advantage of you. People who genuinely care. They are the ones worth keeping in your life. Everyone else is just passing through.

HOW TO MAKE THE
WORLD A **BETTER** PLACE

Once upon a time, a young man and woman met, gazed into each other's eyes, kissed, and knew – for certain – that they were supposed to be together forever. In the subsequent days, weeks, and months everything fell into place just as they had anticipated. He was perfect in her eyes, and she was perfect in his.

Oh, it's the majestic certainty of young love! When two souls who barely know each other believe they know everything that they must know to live happily ever after in their own blissful bubble. They think this because it's what their emotional hearts and minds tell them is true.

But you know what happens next. It's what always happens next in phony fairy tales like this. For one reason or another, logic trumps emotion, their bubble bursts, and the two lovers tumble back down to Earth, bruising themselves along the way and realizing that their perfect partner isn't so perfect after all.

Maybe he learns that she doesn't like rock music – and rock music is extremely important to him. Maybe she learns that he never makes the bed – and making the bed is extremely important to her. Regardless of the specifics, our lovers are finally beginning to see each other for who they really are – imperfect human beings. This is the turning point at which 'falling in love' ends and the test of 'true love' begins.

Either their mindset adjusts and they accept reality – that true love isn't so much about perfection as it is about growth and patience – or they move on to the next short-term fairy tale romance in hopes of finding that one perfect soul mate who does everything just right.

Why am I telling you this story?

Because the fluctuating feelings that steer our romantic relationships are quite similar to those that steer our motivation to make a meaningful impact on the world around us. A little passion is all that's required to start, but only sustained perseverance makes it worthwhile.

Sure, short powerful bursts of effort and seemingly giant leaps in a single bound appear to be remarkable. But they fade as fast as they arrive, and all we're left with in the end is an unfulfilled void.

An enduring dedication – fulfilling promises by marching forward with one foot in front of the other, even when the going gets tough – is what true love is all about. And it's this kind of love, and only this kind of love, that can make the world a better place.

12 THINGS *Happy* People Do DIFFERENTLY

Studies conducted by positivity psychologist Sonja Lyubomirsky point to 12 things

happy people do differently to increase their levels of happiness. These are things that we can start doing today to feel the effects of more happiness in our lives.

I want to honor and discuss each of these 12 points, because no matter what part of life's path we're currently traveling on, these 'happiness habits' will always be applicable.

1 *Express gratitude.*

When you appreciate what you have, what you have appreciates in value. Kinda cool right? So basically, being grateful for the goodness that is already evident in your life will bring you a deeper sense of happiness. And that's without having to go out and buy anything. It makes sense. We're gonna have a hard time ever being happy if we aren't thankful for what we already have.

2 *Cultivate optimism.*

Winners have the ability to manufacture their own optimism. No matter what the situation, the successful diva is the chick who will always find a way to put an optimistic spin on it. She knows failure only as an opportunity to grow and learn a new lesson from life. People who think optimistically see the world as a place packed with endless opportunities, especially in trying times.

3 *Avoid over-thinking and social comparison.*

Comparing yourself to someone else can be poisonous. If we're somehow 'better' than the person that we're comparing ourselves to, it gives us an unhealthy sense of superiority. Our ego inflates – KABOOM – our inner Kanye West comes out! If we're 'worse' than the person that we're

> *"I'd always believed that a life of quality, enjoyment, and wisdom were my human birthright and would be automatically bestowed upon me as time passed. I never suspected that I would have to learn how to live - that there were specific disciplines and ways of seeing the world I had to master before I could awaken to a simple, happy, uncomplicated life."*
>
> -Dan Millman

comparing ourselves to, we usually discredit the hard work that we've done and dismiss all the progress that we've made. What I've found is that the majority of the time this type of social comparison doesn't stem from a healthy place. If you feel called to compare yourself to something, compare yourself to an earlier version of yourself.

4   *Practice acts of kindness.*

Performing an act of kindness releases serotonin in your brain. (Serotonin is a substance that has TREMENDOUS health benefits, including making us feel more blissful.) Selflessly helping someone is a super powerful way to feel good inside. What's even cooler about this kindness kick is that not only will you feel better, but so will people watching the act of kindness. How extraordinary is that? Bystanders will be blessed with a release of serotonin just by watching what's going on. A side note is that the job of most anti-depressants is to release more serotonin. Move over Pfizer, kindness is kicking ass and taking names.

5   *Nurture social relationships.*

The happiest people on the planet are the ones who have deep, meaningful relationships. Did you know studies show that people's mortality rates are DOUBLED when they're lonely? WHOA! There's a warm fuzzy feeling that comes from having an active circle of good friends who you can share your experiences with. We feel connected and a part of something more meaningful than our lonesome existence.

6   *Develop strategies for coping.*

How you respond to the 'craptastic' moments is what shapes your character. Sometimes crap happens – it's inevitable. Forrest Gump knows the deal. It can be hard to come up with creative solutions in the moment when manure is making its way up toward the fan. It helps to have healthy strategies for coping pre-rehearsed, on-call, and in your arsenal at your disposal.

7 *Learn to forgive.*

Harboring feelings of hatred is horrible for your well-being. You see, your mind doesn't know the difference between past and present emotion. When you 'hate' someone, and you're continuously thinking about it, those negative emotions are eating away at your immune system. You put yourself in a state of suckerism (technical term) and it stays with you throughout your day.

8 *Increase flow experiences.*

Flow is a state in which it feels like time stands still. It's when you're so focused on what you're doing that you become one with the task. Action and awareness are merged. You're not hungry, sleepy, or emotional. You're just completely engaged in the activity that you're doing. Nothing is distracting you or competing for your focus.

9 *Savor life's joys.*

Deep happiness cannot exist without slowing down to enjoy the joy. It's easy in a world of wild stimuli and omnipresent movement to forget to embrace life's enjoyable experiences. When we neglect to

appreciate, we rob the moment of its magic. It's the simple things in life that can be the most rewarding if we remember to fully experience them.

10 *Commit to your goals.*

Being wholeheartedly dedicated to doing something comes fully-equipped with an ineffable force. Magical things start happening when we commit ourselves to doing whatever it takes to get somewhere. When you're fully committed to doing something, you have no choice but to do that thing. Counter-intuitively, having no option – where you can't change your mind – subconsciously makes humans happier because they know part of their purpose.

11 *Practice spirituality.*

When we practice spirituality or religion, we recognize that life is bigger than us. We surrender the silly idea that we are the mightiest thing ever. It enables us to connect to the source of all creation and embrace a connectedness with everything that exists. Some of the most accomplished people I know feel that they're here doing work they're "called to do."

12 *Take care of your body.*

Taking care of your body is crucial to being the happiest person you can be. If you don't have your physical energy in good shape, then your mental energy (your focus), your emotional energy (your feelings), and your spiritual energy (your purpose) will all be negatively affected. Did you know that studies conducted on people who were clinically depressed showed that consistent exercise raises happiness levels just as much as Zoloft? Not only that, but here's the double whammy... Six months later, the people who participated in exercise were less likely to relapse because they had a higher sense of self-accomplishment and self-worth.

21 Quick Tricks to Feel Better INSTANTLY

When life gets stressful and you feel like you're losing your emotional balance, use one or more of these simple tricks to help you relax your mind and re-center yourself in an instant.

1 *Wash your hands and face, and brush your teeth.*

The simple act of cleaning these parts of your body is both reinvigorating and relaxing, and gives you that 'fresh start' feeling.

2 *Change your socks for refreshment.*

It's an odd trick, but it works. Bring a change of socks to work, and change your socks midway through the day. You'll be amazed at how much fresher you'll feel. This trick is especially handy on days with lots of walking.

3 *Call a close friend*

Sometimes a quick conversation with someone you care about is just what you need to boost your mood.

4 *Stretch.*

When you feel yourself getting stressed, get up, reach toward the sky, bend down and touch your toes, twist your torso from side to side – stretch it out.

5 *Go outdoors.*

Getting some fresh air outdoors is always a good way to rouse your senses and clear your mind.

6 *Take a light exercise break.*

Do a few sets of jumping jacks to get your blood moving, or take a walk. Even the slightest bit of exercise can reduce momentary stress and re-energize your mind.

7 Dress to feel your best.

When we know we are looking our best, we naturally feel better.

8 Listen to your favorite music.

If it's not too much of a distraction, listening to your favorite upbeat music can be a great way to boost your spirits.

9 Watch or read something that inspires you.

Sometimes all you need is a little pep talk. Watch a motivational video or read something that inspires you.

10 Have a good laugh.

Watch a funny video clip or read your favorite comic strip. A good chuckle will stimulate your mind, giving you a renewed sense of optimism.

11 Take a few really deep, controlled breaths.

Deep breathing helps reduce stress, a source of fatigue, and increases the level of oxygen in the blood. Techniques can be as simple as inhaling for five seconds, holding your breath for four seconds and exhaling for four seconds. You can also try more elaborate techniques which require different positions

12 Clear your stuffed nose.

If allergies have your sinuses blocked, you may be feeling more tired and cranky. Rinse your nasal passages with saline solution.

13 Cook a tasty meal.

Even if you are by yourself, preparing a tasty dinner, setting the table, and treating yourself to a wonderful culinary

experience will lift your spirits. Sharing it with someone you love or respect will make it even more nurturing.

14 Walk away from energy vampires.

Energy vampires are people who always have something to complain about, or a problem that needs to be fixed, and they'll drain your energy by making you listen to them about their problems or by giving them attention.

15 Complete an important piece of unfinished business.

Today is a perfect day to finish what you started. Few feelings are more satisfying than the one you get after an old burden has been lifted off of your shoulders.

16 Work on something that's meaningful to you.

Engage yourself in a meaningful personal project. Or pull the trigger on doing something you've wanted to do for a long time, but haven't yet had the resolve to do.

17 Assist someone in need.

In life, you get what you put in. When you make a positive impact in someone else's life, you also make a positive impact in your own life. Do something that's greater than you, something that helps someone else to be happy or to suffer less. I promise, it will be an extremely rewarding experience.

18 Think about your latest (or greatest) success.

Think about it for at least sixty seconds. Taking in your success as often as possible will help you reach it again and again. Quite simply, it reminds you that if you've done it before, you can do it again.

19 Act like today is already an awesome day.

Do so, and it will be. Research shows that although we think that we act because of the way we feel, in fact, we often feel because of the way we act. A great attitude always leads to great experiences.

20 Notice what's right.

Everything that happens in life is neither good nor bad. It just depends on your perspective. And no matter how it turns out, it always ends up just the way it should. Either you succeed or you learn something. So stay positive, appreciate the pleasant outcomes, and learn from the rest.

21 Take a moment to acknowledge how far you've come.

Look around you, remember that you started with nothing, and know that everything you see, you created. We can all lose our feelings of self-worth, especially when something goes wrong in our world. The truth is that if you have done it before, you can do it again, no matter what.

Finding simple ways to give yourself an emotional boost when you feel like you're stuck in a rut is a vital skill to master. It's a timeless practice that truly happy, productive people use on a regular basis.

12 *Stressful* THINGS to STOP *Tolerating*

Needless tolerations can bleed you dry of energy and make it impossible for you to function effectively. You can't live a happy, successful, fulfilling life if you're spending all your energy tolerating things that shouldn't be tolerated. Sometimes you need to put your foot down.

Here are some things to stop tolerating in your life:

1 *The decision to settle for mediocrity.*

It's not always about trying to fix something that's broken. Sometimes it's about starting over and creating something better. Sometimes you need to distance yourself to see things clearly. Sometimes growing up means growing apart from old habits, relationships, and situations, and finding something new that truly moves you — something that gets you so excited you can't wait to get out of bed in the morning. That's what life is all about. Don't settle.

2 *Your own negative thinking.*

Your mind is your sacred space. You can close the windows and darken your space, or you can open the windows and let light in. It's your choice. The sun is always shining on some part of your life. What do you typically think about? How far you've come, or how far you have to go? Your strengths, or your weaknesses? The best that could happen, or the worst that might come to be? Pay attention to your self-talk. Because maybe, just maybe, the only thing that needs to shift in order for you to experience more happiness, more love, and more success, is your way of thinking.

Other people's negativity.

If you don't value yourself, look out for yourself, and stick up for yourself, you're sabotaging yourself. You do not have

control over what others say and do; but you do have control over whether or not you will allow them to say and do these things to you. You alone can deny their poisonous words and actions from invading your heart and mind. Remember, if you do not respect your sacred inner space, no one else will either.

Unhealthy relationships.

Choose your relationships wisely. Being alone will never cause as much loneliness as the wrong relationships. Be with people who know your worth. You don't need lots of friends to be happy; just a few real ones who appreciate you for who you are. Oftentimes walking away has nothing to do with weakness, and everything to do with strength. We walk away not because we want others to realize our worth, but because we finally realize our own worth.

Dishonesty.

Inner peace is being able to rest at night knowing you haven't used or taken advantage of anyone to get to where you are

in life. Living a life of honesty creates peace of mind, and peace of mind is priceless. Period. Don't be dishonest and don't put up with people who are.

6 A work environment or career field you hate.

If it doesn't feel right, don't settle on the first or second career field you dabble in. Keep searching. Eventually you will find work you love to do. If you catch yourself working hard and loving every minute of it, don't stop. You're on to something big. Because hard work isn't hard when you concentrate on your passions.

7 Being disorganized and unprepared.

Get up 30 minutes earlier so you don't have to rush around like a mad man. That 30 minutes will help you avoid speeding tickets, tardiness and other unnecessary headaches. Clear the clutter. Get rid of stuff you don't use.

8 Inaction.

The acquisition of knowledge doesn't mean you're growing; growing happens when what you know changes how you live. You can't change anything or make any sort of progress by sitting back and thinking about it. If you keep doing what you're doing, you'll keep getting what you're getting. The best time to start is now.

9 The lingering of unfinished business.

There's nothing more stressful than the perpetual lingering of unfinished business. Stop procrastinating. Start taking action to tie loose ends. Putting something off instantly makes it harder and scarier.

10 The choice to mull over past mistakes and regrets.

If you feel like your ship is sinking, it might be a good time to throw out the stuff that's been weighing it down. The next time you decide to unclutter your life and clean up your space, start with the things that are truly useless, like old regrets, shame, and anger. Let it go. You can't start the next chapter of your life if you keep rereading your previous one.

11 A mounting pile of personal debt.

Financial debt causes stress and heartache. Live a comfortable life, not a wasteful one. Do not buy stuff you do not need. Do not spend to impress others. Do not live life trying to fool yourself into thinking wealth

is measured in material objects. Manage your money wisely so your money does not manage you. Always live well below your means.

12 Your reluctance to say what you need to say.

Everyone has this little watchdog inside their head. It's always there watching you. It was born and raised by your family, friends, coworkers and society at large, and its sole purpose is to watch you and make sure you stay in line. And once you become accustomed to the watchdog's presence, you begin to think it's opinion of what's acceptable and unacceptable are absolute truths. But they're not truths; they're just other people's opinions. Remember, the watchdog is just a watchdog, he just watches. He can't actually control you. He can't do anything about it if you decide to rise up and go against the grain. No, you shouldn't start shouting obscenities and acting like a fool. But you must say what you need to say, when you need to say it. It may be your only chance to do so. Don't censor yourself. Speak the truth – your truth – always.

10 ACTIONS that Always Bring *Happiness*

It's important to make someone happy, and it's important to start with yourself. Happiness is not something you postpone for the future; it is something you design into the present.

Starting today...

1 *Appreciate how much you have*

If we counted our blessings instead of our money, we would all be a lot richer. Happiness is there if you want it to be. You just have to see that it's wrapped in beauty and hidden delicately between the seconds of your life. If you never stop for a minute to notice, you might miss it.

2 *Focus on things that truly matter.*

The simple fact that you are even here, alive, on this planet is a divine miracle, and you should not spend the time you have being busy, being miserable. Every moment you get is a gift, so stop focusing on unhappy things, and spend your moments on things that truly matter to your heart.

3 *Define your own meaning of life, and pursue it.*

What is the meaning of life? Whatever you want it to be. Don't fear failure; fear a lifetime of mediocrity due to lack of effort and commitment. There are so many people out there who will tell you that you CAN'T. What you need to do is turn around and say, "Watch me!"

4 *Embrace life's challenges.*

You may think that taking a detour in life is a waste of time and energy, but you can also see the detour as a means of learning more about who you are and where you are heading in your life. Being off the beaten path may be disorienting and confusing at times, yet it challenges your creative spirit to discover new ways to build a stronger YOU. In the end, it's usually the tough situations that feel like your tomb that actually become your cocoon. Hang in there. You're coming out of this stronger and wiser.

5 Find the balance that allows you to be who you truly are.

Your worst battle is between what you know and what you feel. One of the hardest decisions you will ever have to make is when to stay put and try harder or when to just take your memories and move on. Sometimes you have to step outside of the person you've been, and remember the person you were meant to be, the person you are capable of being, and the person you truly are.

6 Love your body enough to take care of it.

You're beautiful; but keep in mind that not everyone is going to see that. Never be ashamed of yourself because you are born into one skin. You can scar it, stretch it, burn it, mark it, tan it, and peel it. But you are always in it, so you might as well take care of it and learn to love it.

7 Limit your time with negative people.

You can't make positive choices for the rest of your life without an environment that makes those choices easy, natural, and enjoyable. So protect your spirit and potential from contamination by limiting your time with negative people.

8 Treat others the way you want to be treated.

Be conscious of your attitude and your actions. You may be on top of the world right now – feeling untouchable. You may have all the tools at your disposal to do and say whatever you want. But remember, life is a circle – what goes around, comes around eventually.

9 Set a good example.

If you want to empower others in your life, you need to start living the most empowered version of yourself first. You are never too old to set another goal or to dream a new dream. Believe in what you want so much that it has no choice but to become your reality. And don't ever compare yourself to anyone else; stay focused on your own journey and leave footprints behind.

10 Accept what is, and live for the possibilities that lie ahead.

Never waste your time wondering about what might have been. Get busy thinking about what still might be, and trusting that however it plays out, it will leave you glad that what might have been, never came to be.

WHERE **HAPPINESS** IS **FOUND**

*There is only one **success**—*
to spend your life in your own way.

\- Christopher Morley

Made Him Happy

I know a man who loves to knit. Blankets, quilts, sweaters... he knits them all. Knitting is his hobby, his escape. He could choose another hobby – something a bit more masculine, like restoring vintage cars or hunting. But this man continues to stick with what makes him happy – knitting. Because he discovered knitting when he was only a little boy who didn't know any better. And now it's a big part of who he is.

As he grew into his teenage years he was made aware of the fact that knitting wasn't a common hobby for a boy – that it's usually a hobby chosen by girls or by "boys who like to wear high heels," as his older brother used to say. Over time, after being ridiculed by his brother and others, he eventually asked himself a question: "Are the opinions others have about knitting at all relevant to my experience of knitting as a hobby?" And he immediately realized the answer was: "No!" So he kept enjoying the hobby that made him happy.

Stories, Fears, and Expectations

It's fascinating how we make certain decisions in life. Sometimes we follow our heart and intuition and we choose the thing that makes the most sense to us – that which makes us happy. Other times we follow our fears and expectations, especially those spawned by the culture and society we live in, and we choose whatever we believe will most appease those fears and expectations – that which makes everyone else (or no one at all) happy.

The man who loves to knit remained open minded and stuck to knitting even when he learned about the cultural and societal expectations that suggested he should give it up. But he didn't always carry forth with this same open minded attitude. For instance, he believed for as long as he could remember that he would someday find the perfect mate. And he knew exactly what she would be like.

The story about her that he inscribed in his head when he was in high school hasn't changed much since. Nor has it changed since he told me a story about her last year over a cup of coffee. The beginning of the story goes something like this:

I've always dreamed that someday I would meet the perfect mate. She would be smart and classy, yet sexy and athletic. And she would be a geek like me. I wouldn't care what her religious background was, so long as she had an open mind and an honest heart. But she would have to be neat and tidy, because I'm not and I need someone who can balance me out.

And she would love to snuggle, like me. Because I would want to hold her at night, and because we would need to be close so we could fool around and giggle and talk softly to each other. We would talk about people, places, our lives and our future together for hours into the night.

And money wouldn't matter to either of us because we'd be in love. She'd know it and I'd know it, and we'd be happy with what we had…

The stories that we tell ourselves and each other sound remarkable, don't they? They romanticize us. They sweep us off our feet. They persuade us to believe that if we dive head first into an intimate relationship, a big financial purchase, greasy foods, imported beers, or whatever it is that temporarily pacifies our worried mind from reality, then we will somehow find what we are truly looking for.

Our obvious dilemma is that reality is not temporary. Reality keeps on coming. That intimate relationship will have our heart blissfully skipping beats until it doesn't any longer. That big financial purchase will be fun and exciting until it isn't any longer. Greasy foods and beer will comfort us until they don't any longer.

Free of Them

The man who loves to knit is aware of the temporary, restrictive nature of the stories we tell ourselves. Because the ending to his story about his perfect mate – the part that comes after the introduction I shared with you above – is about a woman who was amazing – almost perfect – but who didn't quite fit the mold of the woman from the story he inscribed in his head. And he was unable to give up the perfect woman from his story for the amazing woman sitting in front of him. When she eventually realized this, she moved on.

Now, the man is also starting to move on. He's slowly rediscovering his true self – the self he knew when he was younger before he started telling himself stories, or buying into the stories, fears and expectations of those who lurk around him. This self was a blank canvas, free to experience and appreciate everything just the way it was, without the burden of a storyline.

And as he slowly rediscovers himself, he struggles with the notion of life without a storyline. Because he can barely remember what life was like when there was no story, no fears, no expectations. But he knows deep down that he once lived in a world free of them. And when he did, he discovered knitting and fell in love with it. It became one of his greatest sources of happiness. And he knows that if he wants to fall in love like that again, he must get back to that story-free world within himself where happiness is found.

Never let a bad day make you feel like you have a bad life.

Tell the negativity committee that meets inside your head to sit down and shut up.

Life isn't about waiting for the storm to pass, it's about learning to dance in the rain.

You look the best when you wear your smile. There is no beauty like the one that comes from inside you.

Moving on doesn't mean forgetting, it means you choose happiness over hurt.

Grudges are a waste of perfect happiness.

Someone else is happy with far less than what you have.

You are always free to do something that makes you smile.

Happiness QUOTES

to BRIGHTEN your day and move your mindset in a POSITIVE direction.

Talk about your blessings more than you talk about your problems.

Stop looking at what you have lost, so you can see what you have.

Those who bring sunshine to the lives of others cannot keep it from themselves.

If you don't like something, change it. If you can't change it, change the way you think about it.

Life does NOT have to be perfect to be wonderful.

The more you love your decisions, the less you need others to love them.

Just because it didn't last forever, doesn't mean it wasn't worth your while.

A bad attitude is like a flat tire, you can't get very far until you change it.

Happiness
QUESTIONS
to Make You *think*

HAPPINESS

is *a*

_____ **?**

What do you

APPRECIATE

most about your

current situation**?**

What would make you

SMILE

right *now* **?**

What's one

BAD habit

that makes you

*miserable***?**

What do you do when

NOTHING

else seems to make you

*happy***?**

How **OLD** would you be

if you didn't know how

old you are**?**

If **HAPPINESS**

was the national currency,

what kind of work would
make you

*rich***?**

Do you

CELEBRATE

the *things*

you do have**?**

What is your

HAPPIEST

childhood memory?

What makes it so

*special***?**

What

MAKES you

*smile***?**

Part Two
Adversity

A smile doesn't always
mean a person is happy.
Sometimes it simply means
they are strong enough
to face their problems.

WHEN OUR
STORIES
HOLD US BACK

She rarely makes eye contact. Instead, she looks down at the ground.

Because the ground is safer. Because unlike people, it expects nothing in return. She doesn't have to feel ashamed. The ground just accepts her for who she is.

As she sits at the bar next to me, she stares down at her vodka tonic, and then the ground, and then her vodka tonic. "Most people don't get me," she says. "They ask me questions like, 'What's your problem?' or 'Were you beaten as a child?' But I never respond. Because I don't feel like explaining myself. And I don't think they really care anyway."

Just then, a young man sits down at the bar on the opposite side of her. He's a little drunk, and says, "You're pretty. May I buy you a drink?" She stays silent and looks back down at the ground. After an awkward moment, he accepts the rejection, gets up, and walks away.

"Would you prefer that I leave too?" I ask. "No," she says without glancing upward. "But I could use some fresh air. You don't have to come, but you can if you want to." I follow her outside and we sit on a street curb in front of the bar.

"Brrr... It's a chilly night!"

"Tell me about it," she says while maintaining her normal downward gaze. The warm vapor from her breath cuts through the cold air and bounces off of the ground in front of her. "So why are you out here with me? I mean, wouldn't you rather be inside in the warmth, talking to normal people about normal things?"

"I'm out here because I want to be. Because I'm not normal. And look, I can see my breath, and we're in San Diego. That's not normal either. Oh, and you're wearing old

Airwalk shoes, and so am I... Which may have been normal in 1994, but not anymore."

She glances up at me and smirks, this time exhaling her breath upward into the moonlight. "I see your ring. You're married, right?"

"Yeah," I reply.

"Well, you're off the market... and safe, I guess. So can I tell you a story?" I nod my head.

As she speaks, her emotional gaze shifts from the ground, to my eyes, to the moonlit sky, to the ground, and back to my eyes again. This rotation continues in a loop for the duration of her story. And every time her eyes meet mine she holds them there for a few seconds longer than she did during the previous rotation.

I don't interject once. I listen to every word. And I assimilate the raw emotion present in the tone of her voice and in the depth of her eyes.

When she finishes, she says, "Well now you know my story. You think I'm a freak, don't you?"

"Place your right hand on your chest," I tell her. She does. "Do you feel something?" I ask.

"Yeah, I feel my heartbeat."

"Now place both of your hands on your face

and move them around slowly." She does. "What do you feel now?" I ask.

"Well, I feel my eyes, my nose, my mouth... I feel my face."

"That's right," I reply. "But unlike you, stories don't have heartbeats, and they don't have faces. Because stories are not alive... they're not people. They're just stories."

She stares into my eyes for a prolonged moment, smiles and says, "Just stories we live through."

"Yeah... And stories we learn from."

12 THINGS To Know BEFORE Letting Go

Oftentimes letting go has nothing to do with weakness, and everything to do with strength. We let go and walk away not because we want the universe to realize our worth, but because we finally realize our own worth.

And that's what this short article is all about – realizing your worth, and harnessing this realization to identify the negative ideas, habits, and people in your life that you need to let go of. Here are some points to consider:

1. *The past can steal your present if you let it.*

You can spend hours, days, weeks, months, or even years sitting alone in a dark room, over-analyzing a situation from the past, trying to put the pieces together, justifying what could've or should've happened. Or you can just leave the pieces on the floor and walk out the front door into the sunlight to get some fresh air.

2. *Not everyone, and not everything, is meant to stay.*

There are things you don't want to happen, but have to accept, things you don't want to know, but have to learn, and people you can't live without but have to let go. Some circumstances and people come into your life just to strengthen you, so you can move on without them.

3. *Happiness is not the absence of problems, but the ability to deal with them.*

Imagine all the wondrous things your mind might embrace if it weren't wrapped so tightly around your struggles. Always look at what you have, instead of what you have lost. Because it's not what the world takes away from you that counts; it's what you do with what you have left.

Sometimes you just need to do your best and surrender the rest.

Don't be too hard on yourself. There are plenty of people willing to do that for you. Tell yourself, "I am doing the best I can with what I have in this moment. And that is all I can expect of anyone, including me." Love yourself and be proud of everything that you do, even your mistakes. Because even mistakes mean you're trying.

You are in control of one person, and one person only: yourself.

There is only one way to happiness, and that is to cease worrying about things which are beyond the power of your

control. Letting go in your relationships doesn't always mean that you don't care about people anymore; it's simply realizing that the only person you really have control over is yourself.

What's right for you may be wrong for others, and vice versa.

Think for yourself, and allow others the privilege of doing so too. We all dance to the beat of a different drum. There are few absolute 'rights' and 'wrongs' in the world. You need to live your life your way – the way that's right for you.

7 Some people will refuse to accept you for who you are.

Always choose to be true to yourself, even at the risk of incurring ridicule from others, rather than being fake and incurring the pain and confusion of trying to be someone you're not. When you are comfortable in your skin, not everyone in this world will like you, and that's okay. You could be the ripest, juiciest apple in the world, and there's going to be someone out there who hates apples.

8 Relationships can only exist on a steady foundation of truth.

When there is breakdown in a relationship, you must have the hard conversation. It may not be pretty and it may not feel good. But if you are willing to listen and tell the truth, it will open up. When you build relationships based on truth and authenticity, rather than masks, false perfection, and being phony, your relationships will heal, connect, and thrive.

9 The world changes when you change.

Practice really seeing whatever it is you're looking at. You are today where your thoughts and perceptions have brought you; you will be tomorrow where your thoughts and perceptions take you. If you truly want to change your life, you must first change your mind. The world around you changes when you change.

0 You can make decisions, or you can make excuses.

Don't let what you can't do stop you from what you can do. No more excuses, no more wasting precious time. This moment is as good a time as any to begin doing what matters most. Start exactly where you are right now. Do what you can with what you have right now. Stop over-thinking and start DOING!

1 It usually takes just a few negative remarks to kill a person's dream.

Don't kill people's dreams with negative words, and don't put up with those who do. Don't let people interrupt you and tell you that you can't do something. If you have a dream that you're passionate about, you must protect it. When others can't do something themselves, they're going to tell you that you can't do it either; and that's a lie. These people are simply speaking from within the boundaries of their own limitations.

12 Sometimes walking away is the only way to win.

Never waste your time trying to explain yourself to people who have proven that they are committed to misunderstanding you. In other words, don't define your intelligence by the number of arguments you have won, but by the number of times you have said, "This needless nonsense is not worth my time."

10 THINGS

You Must **GIVE UP** to *Move Forward*

If you want to fly and move on to better things, you have to give up the things that weigh you down – which is not always as obvious and easy as it sounds.

Starting today, give up…

1 Letting the opinions of others control your life.

People know your name, not your story. They've heard what you've done, but not what you've been through. So take their opinions of you with a grain of salt. In the end, it's not what others think, it's what you think about yourself that counts. Sometimes you have to do exactly what's best for you and your life, not what's best for everyone else.

2 The shame of past failures.

You will fail sometimes, and that's okay. The faster you accept this, the faster you can get on with being brilliant. Your past does not equal your future. Just because you failed yesterday; or all day today; or a moment ago; or for the last six months; or for the last sixteen years, doesn't have any impact on the current moment. All that matters is what you do right now.

3 Being indecisive about what you want.

You will never leave where you are until you decide where you would rather be. It's all about finding and pursuing your passion. Neglecting passion blocks creative flow. When you're passionate, you're energized. Likewise, when you lack passion, your energy is low and unproductive. Energy is everything when it comes to being successful. Make a decision to figure out what you want, and then pursue it passionately.

■ Procrastinating on the goals that matter to you.

There are two primary choices in life: to accept conditions as they exist, or accept the responsibility for changing them.

Follow your intuition. Don't give up trying to do what you really want to do. When there is love and inspiration, you can't go wrong. And whatever it is you want to do, do it now. There are only so many tomorrows. Trust me, in a year from now, you will wish you had started today.

5 *Choosing to do nothing.*

You don't get to choose how you are going to die, or when. You can only decide how you are going to live, right now. Every day is a new chance to choose. Choose to change your perspective. Choose to flip the switch in your mind from negative to positive. Choose to turn on the light and stop fretting about insecurity and doubt. Choose to do work that you are proud of. Choose to see the best in others, and to show your best to others. Choose to truly LIVE, right now.

6 *Your need to be right.*

If you keep on saying you're right, even if you are right now, eventually you will be wrong. Aim for success, but never give up your right to be wrong. Because when you do, you will also lose your ability to learn new things and move forward with your life.

7 *Running from problems that should be fixed.*

We make life harder than it has to be. The difficulties started when... conversations became texting, feelings became subliminal, sex became a game, the word 'love' fell out of context, trust faded as honesty waned, insecurities became a way of living, jealously became a habit, being hurt started to feel natural, and running away from it all became our solution. Stop running! Face these issues, fix the problems, communicate, appreciate, forgive and LOVE the people in your life who deserve it.

8 *Making excuses rather than decisions.*

Life is a continuous exercise in creative problem solving. A mistake doesn't become a failure until you refuse to correct it. Thus, most long-term failures are the outcome of people who make excuses instead of decisions.

9 *Overlooking the positive points in your life.*

What you see often depends entirely on what you're looking for. Do your best and surrender the rest. When you stay stuck in regret of the life you think you should have had, you end up missing the beauty of what you do have. You will have a hard time ever being happy if you aren't thankful for the good things in your life right now.

10 *Not appreciating the present moment.*

We do not remember days, we remember moments. Too often we try to accomplish something big without realizing that the greatest part of life is made up of the little things. Live authentically and cherish each precious moment of your journey. Because when you finally arrive at your desired destination, I guarantee you, another journey will begin.

16 HARSH TRUTHS that Make Us *Stronger*

It takes more courage to reveal insecurities than to hide them, more strength to relate to people than to dominate them, more manhood (or womanhood) to abide by thought-out principles rather than blind reflex. Toughness is in the soul and spirit, not in muscles and an immature mind. - Alex Karras

1 *Life is not easy.*

Hard work makes people lucky – it's the stuff that brings dreams to reality. So start every morning ready to run farther than you did yesterday and fight harder than you ever have before.

2 *You will fail sometimes.*

The faster you accept this, the faster you can get on with being brilliant. You'll never be 100% sure it will work, but you can always be 100% sure doing nothing won't work. So get out there and do something! Either you succeed or you learn a vital lesson. Win – Win.

3 *Right now, there's a lot you don't know.*

The day you stop learning is the day you stop living. Embrace new information, think about it and use it to advance yourself.

4 *There may not be a tomorrow.*

Not for everyone. Right now, someone on Earth is planning something for tomorrow without realizing they're going to die today. This is sad but true. So spend your time wisely today and pause long enough to appreciate it.

5 *There's a lot you can't control.*

You can't control everything in your life no matter how many safeguards you put into place. But thankfully, you don't have to control everything to find peace and happiness. It lives with you always, deep within. More than getting into the nuances of control itself, you should be more interested in encouraging yourself to commit to giving it up, on purpose. See what happens when you loosen your grip, throw your hands into the air, and allow life to just happen and flow as it does, without constant micromanagement.

6 Information is not true knowledge.

Knowledge comes from experience. You can discuss a task a hundred times, but these discussions will only give you a philosophical understanding. You must experience a task firsthand to truly know it.

7 You can't be successful without providing value.

Don't waste your time trying to be successful, spend your time creating value. When you're valuable to the world around you, you will be successful.

8 Someone else will always have more than you.

Whether it's money, friends or magic beans that you're collecting, there will always be someone who has more than you. But remember, it's not how many you have, it's

how passionate you are about collecting them. It's all about the journey.

9 You can't change the past.

As Maria Robinson once said, "Nobody can go back and start a new beginning, but anyone can start today and make a new ending." You can't change what happened, but you can change how you react to it.

10 The only person who can make you happy is you.

The root of your happiness comes from your relationship with yourself. Sure external entities can have fleeting effects on your mood, but in the long run nothing matters more than how you feel about who you are on the inside.

11 There will always be people who don't like you.

You can't be everything to everyone. No matter what you do, there will always be someone who thinks differently. So concentrate on doing what you know in your heart is right. What others think and say about you isn't all that important. What is important is how you feel about yourself.

12 *You won't always get what you want.*

As Mick Jagger once said, "You won't always get what you want, but if you try sometimes you might find you get what you need." Look around. Appreciate the things you have right now. Many people aren't so lucky.

13 *In life, you get what you put in.*

If you want love, give love. If you want friends, be friendly. If you want money, provide value. It really is this simple.

4 *Good friends will come and go.*

Most of your high school friends won't be a part of your college life. Most of your college friends won't be a part of your 20-something professional life. Most of your 20-something friends won't be there when your spouse and you bring your second child into the world. But some friends will stick. And it's these friends – the ones who transcend time with you – who matter.

5 *Doing the same exact thing every day hinders self growth.*

If you keep doing what you're doing, you'll keep getting what you're getting. Growth happens when you change things – when you try new things – when you stretch beyond your comfort zone.

16 *You will never feel 100% ready for something new.*

Nobody ever feels 100% ready when an opportunity arises. Because most great opportunities in life force us to grow beyond our comfort zones, which means you won't feel totally comfortable or ready for it.

And remember, trying to be someone else is a waste of the person you are. Strength comes from being comfortable in your own skin.

12 WAYS to Get a SECOND CHANCE in Life

We all need second chances. This isn't a perfect world. We're not perfect people. I'm probably on my 1000th second chance right now and I'm not ashamed to admit it. Because even though I've failed a lot, it means I've tried a lot too.

We rarely get things right the first time. Almost every major accomplishment in a person's life starts with the decision to try again and again – to get up after every failed attempt and give it another shot.

The only difference between an opportunity and an obstacle is attitude. Getting a second chance in life is about giving yourself the opportunity to grow beyond your past failures. It's about positively adjusting your attitude toward future possibilities.

Here's how:

1 *Let go of the past.*

What's done is done. When life throws us nasty curveballs it typically doesn't make any sense to us, and our natural emotional reaction might be to get extremely upset and scream obscenities at the top of our lungs. But how does this help our dilemma? Obviously, it doesn't.

The smartest, and oftentimes hardest, thing we can do in these kinds of situations is to be more tempered in our reactions. To want to scream obscenities, but to be wiser and

more disciplined than that. To remember that emotional rage only makes matters worse. And to remember that tragedies are rarely as bad as they seem, and even when they are, they give us an opportunity to grow stronger.

Every difficult moment in our lives is accompanied by an opportunity for personal growth and creativity. But in order to attain this growth and creativity, we must first learn to let go of the past. We must recognize that difficulties pass like everything else in

> ## "Nobody can go back and start a new beginning, but anyone can start today and make a new ending."
> -Maria Robinson

life. And once they pass, all we're left with are our unique experiences and the lessons required to make a better attempt next time.

Identify the lesson.

Everything is a life lesson. Everyone you meet, everything you encounter, etc. They're all part of the learning experience we call 'life.'

Never forget to acknowledge the lesson, especially when things don't go your way. If you don't get a job you wanted or a relationship doesn't work, it only means something better is out there waiting. And the lesson you just learned is the first step towards it.

Lose the negative attitude.

Negative thinking creates negative results. Positive thinking creates positive results. Period.

Every one of the other suggestions in this article is irrelevant if your mind is stuck in the gutter. Positive thinking is at the forefront of every great success story. The mind must believe it can do something before it is capable of actually doing it.

4 Accept accountability for your current situation.

Either you take accountability for your life or someone else will. And when they do, you'll become a slave to their ideas and dreams instead of a pioneer of your own.

You are the only one who can directly control the outcome of your life. And no, it won't always be easy. Every person has a stack of obstacles in front of them. You must take accountability for your situation and overcome these obstacles. Choosing not to is giving up on the life you were meant to create.

5 Focus on the things you can change.

Some forces are out of your control. The best thing you can do is do the best with what's in front of you with the resources you do have access to.

Wasting your time, talent and emotional energy on things that are beyond your control is a recipe for frustration, misery and stagnation. Invest your energy in the things you can change.

6 *Figure out what you really want.*

You'll be running on a hamster wheel forever if you never decide where you want to go. Figure out what's meaningful to you so you can be who you were born to be.

Some of us were born to be musicians – to communicate intricate thoughts and rousing feelings with the strings of a guitar. Some of us were born to be poets – to touch people's hearts with exquisite prose. Some of us were born to be entrepreneurs – to create growth and opportunity where others saw rubbish. And still, some of us were born to be or do whatever it is, specifically, that moves you.

Don't quit just because you didn't get it right on your first shot. And don't waste your life fulfilling someone else's dreams and desires. You must follow your intuition and make a decision to never give up on who you are capable of becoming.

7 *Eliminate the non-essential.*

First, identify the essential – the things in your life that matter most to you. Then eliminate the fluff. This drastically simplifies things and leaves you with a clean slate – a fresh, solid foundation to build upon without needless interferences. This process works with any aspect of your life – work projects, relationships, general to-do lists, etc.

Remember, you can't accomplish anything if you're trying to accomplish everything. Concentrate on the essential. Get rid of the rest.

8 *Be very specific.*

When you set new goals for yourself, try to be as specific as possible. "I want to lose twenty pounds" is a goal you can aim to achieve. "I want to lose weight" is not. Knowing the specific measurements of what you want to achieve is the only way you will ever get to the end result you desire.

Also, be specific with your actions too. "I will exercise" is not actionable. It's far too vague. "I will take a 30 minute jog every weekday at 6PM" is something you can actually do – something you can build a routine around – something you can measure.

9 *Concentrate on DOING instead of NOT DOING.*

"Don't think about eating that chocolate donut!" What are you thinking about now? Eating that chocolate donut, right? When you concentrate on not thinking about something, you end up thinking about it.

The same philosophy holds true when it comes to breaking our bad habits. By relentlessly trying not to do something, we end up thinking about it so much that we subconsciously provoke ourselves to cheat

– to do the exact thing we are trying not to do

Instead of concentrating on eliminating bad habits, concentrate on creating good habits (that just happen to replace the bad ones). For instance, if you're trying to eliminate snacking on junk food, you might create a new mental habit like this: "At 3PM each day, about the time I'm usually ready for a snack, I will eat five whole wheat crackers." After a few weeks or months of concentrating on this good habit it will become part of your routine. You'll start doing the right thing without even thinking about it.

10 *Create a daily routine.*

It's so simple, but creating a daily routine for yourself can change your life. The most productive routines, I've found, come at the start and end of the day – both your workday and your day in general. That means, develop a routine for when you wake up, for when you first start working, for when you finish your work, and for the hour or two before you go to sleep.

Doing so will help you start each day on point, and end each day in a way that prepares you for tomorrow. It will help you focus on the important stuff, instead of the distractions that keep popping up. And most importantly, it will help you make steady progress – which is what second chances are all about.

11 *Maintain self-control and work on it for real.*

The harder you work the luckier you will become. Stop waiting around for things to work out. If you keep doing what you're doing, you'll keep getting what you're getting.

While many of us decide at some point during the course of our lives that we want to answer our calling, only an astute few of us actually work on it. By "working on it," I mean truly devoting oneself to the end result. The rest of us never act on our decision. Or, at best, we pretend to act on it by putting forth an uninspired, half-assed effort.

If you want a real second chance, you've got to be willing to give it all you got. No slacking off! This means you have to strengthen and maintain your self-control. The best way I've found to do this is to take one small bite of the elephant at a time. Start with just one activity, and make a plan for how you will deal with troubles when they arise. For instance, if you're trying to lose weight, come up with a list of healthy snacks you can eat when you get the craving for snacks. It will be hard in the beginning, but it will get easier. And that's the whole point. As your strength grows, you can take on bigger challenges.

Remember, life is not easy, especially when you plan on achieving something worthwhile. Achieving your dreams can be a lot of work, even the second time around. Be ready for it.

12 *Forget about impressing people.*

So many people buy things they don't need with money they don't have to impress people they don't know. Or some variation thereof...

Don't be one of these people. It's a waste of time. And it's probably one of the reasons you need a second chance in the first place.

Just keep doing what you know is right. And if it doesn't work, adjust your approach and try again. You'll get there eventually.

WHY WE MUST
FORGIVE OURSELVES

*To **forgive** is to set a prisoner free and discover the prisoner was you.*

Healing

Once upon a time there lived a woman who had a bad temper. She screamed at and scolded everyone around her. For most of her life she believed the fiery rage inside her was everyone else's fault. But one morning she woke up and realized she had isolated herself from all the people in her life who she cared about. She had no friends, and even her family wanted nothing to do with her. She knew in that moment that she needed to make a change.

She went to see a well respected Buddhist monk to ask for advice. The monk told her to take a large clay jug from his kitchen, fill it with water, and stand outside on the sidewalk in front of his house. "It's hot outside, and that's a busy sidewalk with lots of pedestrians," the monk told her as he pointed out the front window of his house. "When a pedestrian passes, you must offer

them a glass of water. Do this until there is no rage left inside you."

The woman with the bad temper was confused – she didn't understand how this would help her. But she had heard that this monk was known for his unconventional wisdom and avant-garde methods of healing, and she was willing to do anything to heal herself and rebuild her relationships with those she cared about.

The Rage

So she stood outside with a water jug and served water to pedestrians every day for the next several weeks. And every morning she asked herself if rage still pulsed through her veins. And every morning the answer was, "yes." So she continued serving water. Until this afternoon when a burly man walked up, snatched the water jug out of her hand, drank directly out of it, and then tossed the jug on the ground as he continued on his way.

The rage within the woman skyrocketed into an irrepressible fit. Unable to contain herself, she picked-up the clay jug off the ground and, with all her might, threw it at the burly man as he walked away. It was a direct hit. The jug shattered into pieces over the back of his head and he fell to the ground, unconscious and bleeding.

As the woman's rage subsided, she realized the magnitude of what she had done and began to cry. She used a payphone to call 911 and report the incident. An ambulance and two police cars arrived at the scene moments later. As the EMTs strapped the burly man into a stretcher, the police handcuffed his arms and legs to the stretcher. Then one of the police officers walked over to the woman, who was still crying, and said, "The city owes you a big 'thank you.' That man has been on our most wanted list for over a year now. He is a primary suspect in multiple murder cases and violent robberies."

The Moral

The moral of the story is that we simply don't know. We want to believe that if we completely rid ourselves of our inner darkness then we will always make the right choices, and be of service to ourselves and those around us. But life isn't so linear and predicable. Sometimes our darkness inadvertently leads us to do things that impact the world in a positive way, just as our unconditional love sometimes forces us to overlook the criminal standing before us.

I tell you this story not to encourage you to let your anger get the best of you, but rather to provide you with an opening to forgive yourself for your own humanity – your own moments of rage and darkness. Because, even in our darkest moments, there is a light that shines within us that has the potential to be of service to ourselves and others in ways we may never fully comprehend.

12 TOUGH TRUTHS that Help You grow

As you look back on your life, you will often realize that many of the times you thought you were being rejected from something good, you were in fact being redirected to something better. You can't control everything. Sometimes you just need to relax and have faith that things will work out. Let go a little and just let life happen. Because sometimes the truths you can't change, end up changing you and helping you grow.

Here are twelve such truths...

1 Everything is as it should be.

It's crazy how you always end up where you're meant to be – how even the most tragic and stressful situations eventually teach you important lessons that you never dreamed you were going to learn. Remember, oftentimes when things are falling apart, they are actually falling into place.

2 Not until you are lost in this world can you begin to find your true self.

Realizing you are lost is the first step to living the life you want. The second step is leaving the life you don't want. Making a big life change is pretty scary. But you know what's even scarier? Regret. Vision without action is a daydream, and action without vision is a nightmare. Your heart is free, have the courage to follow it.

3. It's usually the deepest pain which empowers you to grow to your full potential.

It's the scary, stressful choices that end up being the most worthwhile. Without pain, there would be no change. But remember, pain, just like everything in life, is meant to be learned from and then released.

!. One of the hardest decisions you will ever face in life is choosing whether to walk away or take another step forward.

If you catch yourself in a cycle of trying to change someone, or defending yourself again someone who is trying to change you, walk away. But if you are pursuing a dream, take another step. And don't forget that sometimes this step will involve modifying your dream, or planning a new one – it's OK to change your mind or have more than one dream.

5. You have to take care of yourself first.

Before befriending others, you have to be your own friend. Before correcting others, you have to correct yourself. Before making others happy, you have to make yourself happy. It's not called selfishness, it's called personal development. Once you balance yourself, only then can you balance the world around you.

6. One of the greatest freedoms is truly not caring what everyone else thinks of you.

As long as you are worried about what others think of you, you are owned by them. Only when you require no approval from outside yourself, can you own yourself.

7. You may need to be single for awhile.

Before you realize that, although the co-owned belongings from your failed relationships might not have been divided equally, the issues that destroyed the relationships likely were. For how can you stand confidently alone, or see the same issues arising in your newest relationship, and not realize which broken pieces belong to you? Owning your issues, and dealing with them, will make you far happier in the long run, than owning anything else in this world.

8. The only thing you can absolutely control is how you react to things out of your control.

The more you can adapt to the situations in life, the more powerful your highs will be, and the more quickly you'll be able to bounce back from the lows in your life. Put most simply: being at peace means being in a state of complete acceptance of all that is, right here, right now.

9 *Some people will lie to you.*

Remember, an honest enemy is better than a friend who lies. Pay less attention to what people say, and more attention to what they do. Their actions will show you the truth, which will help you measure the true quality of your relationship in the long-term.

10 *If you concentrate on what you don't have, you will never have enough.*

If you are thankful for what you do have, you will end up having even more. Happiness resides not in possessions, and not in gold; happiness dwells in the soul. Abundance is not about how much you have, it's how you feel about what you have. When you take things for granted, your happiness gets taken away.

11 *Yes, you have failed in the past.*

But don't judge yourself by your past, you don't live there anymore. Just because you're not where you want to be today doesn't mean you won't be there someday.

You can turn it all around in the blink of an eye by making a simple choice to stand back up – to try again, to love again, to live again, and to dream again.

12 *Everything is going to be alright; maybe not today, but eventually.*

There will be times when it seems like everything that could possibly go wrong is going wrong. And you might feel like you will be stuck in this rut forever, but you won't. Sure the sun stops shining sometimes, and you may get a huge thunderstorm or two, but eventually the sun will come out to shine. Sometimes it's just a matter of us staying as positive as possible in order to make it to see the sunshine break through the clouds again.

12 TRUTHS You Should Know by now

Just a few simple truths we learn on the road of life...

1. The route to our destination is never a straight one.

We take questionable turns and we get lost. But it doesn't always matter which road we embark on; what matters is that we embark. Either way life will likely get a little complicated, and bring unexpected hurdles and changes. But that's okay. Sometimes you have to stumble and feel weak for a little while to realize how strong you really are.

2. Real friends won't ask you to change who you are.

The RIGHT people for you will love all the things about you that the WRONG people are intimidated by. Don't change so people will like you. Be patient, keep being your awesome self, and pretty soon the RIGHT people will love the REAL you.

3. Cheating is a choice, not a mistake, and not an excuse.

If you decide to cheat, and you succeed in cheating someone out of something, don't think that this person is a fool. Realize that this person trusted you much more than you ever deserved, and they learned a lesson about who you really are.

4. The past can't hurt you anymore — not unless you let it.

Forgive and move on! Forgiveness allows you to focus on the future without combating the past. Without forgiveness, wounds can never be healed, and moving on can never be accomplished. What happened in the past is just one chapter. Don't close the book, just turn the page. Cry when you must and push forward. Let your tears water the seeds of your future growth and happiness.

5 Adversity will come to every person at some point.

How you meet it, what you make of it, and what you allow it to take from you and give to you is determined by your mental habits and personal choices. In short, you can't change the cards you were dealt, just how you play the hand.

6 Sometimes things fall apart so better things can fall together.

When things fall apart, consider the possibility that life knocked it down on purpose. Not to bully you, or to punish you, but to prompt you to build something that better suits your personality and your purpose.

7 Someone else doesn't have to be wrong for you to be right.

Keep an open mind. The highest form of ignorance is when you reject something you don't know. We all have our own unique path and feelings. When you judge another, you do not define them, you define yourself. It's one thing to feel that you are on the right path, but it's another to think that yours is the only path.

8 Everything has been just the way it needed to be.

In life, we do lots of things. Some we wish we could take back. Some we wish we could relive a thousand times. All of these things, positive and negative, have taught us important lessons and have collectively made us into the person we are today. If we were to reverse or adjust any of them, we wouldn't be who we are; we would be somebody else. So just live, make mistakes, make memories, and take chances. Never second guess who you are or where you've been.

9 Silence is often the loudest cry.

There's always some truth behind 'just kidding,' knowledge behind 'I don't know,' emotion behind 'I don't care,' and pain behind: 'It's okay.' So pay close attention to how people feel, especially those you care for most. And remember, silence is often the loudest cry. Sometimes what a person needs most is a hand to hold and a heart to understand.

10 The difference between where you are and where you want to be, is what you do.

What you do today is important because you are exchanging a day of your life for it. Don't wait until everything is just right;

it will never be perfect. There will always be challenges, obstacles and less than perfect conditions. But with each step you take, you will grow stronger and stronger, more skilled, more confident, and more successful. So start doing what you need to do today. Life is a courageous journey or nothing at all. We usually can't become who we want to be by continuing to do what we've been doing.

11 | *It's not who you are that holds you back, it's who you think you're not.*

Judging yourself is not the same as being honest with yourself. Don't sell yourself short! You are capable of great things. And don't ever let someone else make you feel like you're not good enough. If they can't see how amazing you are, then they're the one who's not good enough for you. Their approval is not needed.

12 | *Right now is the only moment guaranteed to you.*

Smile through the hard times, even though it doesn't always seem to get any better. A smile is the first step to fixing things. The trick is to enjoy life by noticing what's right. Don't wish away your days waiting for better times ahead. Right now is the only moment guaranteed to you. Right now is life. Don't miss it.

40 LESSONS for **FINDING** *Strength* in Hard Times

Nobody gets through life without losing someone they love, someone they need, or something they thought was meant to be. But it is these losses that make us stronger and eventually move us toward future opportunities for growth and happiness.

Over the past five years Angel and I have dealt with several hardships, including the sudden death of a sibling, the loss of a best friend to illness, betrayal from a business partner, and an unexpected (breadwinning) employment layoff. These experiences were brutal. Each of them, naturally, knocked us down and off course for a period of time. But when our time of mourning was over in each individual circumstance, we pressed forward, stronger, and with a greater understanding and respect for life.

Here are some lessons we've learned along the way:

1 *You are not what happened to you in the past.*

No matter how chaotic the past has been, the future is a clean, fresh, wide open slate. You are not your past habits. You are not your past failures. You are not how others have at one time treated you. You are only who you think you are right now in this moment. You are only what you do right now in this moment.

2 *Focus on what you have, not on what you haven't.*

You are who you are and you have what you have, right now. And it can't be that bad, because otherwise you wouldn't be able to read this. The important thing is simply to find one POSITIVE thought that inspires and helps you move forward. Hold on to it strongly, and focus on it. You may feel like you don't have much, or anything at all, but you have your mind to inspire you. And that's really all you need to start moving forward again.

Sometimes you have to die a little on the inside first in order to be reborn and rise again as a stronger, smarter version of yourself.

3 Struggling with problems is a natural part of growing.

Part of living and growing up is experiencing unexpected troubles in life. People lose jobs, get sick, and sometimes die in car accidents. When you are younger, and things are going pretty well, this harsh reality can be hard to visualize. The smartest, and oftentimes hardest, thing we can do in these kinds of situations is to be tempered in our reactions. To want to scream obscenities, but to wiser and more disciplined than that. To remember that emotional rage only makes matters worse. And to remember that tragedies are rarely as bad as they seem, and even when they are, they give us an opportunity to grow stronger.

4 It's okay to fall apart for a little while.

You don't always have to pretend to be strong, and there is no need to constantly prove that everything is going well. You shouldn't be concerned with what other people are thinking either – cry if you need to – it's healthy to shed your tears. The sooner you do, the sooner you will be able to smile again. And a smile doesn't always mean a person is happy. Sometimes it simply means they are strong enough to face their problems.

5 Life is fragile, sudden, and shorter than it often seems.

There may not be a tomorrow – not for everyone. Right now, someone on Earth is planning something for tomorrow without realizing they're going to die today. This is sad but true. So spend your time wisely today and pause long enough to appreciate it. Every moment you get is a gift. Don't waste time by dwelling on unhappy things. Spend it on things that move you in the direction you want to go.

6 You will fail sometimes.

The faster you accept this, the faster you can get on with being brilliant. You'll never be 100% sure it will work, but you can always be 100% sure doing nothing won't work.

Doing something and getting it wrong is at least ten times more productive than doing nothing. So get out there and try! Either you succeed or you learn a vital lesson. Win – Win.

7 You have the capacity to create your own happiness.

Feelings change, people change, and time keeps rolling. You can hold onto past mistakes or you can create your own happiness. A smile is a choice, not a miracle. Don't make the mistake of waiting on someone or something to come along and make you happy. True happiness comes from within.

8 Emotionally separate yourself from your problems.

You are far greater than your problems. You are a living, breathing human being who is infinitely more complex than all of your individual problems added up together. And that means you're more powerful than them – you have the ability to change them, and to change the way you feel about them.

9 Don't make a problem bigger than it is.

You should never let one dark cloud cover the entire sky. The sun is always shining on some part of your life. Sometimes you just have to forget how you feel, remember what you deserve, and keep pushing forward.

10 Everything that happens is a life lesson.

Everyone you meet, everything you encounter, etc. They're all part of the learning experience we call 'life.' Never forget to acknowledge the lesson, especially when things don't go your way. If you don't get a job that you wanted or a relationship doesn't work, it only means something better is out there waiting. And the lesson you just learned is the first step towards it.

11 View every challenge as an educational assignment.

Ask yourself: "What is this situation meant to teach me?" Every situation in our lives has a lesson to teach us. Some of these lessons include: To become stronger. To communicate more clearly. To trust your instincts. To express your love. To forgive.

To know when to let go. To try something new.

12 *Things change, but the sun always rises the next day.*

The bad news: nothing is permanent. The good news: nothing is permanent.

13 *Giving up and moving on are two very different things.*

There comes a point when you get tired of chasing everyone and trying to fix everything, but it's not giving up, and it's not the end. It's a new beginning. It's realizing, finally, that you don't need certain people and things and the drama they bring.

14 *Distance yourself from negative people.*

Every time you subtract negative from your life you make room for more positive. Life is too short to spend time with people who suck the happiness out of you. Let go of negative people, for they are the greatest destroyers of self confidence and self esteem. Surround yourself with people who bring out the best in you.

15 *Perfect relationships don't exist.*

There's no such thing as a perfect, ideal relationship. It's how two people deal with the imperfections of a relationship that make it ideal.

16 *You must love yourself too.*

One of the most painful things in life is losing yourself in the process of loving someone too much, and forgetting that you are special too. When was the last time someone told you that they loved you just the way you are, and that what you think and how you feel matters? When was the last time someone told you that you did a good job, or took you someplace, simply because they know you feel happy when you're there? When was the last time that 'someone' was YOU?

17 *Don't let others make decisions for you.*

Sometimes you just have to live not caring what they think of you, shake off the drama, and prove to YOURSELF that you're better than they think you are.

18 Resentment hurts you, not them.

Always forgive people and move on, even if they never ask for your forgiveness. Don't do it for them – do it for you. Grudges are a waste of happiness. Get that unnecessary stress out of your life right now.

19 You're not alone. Everyone has problems.

To lose sleep worrying about a friend. To have trouble picking yourself up after someone lets you down. To feel like less because someone didn't love you enough to stay. To be afraid to try something new for fear you'll fail. None of this means you're dysfunctional or crazy. It just means you're human, and that you need a little time to right yourself. You are not alone. No matter how embarrassed or pathetic you feel about your own situation, there are others out there experiencing the same emotions. When you hear yourself say, "I am all alone," it is your mind trying to sell you a lie.

20 You still have a lot to be thankful for.

Although the world is full of suffering, it is also full of brave people who are overcoming it. Sometimes you have to forget what's gone, appreciate what still remains, and look forward to what's coming next. Henry David Thoreau once said, "Wealth is the ability to fully experience life." Even when times are tough, it's always important to keep things in perspective. You didn't go to sleep hungry last night. You didn't go to sleep outside. You had a choice of what clothes to wear this morning. You hardly broke a sweat today. You didn't spend a minute in fear. You have access to clean drinking water. You have access to medical care. You have access to the Internet. You can read. Some might say you are incredibly wealthy, so remember to be grateful for all the things you do have.

21 Consciously nurture your inner hope.

A loss, a worry, an illness, a dream crushed – no matter how deep your hurt or how high your aspirations, do yourself a favor and pause at least once a day, place your hands over your heart and say aloud, "Hope lives here."

22 It's better to be hurt by the truth, than comforted by a lie.

You must see things how they are instead of how you hoped, wished, or expected them to be. It's always better to be slapped with the truth than kissed with a lie.

23 It's hard to tell exactly how close you are to success.

Connecting the dots going forward is nearly impossible, but when you look backward it always makes perfect sense. Success is often closer than it seems, and arrives suddenly, when you least expect it.

24 Not getting what you want can be a blessing.

Not getting what you want is sometimes a wonderful stroke of good luck, because it forces you reevaluate things, opening new doors to opportunities and information you would have otherwise overlooked.

25 Laughter is the best medicine for stress.

Laugh at yourself often. Find the humor in whatever situation you're in. Optimism is a happiness magnet. If you stay positive, good things and good people will be drawn to you.

26 Mistakes are important to make.

We've all made mistakes. We've let people take advantage of us, and we've accepted way less than we deserve. But if you think about it, we've learned a lot from our bad choices, and even though there are some things we can never recover and people who will never be sorry, we now know better for next time. We now have more power to shape our future. Remember, failure is not falling down; failure is staying down when you have the choice to get back up. Get back up! Oftentimes good things fall apart so better things can fall together.

27 Worrying is literally a waste of energy.

Worry will not drain tomorrow of its troubles, it will drain you of your strength today.

28 Even when it's hard to move, take small steps forward.

Especially in trying times, it's important to continuously push yourself forward. Because momentum is everything! As long as you keep the momentum positive – even if you're moving at a snail's pace – you'll eventually get to the finish line. So celebrate every step you take today, no matter how small. Because every step will lead you farther away from where you were yesterday and closer to where you want to be tomorrow. Be it a better life or a dream we long to realize, we reach our destinations by taking many, many small steps in the same direction, one at a time.

29 There will always be people who dislike you.

You can't be everything to everyone. No matter what you do, there will always be someone who thinks differently. So concentrate on doing what you know in your heart is right. What others think and say about you isn't all that important. What is important is how you feel about yourself.

30 You are better off without some people you thought you needed.

The sad truth is, there are some people who will only be there for you as long as you have something they need. When you no longer serve a purpose to them, they will leave. The good news is, if you tough it out, you'll eventually weed these people out of your life and be left with some great friends you can always count on.

31 You are ONLY competing against yourself.

When you catch yourself comparing yourself to a colleague, neighbor, friend, or someone famous, stop! Realize that you are different, with different strengths – strengths these other people don't possess. Take a moment to reflect on all the awesome abilities you have and to be grateful for all the good things in your life.

32 You can't control everything that happens to you.

But you can control how you react to things. Everyone's life has positive and negative aspects — whether you're happy or not depends greatly on which aspects you focus on. For instance: Did you catch a head cold? At least it's only a temporary virus and nothing life-threatening. Did you lose a basketball game? Thankfully you got to spend the afternoon with friends doing something fun and healthy. Did your stock market savings go down? It'll bounce back in the long-term. And besides, it's great that you've been diligent and fortunate enough to save a nest egg of savings when many people are barely making ends meet. You get the idea.

33 *Life is NOT easy.*

If you expect it to be, you will perpetually disappoint yourself. Achieving anything worthwhile in life takes effort. So start every morning ready to run farther than you did yesterday and fight harder than you ever have before. Above all, make sure you properly align your efforts with your goals. It won't be easy, but it will be worth it in the end.

34 *Your future is spotless.*

Regardless of how filthy your past has been, your future is still spotless. Don't start your day with the broken pieces of yesterday. Don't look back unless it's a good view. Every day is a fresh start. Each day is a new beginning. Every morning we wake up is the first day of the rest of our life. One of the very best ways to get beyond past troubles is to concentrate all of your attention and effort on doing something that your future self will thank you for.

35 *You are not trapped; you just need to re-learn a few things.*

We all have doubts that make us feel trapped at times. If you doubt your ability to make a life-altering decision, to take on a new chapter in your life, or to fend for yourself after years of being overly-fostered, consider this: Surely if a bird with healthy wings is locked in a cage long enough, she will doubt her own ability to fly. You still have your wings, but your muscles are weak. Train them and stretch them slowly. Give yourself time. You'll be flying again soon.

36 *Everything in life is two-sided.*

There is good reason why we can't expect to feel pleasure without ever feeling pain; joy without ever feeling sorrow; confident without ever feeling fear; calm without ever feeling restless; hope without ever feeling despair: There is no such thing as a one-sided coin in life, with which one can buy a pain-free, trouble-free existence.

37 *You always have a choice.*

No matter what, there are always at least two options. If you can't physically change something, you can change the way you think about it. You can sit in the dark, or you can find your inner light and discover powerful pieces of yourself you never knew existed. You can view a crisis as an invitation to learn something new, viewing the shake-up in your outer world as an enlightening opportunity to wake-up your inner world.

38 Let others in when you're in a dark place.

No, they won't always be able to pull you out of the dark place you're in, but the light that spills in when they enter will at least show you which way the door is.

39 If you ask negative questions, you will get negative answers.

There are no positive answers to, "Why me?" "Why didn't I?" "What if?" etc. Would you allow someone else to ask you the demoralizing questions you sometimes ask yourself? I doubt it. So stop and swap them for questions that push you in a positive direction. For instance, "What have I learned from this experience?" "What do I have control over?" "What can I do right now to move forward?"

40 The end is a new beginning.

Say to yourself: "Dear Past, thank you for all the life lessons you have taught me. Dear Future, I am ready now!" Because a great beginning always occurs at the point you thought would be the end of everything.

12 Happy ☺ Thoughts

for **TROUBLED** Times

People and circumstances will occasionally break you down. But if you keep your mind focused, your heart open to possibility, and continue to put one foot in front of the other, you will be able to quickly recover the pieces, rebuild, and come back much stronger than you ever would have been otherwise.

Here are a few happy thoughts to ponder on those days when the whole world seems like it's crashing down around you.

Down days are completely normal, and not something you should feel guilty about having.

Happiness is never constant. Surrendering to your sadness, or whatever negative emotion is trying to come to the surface, does not make you a bad person. But remember, if you aren't sincerely thankful for every smile, don't be totally shocked by every tear. Keep things in perspective.

2 *When you are at your lowest point, you are open to the greatest positive change.*

Happiness is not the absence of problems, but the strength to deal with them. Strength doesn't come from what you can do; it comes from overcoming the things you once thought you couldn't do.

3 *There is a huge difference between giving up and moving on.*

Moving on doesn't mean giving up, but rather accepting that there are some things that cannot be. Moving on can mean that you're making a choice to be happy rather than hurt. For some folks, good situations last a lifetime, but for many, not knowing when to move on can hold them back forever.

4 *Life rarely turns out exactly the way you want it to, but you still have an opportunity to make it great.*

You have to do what you can, with what you have, exactly where you are. It won't always be easy, but it will be worth it in the end. Remember that there is no perfect life, just perfect moments. And it's these moments you must cherish; it's these moments that make the whole journey worthwhile.

5 *Most people ask for happiness on condition, but long-term happiness can only be felt if you don't set conditions.*

Accept life unconditionally. Realize that life balances itself between the ideal and the disappointing. And the disappointments are just life's way of saying, "I've got something better for you right around the corner." So be patient, live life, accept what is, and have a little faith.

6 *Too often, we carry around things from our past that hurt us*

– regrets, shame, anger, pain, etc. Don't let these negative points from the past rob your present happiness. You had to live though these things in the past, and although unfortunate, they can't be changed. But if the only place they live today is in your mind, then let go, move on, and be happy.

7 *You can choose to view things differently.*

Pick one part of your life that you are unhappy with and look at it from a different point of view. See the rain as nourishment for future growth. Consider being alone for awhile to create the solitude you need to hear your inner voice. Think of your lack of funds as an opportunity to experience the simple things in life. Right now, you can choose to allow the light to shine in your life. It is a choice. Why not allow it?

8 *Once you embrace unpleasant news, not as a negative but as evidence of a need for positive change, you're learning from it and growing.*

Whatever life throws at you, even if it hurts, be strong and fight through it. Remember, strong walls shake but never collapse. Life always offers you another chance – it's called tomorrow.

9 *When your flaws are stitched together with good intentions, your flaws make you beautiful.*

It's better to be true to yourself and risk being ridiculed by others, than to be false, and miss out on the beauty of being YOU. Never be bullied into silence. Never let someone else tell you who you are. Accept no one's definition of your life, except your own.

10 *You have the ability to heal yourself.*

Just like lava flowing slowly out of a volcano, you must create a healthy outlet for your pain and anger. It's important after you've been hurt to take some time to think about your pain, and address it calmly and consciously, so you can thwart the possibility of more pain brewing from your own negativity.

11 *There's a lot of life left to be lived.*

The real tragedy in life is not death, but the passion we let die inside of us while we still live. Remember, troubles from the past cannot define you, destroy you, or defeat you all by themselves. As long as you keep pushing forward, they can only strengthen you.

12 *You are a work in progress; which means you get there a little at a time, not all at once.*

Today is a brand new day – a fresh start. Replace negativity with positivity. Think happy thoughts. Exercise. Drink lots of water. Fill your body with fuel. Healthy is happy. Inspire yourself. Create. Laugh. Play. Love. Learn. Give someone a compliment. Perform a random act of kindness. Take a chance on an idea you believe in. You have the opportunity to do these things every single day – to make the necessary changes and slowly become the person you want to be. You just have to decide to do it. Decide that today is the day. Say it: "This is going to be my day!"

WHAT YOU NEED TO KNOW WHEN
TRAGEDY STRIKES

The Accident

Tragedy strikes a man who isn't yet old. A mini-van traveling toward him on a dark mountain highway hits his car nearly head-on just after sunset. He grasps his steering wheel hard and veers into the rocky mountainside until his car screeches to a halt. The mini-van flips onto its side and skids in the other direction off the cliff, plummeting 500 feet to the ground. Inside is a young family of five.

He doesn't recall the events that followed during the next few days. He doesn't recall the three eye witnesses who comforted him and assured him that it wasn't his fault — that the other driver had swerved into his lane. He doesn't recall how he got to the emergency room or the fact that he stayed there for five days to treat a concussion and a broken collar bone.

The Guilt

What he does know — and clearly recalls — are the endless string of days he passes sitting alone in his bedroom, crying, and thinking, "Why me?" Why after forty-eight years of Sunday church attendance, unwavering faith, and regular community volunteering and charity, would God ask him to spend the rest of his life knowing that he singlehandedly killed an entire family?

He has a loving, supporting family that tries to comfort his ailing heart, but he can only see them as the loving family he has taken from the world. He also has an overflowing network of close friends who want to see him smile again, but they now represent friends that others have lost because of him.

The man who isn't yet old begins to age more rapidly. Within a few short months, he is a shell of his former self — skin and bones, wrinkles creasing across his face, a despondent downward gaze, and a hole in his heart that has grown so wide he feels like there's nothing left at all.

All of the people around him – those family members and friends who care so much – have done everything in their power to revive him to his former self. When love didn't work, they tried relaxing vacations. When vacations didn't work, they tried getting him involved in community activities. When the community activities didn't work, they tried doctors. And now they have resigned from trying. Because the man who is now an old man has completely resigned from everything.

The Dream

A night comes when he decides that it's just not worth it any more – that it's time to leave this world behind. Perhaps to go somewhere better. Perhaps to go nowhere at all. Luckily, he decides to sleep on it, because he barely has the strength to keep his eyelids open. So he closes his eyes and instantly falls into a deep sleep.

And he begins to dream. In it, he is sitting in a dimly lit room at a round table across from an elderly woman who looks much like his late mother. They stare at each other in silence for several minutes and then the elderly woman speaks.

"My son, tragedy is simply a miracle waiting to be discovered. Because within tragedy lie the seeds of love, learning, forgiveness, and empathy. If we choose to plant these seeds, they grow strong. If, on the other hand, we choose to overlook them, we prolong our tragedy and let somebody else discover the miracle."

The old man cries in his dream and in his sleep. He thinks about his wife, and his children, and all of the wonderful people who care for him. And he suddenly realizes that instead of using the tragic accident to notice how precious life is, he has prolonged the tragedy and essentially ceased to live his life. And he is very close, now, to passing all of his pain and sorrow over to the people he loves most in this world.

A New Beginning

He opens his eyes and takes a deep breath. He is alive. He realizes that he still has an opportunity to change things... To mend the broken pieces and experience the miracle that comes after the tragedy... To plant the seeds of love, learning, forgiveness, and empathy, and water these seeds until they grow strong.

He rolls over and kisses his wife on the cheek and ruffles her hair until her eyelids begin to flutter. She opens her eyes and looks at him, totally confused. There's a spark in his eyes that she hasn't seen in a long while – a spark that she thought had died with his youth on the day of the accident. "I love you so much," he says. "I've missed you," she replies. "Welcome back."

You can press forward long after you can't. It's just a matter of wanting it bad enough.

If you awake every morning with the thought that something wonderful will happen in your life today, and you pay close attention, you'll often find that you're right.

Crying doesn't indicate that you're weak. Since birth, it has always been a sign that you're alive and full of potential.

Give up worrying about what others think of you. What they think isn't important. What is important is how you feel about yourself.

You must see things how they are instead of how you hoped, wished, or expected them to be.

You never know how strong you really are until being strong is the only choice you have.

A problem is a chance for you to learn.

Reminders to help **MOTIVATE** you when you need it most

Grudges are a waste of perfect happiness. Let it go.

Tough times never last, but tough people do.

Not getting what you want is sometimes a wonderful stroke of good luck.

Giving up doesn't always mean you're weak, sometimes it means you are strong enough and smart enough to let go.

Mistakes teach you important lessons. Every time you make one, you're one step closer to your goal. The only mistake that can truly hurt you is choosing to do nothing simply because you're too scared to make a mistake.

If it's out of your control, why fret about it? Concentrating on things you can control is how you make good things happen.

Don't pray when it rains if you don't pray when the sun shines.

If you keep doing what you're doing, you'll keep getting what you're getting.

Adversity
QUESTIONS
to Make You *think*

What **STANDS** between
you
and
happiness?

Are you holding on to
SOMETHING
you need to
let go?

Decisions are being made
right now. The question is
are you **MAKING** them
yourself
or are you letting others
make them
for you?

Do you **REMEMBER**
that time 5 years ago when
you were extremely upset?
Does it really
matter now?

What is the biggest
CHALLENGE
you face
right now?

If the average human life span
was 40 years, how would you
LIVE your life
differently?

What's
SOMETHING
bad that happened to you
that made you
stronger?

What is
WORTH
the
pain?

Are you
AWARE .
that *someone*
has it *worse*
than you?

What's
MISSING in your
life?

Part Three
Relationships

In life you'll realize there is a purpose for everyone you meet. Some will test you, some will use you, and some will teach you. But most importantly, some will bring out the best in you.

WHO WILL
SAVE YOUR **LIFE?**

In the summer of 1997, at the age of fifteen, I learned a valuable life lesson.

And I learned it the hard way.

Leave It There For Now

"Go deep!" Roger shouts. I sprint as fast as I can, but not fast enough. The football flies over my head, bounces off the ground, and takes a massive leap over the schoolyard's fence. It lands in private property on the opposite side.

"Ahh... jeez!" I yelp. "That's the witch lady's yard! You're going to go get that!"

"No I'm not!" Roger insists. "I had to deal with that freak last week. So this time it's your turn."

"Man, she creeps me out! The way she speaks... and that hairy mole on her nose... yuck! I don't feel like dealing with her. It's my football, and I'd rather just leave it there for now and get it later."

"Fair enough, I'm ready to do something else anyway," Roger replies. "Let's head

over to the arcade. I wouldn't mind whooping your butt in a few rounds of Street Fighter."

"Ha, you wish! I'll destroy you, but not today. I promised my mom I wouldn't leave the schoolyard."

Roger rolls his eyes. "Dude, you're such a goody-goody. The arcade is practically across the street. We'll be back here long before your mom comes looking for us."

I think for a second. "Well... alright, screw it. Let's go."

We jump on our bikes and peddle off to the arcade.

It's Too Late

Thirty minutes later, Roger is begging for mercy. "Ah, today is just your lucky day," he gripes. "Don't let it get to your head."

I chuckle. "Yeah, yeah... I didn't say a word. But we do need to get back to the schoolyard so I can get my football."

We jump back on our bikes, peddle to the crosswalk, and wait for the 'walk' signal. "Okay, 'walk,' we're good! Last one to the witch's house is a rotten egg!" Roger shouts. I have about a six foot head start on him, so I begin peddling as fast as I can.

"No Marc! Watch out!" Roger squeals in a panic. I look up just in time to see a black car speeding directly at me through the red light. I leap from my bike. But it's too late.

My lanky fifteen year old body smashes into the windshield, flips lifelessly over the roof of the car, and strikes the concrete with a sickening thud.

Barely conscious, bloody, and broken.

I vaguely hear Roger's voice crying for help over the sound of screeching tires... as the black car speeds away from the scene of the accident.

He's Our Guardian Angel

I open my eyes slowly and my vision gradually comes into focus. "Hey honey," my mom says.

"Where am I?"

"You're in the hospital, dear. But the surgeon said you're going to be just fine."

"Surgery?"

"It's okay, you've already been through surgery in the ER," my mom replies as she grasps my hand. "You cracked four of your ribs, which punctured your lungs. But they went in and stitched you back together."

"That... That..." My mom interrupts me as tears begin rolling down her cheeks.

"We just need to be grateful... because you were barely breathing, honey. The surgeon said your lungs were filled with blood. He said it could have been a lot worse had the ambulance not gotten to you in time."

"That car... that black car... it ran the red light," I whisper restlessly.

"Shhh... It's okay," my mom reassures me. "The same wonderful man that called the ambulance also called the police with the license plate number of the black car. The driver was drunk. It was a hit and run. But the police already have him in custody."

"Do you know who made the calls?"

My mom reaches into her jeans pocket, pulls out a post-it note, and holds it up so I can read it. "Chris Evans – 305-555-8362" is written in red ink. "Chris Evans," my mom says as she takes a deep breath. "Whoever he is, he's our guardian angel."

"How'd you get his name and number?"

"I asked the paramedics for it. They told me they weren't supposed to give out this kind of information, but I begged," my mom says. "I told them I needed to know who saved my baby's life."

"Have you called him?"

"Yeah, but he doesn't answer my calls. It rings four times and goes straight to a voicemail beep. There's not even a voice greeting. I've already left three messages over the last forty-eight hours. But he hasn't called me back, and I suspect he may never."

How Do You Know?

Six months later, after a grueling recovery process, my doctor finally gives me the nod to partake in regular physical activity again. Roger and I jump at the chance to toss his new Nerf football around at the schoolyard.

"Go deep!" Roger shouts.

"Not yet, dude. I'm still not 100%. My doctor says I need to ease into it slowly. Cool?"

Roger smiles. "Yeah, of course, bro. My bad, I didn't mean to..." He is suddenly interrupted.

"Marc! Marc Andrew something!" a raspy female voice hollers from behind us. Roger and I turn around and are shocked to see the witch lady peeking her head over the schoolyard's fence. "I believe this belongs to you." She holds up an old football and tosses it towards me. The ball bounces across the ground and rolls up to my feet. Sure enough, it's the ball I left on her property the day of the accident.

"Thanks, but... how... how do you know my name? And my middle name?" I ask.

"About six months ago, your mom left me a few voicemail messages. My name is Chris Evans," she says.

11 THINGS

Everyone NEEDS You to *Know*

A silhouette of a human being stands before you.

Perhaps an old friend. Perhaps a neighbor. Perhaps a perfect stranger, like me.

Here are 11 things we all need you to keep in mind...

1. *You never really know how much the people around you are hurting.*

You could be standing next to someone who is completely broken inside and you wouldn't even know it. So never deprive someone of hope; it might be all they have. And remember that there are two ways to spread light in this world: You can either be a flame of hope, or a mirror that reflects it. Be one of the two every chance you get.

2. *The most important trip you will likely take in life is meeting others half way.*

You will achieve far more by working with people, rather than against them. Giving someone else a voice, and showing them that their ideas matter, will have a long-lasting, positive impact on the both of you.

3. *Relationships don't create happiness, they reflect it.*

Happiness is an inside job.

Relationships are simply the mirrors of your happiness; they reflect it and help you celebrate it. They are mirrors because they are a perfect reflection of your thoughts and beliefs. To reflect means to encourage you when you feel weak and challenge you when you feel strong, thereby returning you to your center. And to celebrate is to share the natural ease and joy of living from your center – of living in the now with clarity.

> ### *"One love, one heart, one destiny."*
> -Bob Marley

4   *Compassion comes back around.*

The son who tends to his chronically ill mother, ignoring his own exhaustion; the neighbor who gives a helping hand, even as his own needs go unanswered; the one who donates a couple dollars to someone in need, even if she has to break her last five dollar bill to do it. Maybe you don't hear the names of these unsung heroes in the news, but surely the universe hears their names and treats them accordingly.

5   *Timing is everything.*

There is a time for silence, a time to let go and allow your friends to launch themselves into their own destiny, and a time to cheer for their victories, or help them pick up the pieces, when it's all over.

6   *Actions are the loudest form of communication.*

What you do speaks so loud that others will have a hard time hearing what you say. So practice what you preach or don't preach at all – walk the talk. And remember that there is often a major gap between what someone says and what they do. Characterize people by their actions and you will never be fooled by their words.

7   *A loving relationship creates freedom and abundance.*

Love doesn't hurt. Love is not the problem. Don't blame love if a failed relationship interfered with your other important relationships, or robbed you of your self-esteem and personal freedoms. No, don't blame love. For it wasn't love that stole from you. It was possession. It was obsession. It was manipulation. It was confusion. Love had nothing to do with your situation. For love doesn't close the door against all that is good. It opens it wide to let more goodness in. Love creates freedom and abundance.

8   *People are more of what they keep silent than what they say.*

Pay attention to their quiet gestures. If you cannot understand someone's silence, you will have a hard time understanding their words.

9   *What others say and do is often based entirely on their own self-reflection.*

When you have people speaking to you who are angry and upset, and you nevertheless remain present and continue to treat them with kindness and respect, you place yourself in a position of great power. You become a means for the situation to be graciously diffused and healed. A Zen teacher once said, "When somebody backs themselves into a corner, look the other way until they get themselves out; and then act as though it never happened." Allowing people to save face in this way, and not reminding them of what they already know is not their most intelligent behavior, is an act of great kindness. This is possible when we realize that people behave in such ways because they are in a place of great suffering. People react to their own thoughts and feelings and their behavior often has nothing directly to do with you.

10 *Sincerity is giving without expectation.*

Good character and true friendship is all about how a person nurtures another person who is vulnerable and can give nothing in return. So when you have been through tough times and come out the other side, look around you. The people still standing beside you are your true friends.

11 *Not every relationship is meant to last forever.*

Some people aren't meant to stay in your life. Some people are just passing through to bring you something – perhaps a lesson you need to learn, or memory that makes you smile years later. When the time comes, it's okay to let go and move on with your life.

20 THINGS to STOP Doing to Others

There is one key factor that can either damage your relationships or deepen them. That factor is your attitude. If you're hoping to grow and maintain positive relationships in your life, read on. Below you will find a 20 step attitude adjustment guaranteed to help you do just that.

1 *Stop holding grudges.*

Grudges are a waste of perfect happiness.

2 *Stop complaining.*

Instead, use your time and energy to do something about it.

3 *Stop meaning what you don't say.*

People can't read minds. Communicate regularly and effectively.

4 *Stop making it all about you.*

The world revolves around the sun, not you. Take a moment to acknowledge this truth on a regular basis.

5 *Stop lying.*

In the long-run the truth always reveals itself. Either you own up to your actions or your actions will ultimately own you.

6 *Stop blaming.*

Blaming others accomplishes nothing. Either you own your problems, or they will own you. Your choice. When you blame others for what you're going through, you deny responsibility – you give-up your power over that part of your life, and you annoy everyone around you in the process.

7 *Stop doubting.*

If you think that you can't achieve something, I have some news for you, you're probably right. But don't let your self-doubt interfere with other people's dreams. Remember, the one who says it can't be done should never interrupt the one doing it.

8 Stop interrupting.

Correcting someone when they're blatantly wrong is one thing, but always interjecting your opinions out of turn gets old fast.

9 Stop being selfish.

You get what you put into a relationship. Nothing less, nothing more.

10 Stop judging.

Everyone is fighting their own unique war. You have no clue what they are going through, just like they have no clue what you're going through.

11 Stop gossiping.

Gossiping about others is a lose/lose situation. It hurts them, and then it hurts your reputation.

12 Stop making promises you can't keep.

Don't over-promise. Over-deliver on everything you do.

13 Stop being defensive.

Just because someone sees something differently than you doesn't mean either one of you is wrong. Keep an open mind. Open minds discover great things.

14 Stop comparing people to others.

No two people are alike. Everyone has their own strengths. We are only competing against our own selves.

15 Stop expecting people to be perfect.

'Perfect' is the enemy of 'good.' And genuine 'goodness' is hard to find in this world. Don't overlook it.

16 Stop trying to be everything to everyone.

It's impossible. But making one person smile can change the world. Maybe not the whole world, but their world. So narrow your focus.

17 Stop screwing people over just because you can get away with it.

Just because you can get away with something doesn't mean you should do it. Think bigger. Do what you know in your heart is right.

18 *Stop making mountains out of molehills.*

People make mistakes. Crap happens.
There's no reason to stress out yourself and
everyone around you because of it. One
way to check if something is worth mulling
over is to ask yourself this question: "Will
this matter in one year's time?" If not, then
it's not worth worrying about.

19 *Stop being dramatic.*

Stay out of other people's drama and don't
needlessly create your own.

20 *Stop giving out advice, and just listen.*

Less advice is often the best advice.
People don't need lots of advice, they
need a listening ear and some positive
reinforcement. What they want to know is
already somewhere inside of them. They
just need time to think, be and breathe,
and continue to explore the undirected
journeys that will eventually help them find
their direction.

And remember, your relationship with
yourself is the closest and most important
relationship you will ever have. So pay
attention to it, develop it, nurture it, and
never, ever stop.

20 THINGS to START Doing in Your *Relationships*

Family isn't always blood. They're the people in your life who appreciate having you in theirs – the ones who encourage you to improve in healthy and exciting ways, and who not only embrace who you are now, but also embrace and embody who you want to be. These people – your real family – are the ones who truly matter.

Here are twenty tips to help you find and foster these special relationships.

1 *Free yourself from negative people.*

Spend time with nice people who are smart, driven and likeminded. Relationships should help you, not hurt you. Surround yourself with people who reflect the person you want to be. Choose friends who you are proud to know, people you admire, who love and respect you – people who make your day a little brighter simply by being in it. Life is too short to spend time with people who suck the happiness out of you. When you free yourself from negative people, you free yourself to be YOU – and being YOU is the only way to truly live.

2 *Let go of those who are already gone.*

The sad truth is that there are some people who will only be there for you as long as you have something they need. When you no longer serve a purpose to them, they will leave. The good news is, if you tough it out, you'll eventually weed these people out of your life and be left with some great people you can count on. We rarely lose friends and lovers, we just gradually figure out who our real ones are. So when people walk away from you, let them go. Your destiny is never tied to anyone who leaves you. It doesn't mean they are bad people; it just means that their part in your story is over.

3 Give people you don't know a fair chance.

When you look at a person, any person, remember that everyone has a story. Everyone has gone through something that has changed them, and forced them to grow. Every passing face on the street represents a story every bit as compelling and complicated as yours. We meet no ordinary people in our lives. If you give them a chance, everyone has something amazing to offer. So appreciate the possibility of new relationships as you naturally let go of old ones that no longer work. Trust your judgment. Embrace new relationships, knowing that you are entering into unfamiliar territory. Be ready to learn, be ready for a challenge, and be ready to meet someone that might just change your life forever.

4 Show everyone kindness and respect.

Treat everyone with kindness and respect, even those who are rude to you – not because they are nice, but because you are. There are no boundaries or classes that define a group of people that deserve to be respected. Treat everyone with the same level of respect you would give to your grandfather and the same level of patience you would have with your baby brother. People will notice your kindness.

5 Accept people just the way they are.

In most cases it's impossible to change them anyway, and it's rude to try. So save yourself from needless stress. Instead of trying to change others, give them your support and lead by example.

6 Encourage others and cheer far them.

Having an appreciation for how amazing the people around you are leads to good places – productive, fulfilling, peaceful places. So be happy for those who are making progress. Cheer for their victories. Be thankful for their blessings, openly. What goes around comes around, and sooner or later the people you're cheering for will start cheering for you.

7 Be your imperfectly perfect self.

In this crazy world that's trying to make you like everyone else, find the courage to keep being your awesome self. And when they laugh at you for being different, laugh back at them for being the same. Spend more time with those who make you smile and less time with those who you feel pressured to impress. Be your imperfectly perfect self around them. We are not perfect for everyone, we are only perfect for those select few people that really take the time to get to know us and love us for who we really are. And to those select few, being our imperfectly perfect self is what they love about us.

8 Forgive people and move forward.

Don't live your life with hate in your heart. You will end up hurting yourself more than the people you hate. Forgiveness is not saying, "What you did to me is okay." It is saying, "I'm not going to let what you did to me ruin my happiness forever." Forgiveness is the remedy. It doesn't mean you're erasing the past, or forgetting what happened. It means you're letting go of the resentment and pain, and instead choosing to learn from the incident and move on with your life. Remember, the less time you spend hating the people who hurt you, the more time you'll have to love the people who love you.

9 Do little things every day for others.

Sometimes those little things occupy the biggest part of their hearts. You can't be everything to everyone, but you can be everything to a select few. Decide who these people are in your life and treat them like royalty.

10 Pay attention to who your real friends are.

There are fake people, and then there are those who are real friends. There are people who take the heart out of you, and those who put it back. You have a choice of who to spend time with. Stick with the people who never let you down and keep their promises; you can't fake that. Real friends have an honest heart, and will go out of their way to help you when you need it most. Real friends are the ones who know you as you are, understand where you have been, accept who you have become, and still encourage you to grow.

11 Always be loyal.

True love and real friendship aren't about being inseparable. These relationships are about two people being true to each other even when they are separated. When it comes to relationships, remaining faithful is never an option, but a priority. Loyalty is everything.

12 Stay in better touch with people who matter to you.

In human relationships distance is not measured in miles, but in affection. Two people can be right next to each other, yet miles apart. So don't ignore someone you care about, because lack of concern hurts more than angry words. Stay in touch with those who matter to you. Not because it's convenient, but because they're worth the extra effort. Remember, you don't need a certain number of friends, just a number of friends you can be certain of. Paying attention to these people is a priority.

13 *Keep your promises and tell the truth.*

If you say you're going to do something, DO IT! If you say you're going to be somewhere, BE THERE! If you say you feel something, MEAN IT! If you can't, won't, and don't, then DON'T LIE. It's always better to tell people the truth up front. Don't play games with people's heads and hearts. Don't tell half-truths and expect people to trust you when the full truth comes out; half-truths are no better than lies. Remember, love and friendship don't hurt. Lying, cheating and screwing with people's feelings and emotions hurts. Never mess with someone's feelings just because you're unsure of yours. Always be open and honest.

14 *Give what you want to receive.*

Don't expect what you are not willing to give. Start practicing the golden rule. If you want love, give love. If you want friends, be friendly. If you want money, provide value. It works. It really is this simple.

15 *Say what you mean and mean what you say.*

Give the people in your life the information they need, rather than expecting them to know the unknowable. Information is the grease that keeps the engine of communication functioning. Start communicating clearly. Don't try to read other people's minds, and don't make other people try to read yours. Most problems, big and small, within a family, friendship, or business relationship, start with bad communication.

16 *Allow others to make their own decisions.*

Do not judge others by your own past. They are living a different life than you are. What might be good for one person may not be good for another. What might be bad for one person might change another person's life for the better. Allow people to make their own mistakes and their own decisions.

17 *Talk a little less, and listen more.*

Less advice is often the best advice. People don't need lots of advice, they need a listening ear and some positive reinforcement. What they want to know is often already somewhere inside of them. They just need time to think, be and breathe, and continue to explore the undirected journeys that will eventually help them find their direction.

18 *Leave petty arguments alone.*

Someone else doesn't have to be wrong for you to be right. There are many roads to what's right. And most of the time it just doesn't matter that much.

9 *Ignore unconstructive, hurtful commentary.*

No one has the right to judge you. They might have heard your stories, but they didn't feel what you were going through. No matter what you do, there will always be someone who thinks differently. So concentrate on doing what you know in your heart is right. What most people think and say about you isn't all that important. What is important is how you feel about yourself.

20 *Pay attention to your relationship with yourself.*

One of the most painful things in life is losing yourself in the process of loving others too much, and forgetting that you are special too. When was the last time someone told you that they loved you just the way you are, and that what you think and how you feel matters? When was the last time someone told you that you did a good job, or took you someplace, simply because they know you feel happy when you're there? When was the last time that 'someone' was YOU?

15 THINGS REAL Friends Do *Differently*

As we mature, we realize it becomes less important to have more friends and more important to have real ones.

Remember, life is kind of like a party. You invite a lot of people, some leave early, some stay all night, some laugh with you, some laugh at you, and some show up really late. But in the end, after the fun, there are a few who stay to help you clean up the mess. And most of the time, they aren't even the ones who made the mess. These people are your real friends in life. They are the ones who matter most.

Here are 15 things real friends do differently:

1 *They face problems together.*

A person who truly knows and loves you – a real friend – is someone who sees the pain in your eyes while everyone else still believes the smile on your face. Don't look for someone who will solve all your problems; look for someone who will face them with you.

2 *They give what they can because they truly care.*

One of the biggest challenges in relationships comes from the fact that many of us enter a relationship in order to get something. We try to find someone who's going to make us feel good. In reality, the only way a relationship will last, and give us joy in the long-term, is if we see our relationship as a place we go to give, and not just a place we go to take. Yes, of course it is okay to take something from a relationship too. But both sides should be giving. It can only be a 'give and take' if BOTH SIDES are GIVING. That's the key.

They make time for each other.

It's obvious, but any relationship without any face time is going to have problems. You shouldn't have to fight for a spot in someone's life. Never force someone to make a space in their life for you, because if they truly care about you, they will create one for you.

They offer each other freedom.

A healthy relationship keeps the doors and windows wide open. Plenty of air is circulating and no one feels trapped. Relationships thrive in this environment. Keep your doors and windows open. If this person is meant to be in your life, all the open doors and windows in the world won't make them leave.

They communicate effectively.

It's been said many times before, but it's true: great communication is the cornerstone of a great relationship. If you have resentment, you must talk it out rather than let the resentment grow. If you

are jealous, you must communicate in an open and honest manner to address your insecurities. If you have expectations of your partner, you must communicate them. If there are any problems whatsoever, you must communicate them and work them out. And communicate more than just problems – communicate the good things too.

6 They accept each other as is.

Trying to change a person never works. People know when they are not accepted in their entirety, and it hurts. A real friend is someone who truly knows you, and loves you just the same. Don't change so people will like you. Be yourself and the right people will love the real you. If you feel like changing something about your friend, ask yourself what change you can make in yourself instead.

7 They are genuine, and expect genuineness.

As Leo F. Buscaglia once said, "Never idealize others. They will never live up to your expectations. Don't over-analyze your relationships. Stop playing games. A growing relationship can only be nurtured by genuineness." Don't play games with people's heads and hearts. Remember, love and friendship don't hurt. Lying, cheating and screwing with people's feelings and emotions hurts. Always be open, honest, and genuine.

8 *They compromise.*

Real friends meet in the middle. When there's a disagreement, they work out a solution that works for both parties – a compromise, rather than a need for the other person to change or completely give in.

9 *They support each other's growth changes.*

Our needs change with time. When someone says, "You've changed," it's not always a bad thing. Sometimes it just means you grown. Don't apologize for it. Instead, be open and sincere, explain how you feel, and keep doing what you know in your heart is right.

10 *They believe in each other.*

Simply believing in another person, and showing it in your words and deeds, can make a huge difference in their life. Studies of people who grew up in dysfunctional homes but who grew up to

be happy and successful show that the one thing they had in common was someone who believed in them. Do this for those you care about. Support their dreams and passions and hobbies. Participate with them. Cheer for them. Be nothing but encouraging. Whether they actually accomplish these dreams or not, your belief is of infinite importance to them.

11 *They maintain realistic expectations of their relationship.*

No one is happy all the time. Friends must keep realistic expectations of each other. Notice when you're projecting something onto the other person that has nothing to do with them, like a fear from a past relationship, and then make an effort to let it go. Recognize when you're looking for that person to do something for you that you need to do for yourself, like making you feel lovable or take care of your needs, and then release those expectations and do it for yourself.

12 *They honor each other in small ways on a regular basis.*

Honor your important relationships in some way every chance you get. Every day you have the opportunity to make your relationship sweeter and deeper by making small gestures to show your appreciation and affection. Remember, making one person smile can change the world. Maybe not the whole world, but their world. Your kindness and gratitude matters. Make an effort to really listen – not just wait to talk. See the other person as if for the first time. It's all too easy to take someone for granted. Really notice all the wonderful things they do, and let them know what you see.

13 *They listen, and they hear every word.*

Giving a person a voice, and showing them that their words matter, will have a long-lasting impact on them. Less advice is often the best advice. People don't need lots of advice, they need a listening ear and some positive reinforcement. What they want to know is often already somewhere inside of them. They just need time to think, be and breathe, and continue to explore the undirected journeys that will eventually help them find their direction.

14 *They keep their promises.*

Your word means everything. If you say you're going to do something, DO IT! If you say you're going to be somewhere, BE THERE! If you say you feel something, MEAN IT! If you can't, won't, and don't, then DON'T LIE. Real friends keep promises and tell the truth upfront.

15 *They stick around.*

The sad truth is that there are some people who will only be there for you as long as you have something they need. When you no longer serve a purpose to them, they will leave. The good news is, if you tough it out, you'll eventually weed these people out of your life and be left with some great people you can count on. We rarely lose friends and lovers, we just gradually figure out who our real ones are.

WHAT WE HAVE BEEN
SEARCHING FOR **ALL** ALONG

Far From Perfect

About a year ago on his 30th birthday, after spending his entire adult life loosely dating different women, he suddenly decided he was ready to settle down. He wanted to find a real mate... a lover... a life partner – someone who could show him what it meant to be in a deep, monogamous, trusting relationship.

So he searched far and wide. There were so many women to choose from, all with great qualities, but none with everything he was looking for. And then, finally, just when he thought that he would never find her, he found her. And she was perfect. She had everything he ever wanted in a woman. And he rejoiced, for he knew how rare a find she was. "I've done my research," he told her. "You are the one for me."

But as the days and weeks turned into months and years, he started to realize that she was far from perfect. She had issues with trust and self-confidence, she liked to be silly when he wanted to be serious, and she was much messier than he was. So he started to have doubts – doubts about her, doubts about himself, doubts about everything.

And to validate these doubts, he subconsciously tested her. He constantly looked around the apartment for things that weren't clean just to prove that she was messy. He decided to go out alone to parties with his single guy friends just to prove that she had trust issues. He set her up and waited for her to do something silly just to prove that she couldn't be serious. It went on like this for awhile.

As the tests continued – and as she, clearly shaken and confused, failed more and more often – he became more and more convinced that she was not a perfect fit for him after all. Because he had dated women in the past who were more mature, more confident, and more willing to have serious conversations.

Inevitably, he found himself at a crossroads. Should he continue to be in a relationship with a woman who he once thought was perfect, but now realizes is lacking the qualities that he already found in the other women that came before her? Or should he return to the lifestyle he had come from, drifting from one empty relationship to the next?

Every Light Casts A Shadow

When he showed up at my door this evening looking for answers, this is what I told him:

One of the greatest lessons we get to learn in life is that we are often attracted to a bright light in another person. Initially, this light is all we see. It's so bright and beautiful. But after awhile, as our eyes adjust, we notice that this light is accompanied by a shadow – and usually a fairly large one.

When we see this shadow, we have two choices: We can either shine our own light on the shadow or we can run from it and continue searching for a shadowless light.

If we decide to run from the shadow, we must also run from the light that created it. And we soon find out that our light is the only light illuminating the space around us. Then, at some point, as we look closer at our own light, we notice something out of the ordinary. Our light is casting a shadow too. And our shadow is a bigger and darker than some of the other shadows we've seen.

If, on the other hand, instead of running from the shadow, we decide to walk towards it, something amazing happens. We inadvertently cast our own light on the shadow, and likewise, the light that created this shadow casts its light on ours. Suddenly, both shadows begin to disappear. Not completely, of course, but every part of the two shadows that are touched by the other person's light illuminate and disappear.

And as a result, we each find more of that bright beautiful light in the other person – which is precisely what we have been searching for all along.

12 Relationship TRUTHS We Often *Forget*

It's easy to make your relationships more complicated than they are. Here are twelve simple reminders to help you keep them on course.

1 *All successful relationships require some work.*

They don't just happen, or maintain themselves. They exist and thrive when the parties involved take the risk of sharing what it is that's going on in their minds and hearts. Open communication and honesty is the key.

2 *Most of the time you get what you put in.*

If you want love, give love. If you want friends, be friendly. If you'd like to feel understood, try being more understanding. It's a simple practice that works.

3 *You shouldn't have to fight for a spot in someone's life.*

Never force someone to make a space in their life for you, because if they know your worth, they will create one for you.

4 *There is a purpose for everyone you meet.*

Some people will test you, some will use you, and some will teach you; but most importantly some will bring out the best in you. Learn to see and accept the differences between these people, and carry on accordingly.

5 *We all change, and that's okay.*

Our needs change with time. When someone says, "You've changed," it's not always a bad thing. Sometimes it just means you stopped living your life their way. Don't apologize for it. Instead, be open and sincere, explain how you feel, and keep doing what you know in your heart is right.

6 *You are in full control of your own happiness.*

If your relationship with yourself isn't working, don't expect your other relationships to be any different. Nobody else in this world can make you happy. It's something you have to do on your own. And you have to create your own happiness first before you can share it with someone else. If you feel that it's your partner's fault, think again, and look within yourself to find out what piece is missing. Your partner can never 'complete' you because you are already whole. The longing for completion that you feel inside comes from being out of touch with who you are.

7 *Forgiving others helps YOU.*

Forgiveness is not saying, "What you did to me is okay." It is saying, "I'm not going to let what you did to me ruin my happiness forever." Forgiveness is the answer. It doesn't mean you're erasing the past, or forgetting what happened. It means you're letting go of the resentment and pain, and instead choosing to learn from the incident and move on with your life.

8 *You can't change people; they can only change themselves.*

Instead of trying to change others, give them your support and lead by example. If there's a specific behavior someone you love has that you're hoping disappears over time, it probably won't. If you really need them to change something, be honest and put all the cards on the table so this person knows what you need them to do.

9 *Heated arguments are a waste of time.*

The less time you spend arguing with the people who hurt you, the more time you'll have to love the people who love you. And if you happen to find yourself arguing with someone you love, don't let your anger get the best of you. Give yourself some time to calm down and then gently discuss the situation.

10 You are better off without some people.

When you have to start compromising yourself and your morals for the people around you, it's probably time to change the people around you. If someone continuously mistreats you or pushes you in the wrong direction, have enough respect for yourself to walk away from them. It may hurt for a little while, but it'll be ok. You'll be ok, and far better off in the long run.

11 Small gestures of kindness go a long way.

Honor your important relationships in some way every chance you get. Every day you have the opportunity to make your relationship sweeter and deeper by making small gestures to show your appreciation and affection. Remember, making one person smile can change the world. Maybe not the whole world, but their world. Your kindness and gratitude matters.

12 Even the best relationships don't last forever.

People don't live forever. Appreciate what you have, who loves you and who cares for you. You'll never know how much they mean to you until the day they are no longer beside you. And remember, just because something doesn't last forever, doesn't mean it wasn't worth your while.

15 Relationship TRUTHS for *Tough times*

These 15 relationship truths may be a bit difficult to accept at times, but in the end, they will help you weed out the wrong relationships, make room for the right ones, and nurture the people who are most important to you.

1 ***Some relationships will be blessings, others will serve as lessons.***

Either way, never regret knowing someone. Everyone you encounter teaches you something important. Some people will test you, some will use you, and some will teach you; but most importantly some will bring out the best in you.

2 ***When times get tough, some people will leave you.***

When you are up in life, your friends get to know who you are. When you are down in life, you get to know who your true friends are. There will be lots of people around when times are easy, but take note of who remains in your life when times get tough, especially the people who sacrifice the resources they have in their life to help you improve yours when you need it most. These people are your real friends.

3 ***Life is full of fake people.***

Sometimes the person you'd take a bullet for ends up being the one behind the gun. It's so easy to believe someone when they TELL you exactly what you want to hear. But when a person SHOWS you who they really are, believe them the first time. Some people are only nice for their own convenience – the type of people who only call when they need something or come around when it's beneficial to them. Not everyone has your best interests at heart. But sometimes you have to be tricked and mislead by the wrong lovers and friends once or twice in your life in order to find and appreciate your soul mate and real friends when they arrive.

4 People can easily be insincere with their words.

When someone truly loves you, they don't have to say a word. You will be able to tell simply by the way they treat you over the long-term. Remember, actions speak much louder than words. A person can say sorry a thousand times, and say "I love you" as much as they want. But if they're not going to prove that the things they say are true, then they're not worth listening to. Because if they can't show it, their words are not sincere.

5 The less you associate with some people, the more your life will improve.

Don't settle to just be someone's downtime, spare time, part time, or sometime. If they can't be there for you all of the time, especially when you need them most, then they're not worth your time.

6 Harsh words can hurt a person more than physical pain.

Taste your own words before you spit them out. Words hurt and scar more than you think, so THINK before you speak. And remember, what you say about others also says a whole lot about YOU.

7 A mistake is an accident. Cheating and lying are not mistakes.

They are intentional choices. Stop hiding behind the words "mistake" and "sorry" and stop putting up with those who do.

8 Excessive jealousy doesn't tell someone how much you love them.

It tells them how much you dislike yourself. And no amount of love, or promises, or proof from them will ever be enough to make you feel better. For those broken pieces you carry, are pieces you must mend for yourself. Happiness is an inside job.

9 When people get nasty with you, it's usually best to walk away.

When someone treats you like dirt, don't pay attention and don't take it personally. They're saying nothing about you and a lot about themselves. And no matter what they do or say, never drop down to their level and sling dirt back. Just know you're better than that and walk away.

10 People will treat you the way you let them treat you.

You can't control them, but you can control what you tolerate. Beautiful things happen when you distance yourself from negative people. Doing so does not mean you hate them, it simply means you respect yourself.

11 One of the most difficult tasks in life is removing someone from your heart.

But remember, no relationship is a waste of time. The wrong ones teach you the lessons that prepare you for the right ones.

12 Resentment hurts you, not them.

Whisper a small prayer of gratitude for the people who have stuck by your side, and send a prayer of good will for those who didn't. For should these people hear your prayers, those who have been there will know how much you appreciate them, and those who left will know that you appreciate your own happiness enough to not let resentment destroy your capacity to live with a compassionate heart.

13 Silence and a half smile can hide a lot of pain from the world.

Pay close attention to those you care about. Sometimes when a friend says, "I'm okay," they need you to look them in the eyes, hug them tight, and reply, "I know you're not."

14 True love comes when manipulation stops.

True love comes when you care more about who the other person really is than about who you think they should become, when you dare to reveal yourself honestly, and when you dare to be open and vulnerable. It takes two to create a sincere environment where this is possible. If you haven't found true love yet, don't settle. There is someone out there who will share true love with you, even if it's not the person you were initially hoping for.

15 Even the best relationships don't last forever.

Nobody gets through life without losing someone they love, someone they need, or something they thought was meant to be. People don't live forever. Appreciate what you have, who loves you and who cares for you. You'll never know how much they mean to you until the day they are no longer beside you. And remember, just because something doesn't last forever, doesn't mean it wasn't worth your while.

10 it's **TIME** to *Let Go*
SIGNS

Holding on is being brave, but letting go and moving on is often what makes us stronger and happier.

Here are ten signs it's time to let go:

1 *Someone expects you to be someone you're not.*

Don't change who you are for anyone else. It's wiser to lose someone over being who you are, than to keep them by being someone you're not. Because it's easier to mend a broken heart, than it is to piece together a shattered identity. It's easier to fill an empty space in your life where someone else used to be, than it is to fill the empty space inside yourself where YOU used to be.

2 *A person's actions don't match their words.*

Everybody deserves somebody who helps them look forward to tomorrow. If someone has the opposite effect on you, because they are consistently inconsistent

and their actions don't match up with their words, it's time to let them go. It's always better to be alone than to be in bad company. True friendship is a promise made in the heart – silent, unwritten, unbreakable by distance, and unchangeable by time. Don't listen to what people say; watch what they do. Your true friends will slowly reveal themselves over time.

3 *You catch yourself forcing someone to love you.*

Let us keep in mind that we can't force anyone to love us. We shouldn't beg someone to stay when they want to leave. That's what love is all about – freedom. However, the end of love is not the end of life. It should be the beginning of an understanding that love sometimes leaves for a reason, but never leaves without a lesson. If someone truly loves you, they will never give you a reason to doubt it. Anyone can come into your life and say how much they love you, but it takes someone really special to stay in your life and prove how much they love you. Sometimes it takes awhile to find the right person, but the right person is always worth the wait.

4 An intimate relationship is based strictly on physical attraction.

Being beautiful is more than how many people you can get to look at you, or how others perceive you at a single glance. It's about what you live for. It's about what defines you. It's about the depth of your heart, and what makes you unique. It's about being who you are and living out your life honestly. It's about those little quirks that make you, you. People who are only attracted to you because of your pretty face or nice body won't stay by your side forever. But the people who can see how beautiful your heart is will never leave you.

5 Someone continuously breaks your trust.

Love means giving someone the chance to hurt you, but trusting them not to. When you completely trust a person, without any doubt, you'll automatically get one of two results - a FRIEND for life or a LESSON for

life. Either way there's a positive outcome. Either you confirm the fact that this person cares about you, or you get the opportunity to weed them out of your life and make room for those who do. In the end you'll discover who's fake, who's true, and who would risk it all for you. And trust me, some people will totally surprise you.

6 Someone continuously overlooks your worth.

Know your worth! When you give yourself to someone who doesn't respect you, you surrender pieces of your soul that you'll never get back. There comes a point when you have to let go and stop chasing some people. If someone wants you in their life, they'll find a way to put you there. Sometimes you just need to let go and accept the fact that they don't care for you the way you care for them. Let them leave your life quietly. Letting go is oftentimes easier than holding on. We think it's too hard to let go, until we actually do. Then we ask ourselves, "Why didn't I do this sooner?"

7 You are never given a chance to speak your mind.

Sometimes an argument saves a relationship, whereas silence breaks it. Speak up for your heart so that you won't have regrets. Life is not about making others happy. Life is about being honest and sharing your happiness with others.

8 | You are frequently forced to sacrifice your happiness.

If you allow people to make more withdrawals than deposits in your life, you will be out of balance and in the negative before you know it. Know when to close the account. It's always better to be alone with dignity than in a relationship that constantly requires you to sacrifice your happiness and self-respect.

9 | You truly dislike your current situation, routine, job, etc.

It's better to be a failure at something you love than to succeed at doing something you hate. Don't let someone who gave up on their dreams talk you out of going after yours. The best thing you can do in life is follow your heart. Take risks. Don't just make the safe and easy choices because you're afraid of what might happen. If you do, nothing will ever happen. Chances must be taken, mistakes must be made, and lessons must be learned. It might be an uphill climb, but when you reach that mountaintop it will be worth every ounce of blood, sweat and tears you put into it.

10 | You catch yourself obsessing over, and living in, the past.

Eventually you will overcome the heartache, and forget the reasons you cried, and who caused the pain. Eventually you will realize that the secret to happiness and freedom is not about control or revenge, but in letting things unfold naturally, and learning from your experiences over the course of time. After all, what matters most is not the first, but the final chapter of your life, which unveils the details of how well you wrote your story. So let go of the past, set yourself free, and open your mind to the possibility of new relationships and priceless experiences.

And the one thing you should never let go of is hope. Remember what you deserve and keep pushing forward. Someday all the pieces will come together. Unimaginably good things will transpire in your life, even if everything doesn't turn out exactly the way you had anticipated. And you will look back at the times that have passed, smile, and ask yourself, "How did I get through all of that?"

12 Relationship TRUTHS I wish I Knew 12 Years Ago

Twelve years ago I was eighteen and just entering college. Since then, friends and acquaintances have come and gone, girlfriends have come and gone, and I met the love of my life, Angel. I've found through my years – through my experience with my own personal relationships – that there are certain undeniable truths that affect the quality and longevity of our relationships, and the resulting impact they have on us. I share them with you today in hopes that they save you from a little heartache and confusion.

1 You have to love yourself first.

In order to truly have a loving, supportive, and long-lasting relationship with someone else, you need to learn how to be your own best friend first. It's all about falling in love with yourself and sharing that love with someone who appreciates you, rather than looking for love to compensate for a self love deficit.

2 You get what you put in.

In twelve years, people won't remember what clothes you wore, which car you drove, and maybe not even your full name. But in twelve years, they will remember how you made them feel and the positive memories you gave them. The true impact you make on people will depend on the time and attention you give to teaching those who know less, caring for those who have less, supporting those who are striving, and tolerating those who are different than you.

3 What people think of you doesn't matter.

You wouldn't worry so much about what people thought of you if you knew just how seldom they do. No one is ever going to care about your life and the way you choose to live it more than you will. That is a beautiful thing – never forget how beautiful. Follow your heart, and take your brain with you every step of the way. Get to know your true self. When you are truly comfortable in your own skin, not everyone will like you, but you won't care about it one bit.

4 Friends and family won't always support your goals, but you must pursue them anyway.

Follow your intuition. Following your intuition means doing what feels right, even if it doesn't look or sound right to others. Only time will tell, but our human instincts are rarely ever wrong. So don't worry about what everyone else thinks; keep living and speaking your truth. The only people that will get mad at you for doing so are those who want you to live a lie.

5 Life doesn't always change as fast as people do.

Learn to accept that not everyone is who you once knew. And realize that sometimes it's not the person you miss, it's the feeling you had when you were with them.

6 Some people are meant to stay in your heart, but not in your life.

If you're having a tough time letting go of someone who left you, realize that if they wanted to stay they would still be there. Sometimes you have to forget what's gone, appreciate what still remains, and look forward to what's coming next. It sucks when you know that you need to let go, but you can't because you're still hoping for the impossible to happen. Yes, it will hurt for awhile, but you have to forget about the person who forgot about you, and move on.

7 Everyone has baggage, just like you.

The minute someone decides to walk out of your life, that is the same moment in which the opportunity and space opens up for someone who actually deserves your love to finally walk in. Remember, everyone has baggage, so don't be ashamed of yours. Be patient and find someone who loves you enough to help you unpack.

8 Love doesn't hurt.

Don't blame love if a failed relationship interfered with your other important relationships, or robbed you of your self-esteem and personal freedoms. No, don't blame love. For it wasn't love that stole from you. It was possession. It was obsession. It was manipulation. It was confusion. Love had nothing to do with your situation. For love doesn't close the door against all that is good. It opens it wide to let more goodness in. Love creates freedom and abundance.

9 Forgiveness is always the right choice.

Anyone can hold a grudge, but it takes a person with strong character to forgive. When you forgive, you release yourself from a painful burden. And no, forgiveness doesn't mean what happened was OK; and it doesn't mean that person should still be welcome in your life. It simply means you have made peace with the pain, and are ready to let it go and move on with your life.

10   *Love requires three things: acceptance, honesty, and commitment.*

Love comes when you care more about who the other person really is, rather than about who you think they should become. It's about daring to reveal yourself honestly, and daring to be open and vulnerable over the long-term. It's about sticking by each other's side through thick and thin, and truly being there in the flesh and spirit when you're needed most. Remember, the most romantic love story is not Romeo and Juliet who died young together; it's the story of grandma and grandpa who helped each other through life, and grew old together.

11   *A big part of who you become is who you choose to surround yourself with.*

Fate controls who walks into your life, but you decide who you let walk out, who you let stay, and who you refuse to let go. Surround yourself with people who make

you a better person, and let go of those who don't.

12   *A soul mate is a person who brings out the best in you.*

They are far from perfect, but they are a perfect fit for you. Remember, every relationship has its problems, but what makes it perfect is when you wouldn't want to be anywhere else, even when times are tough.

THE **UNWRITTEN LOVE** POEM

Almost ten years ago, I wrote an unsigned love poem to a girl I hardly knew. I told Brianna, among other things, that life was a blaze of magnificence, that she made it even brighter, and that someday I would spend everyday with the prettiest girl in the world.

When she read the poem she got goose bumps, smiled from ear to ear, and daydreamed about the gentleman behind the poetic prose. She showed it to her sister who sighed and said, "How romantic... I wish someone would write me a poem like that." Then she showed it to her parents. Her mom smirked, but her dad frowned and said, "Don't waste your thoughts on a foolish boy hiding behind a silly poem." Finally, she let her new boyfriend read it. In a grim voice he said, "Let me know when you find out who wrote it, because I'd like to give him a piece of my mind!"

Despite reactions ranging from enthusiasm to aggravation, she kept the poem and still has it in her possession today... nearly ten years later. Her younger brother, Jose, recently found it neatly folded and tucked between two pages of a photo album she keeps in her den.

I know all this because Jose told me. He and I met in school ten years ago and we have been best friends ever since. He was, frankly, the reason I wrote the poem.

A Second Glance

"Your sister is pretty," I told Jose during my first visit to his home.

"Forget about it," he said. "Brianna has buff guys fighting for her affection everyday. You couldn't hold her attention long enough to get a second glance."

"I could if I wrote her a poem," I replied.

"She has guys writing her romantic crap all the time," he said. "She'll just toss it out with all the other failed attempts."

"Not mine," I insisted.

"You're crazy," he chuckled. "Go ahead and try. Make me laugh!"

I wrote the poem that evening and mailed it anonymously the next morning.

I Thought I Was Special

The poem I wrote Brianna wasn't genuine, at least not in my mind. I wrote it because Jose doubted me. Sure, I thought Brianna was pretty, but I didn't want to settle down with her. At the time, I didn't even know her. And as it turns out, she and I have almost nothing in common.

The last genuine love poem I wrote went to a girl I met a month before I met Brianna. She was on the varsity soccer team, and her beauty was majestic. I wrote Sara a poem and slipped it into her locker the same afternoon. I confessed my desire to be a soccer ball, and risk being kicked around, if it was the only way I could catch her attention. She caught up with me the next morning and told me I didn't need to transform into a soccer ball to catch her attention. I asked her out on a date a few minutes later.

Our first date went well. But the next afternoon Sara spoke to a few of her teammates, two of which I had previously dated. She was appalled when she found out that I had written Jackie a poem about innocent kisses blown her way in

the breeze, and Carol a poem about the lucky sunshine that glistens off her skin. Needless to say, a second date was not in our future.

"Stupid me... When I read the poem I actually believed you were being sincere! I thought I was special," Sara screamed!

"I was... and you are," I mumbled as she walked away.

But Sara had a point. Although I had never summoned the desire to be a soccer ball in any of my previous poems, I did use similar analogies that carried the same fundamental connotations of flirtatious affection.

I wasn't trying to hurt her. I thought she was gorgeous. I thought she carried herself with amazing grace. I wanted to be around her. I wanted to be hers. She was the most perfect girl in the entire world... and I felt this way a hundred times before.

No Two Words Would Rhyme

Roughly six months after I met Brianna, I met Angel. I realized shortly thereafter that she moved me in a way the others had not. I couldn't consciously pinpoint it, but I knew our relationship felt special. Even after the initial excitement fatigued, she kept me captivated in awe. I was wide awake in the second inning for the first time in my life.

Angel and I have been together for nine years now and I appreciate her more and more with each passing day. Yet despite my love for her, she's never received a love poem.

It's not that I haven't tried. I tried, once, to write her a poem about the depth and beauty of her hazel-green eyes. I stumbled over my words. Another time I tried to write her a poem about the mornings I wake up early just to watch her sleep. I failed again. And just last month I tried to write her a poem entitled "Amidst an Angel." But no two words would rhyme.

Nine years and not a single love poem written. Of course, Angel knows I love to write, so she has periodically questioned my motives for never writing her a romantic piece.

Yesterday afternoon I found myself trying again. I tried to poetically recreate the story of our first encounter. I wanted to make it cute. I wanted to make her smile. I wanted to make her cry. I wanted to typify our tale in exquisite prose. Nothing came.

The Most Profound Affirmation

I fell asleep last night thinking about my predicament. Have I lost my touch? Has someone cast an evil spell on me? Or is there a more profound, philosophical explanation?

Zzzz…

I dreamt I was sitting at round table in a dimly lit room. There was a man sitting across the table from me. He looked a lot like me, only his hair was peppered with silver and his skin was worn.

"I'm here to answer your question," he said.

"What question?" I asked.

"The one you've been asking yourself for years," he replied.

"What's wrong with me?" I huffed. "Why can't I write Angel a love poem?"

"Perhaps you can't write her a love poem because you realize, subconsciously, that leaving it unwritten is the most profound affirmation of love you can make. Because you truly do love her, and true love cannot be translated into words. Because words alone could never do her any justice."

I nodded in agreement.

He went on: "The sad truth, of course, is that this affirmation of love will always remain unnoticed. Because there is no visible output to notice… no poem to read."

My eyes popped open.

Inspired to Write

It was 4AM, but I was wide awake and inspired to write about the epiphany I had in my dreams. I leaned over, kissed

Angel on the forehead, and rolled out of
bed. I powered on my laptop and opened
the word processor I use for blogging.
After gazing at the blank white screen
for several minutes, I placed my fingers
on the keyboard and titled the page "The
Unwritten Love Poem."

A silhouette of a human being stands before you.

Perhaps a friend. Perhaps a lover. Perhaps a perfect stranger.

They need you to connect with them. They need you to share this moment.

They need you to be you – just the way you are.

And they need you to respect them – just the way they are.

Relationship QUESTIONS to Make You *think*

Have you been the **KIND** of friend you want as a *friend*?

Have you ever been with someone, said nothing, and walked away feeling like you just had the **BEST** *conversation* ever?

Which is **WORSE**, when a *good* friend moves away, or losing touch with a *good* friend who lives right near you?

Who do you **LOVE?** What are you *doing* about it?

What can you do **TODAY** to become a *person* others want to be around?

Is it **POSSIBLE** to *lie* without saying a word?

What are the top three **QUALITIES** you look for in a *friend*?

Would you break the law to **SAVE** a *loved* one?

What are you known for by your **FRIENDS** and *family*?

If you knew that everyone you know was going to die tomorrow, **WHO** would you *visit* today?

Part Four
Self Love

Never forget,
YOU deserve YOUR love
and affection just as much,
if not more, than anyone
else in the universe.

I AM MY OWN
WORST ENEMY

A petite, light-skinned Jamaican woman sits with her husband in a crowded beachside ice cream shop in San Diego. Although she doesn't speak loudly or occupy much space in the room, people notice her.

Her hair is long, flowing and black like a windy night. Her lips are soft and red like rose petals. Her curves are subtle, yet they dip and bend in all the right places. Her skin is smooth, brown, maple cream. And her clothes are modest, accentuating everything, while exposing nothing at all.

She knows why they're looking at her. "It's because I'm not white," she says. "It's because we're an interracial couple and they don't understand why you're with me."

Her husband groans and closes his eyes. There's nothing he can say. They've already had this conversation a hundred times before. He threads his fingers through his hair in frustration and watches as his chocolate ice cream begins to melt.

Three tables over, two white college kids eat their ice cream cones and check out 'the scene.' As usual, they're not impressed. The women around here are too old, too fat, too ugly, or..., "Wow, look at her," the pimple-faced one says as he nods his head towards the Jamaican woman.

The prematurely balding one turns around to look. "Oh yeah, she must be a model," he replies. "She's way out of our league, bro..."

"I don't think I should have to explain why this is so painful for me," the Jamaican woman continues. "The media portrays white, blonde females as the essence of beauty and perfection. My color is simply a genetic defect."

A chubby white girl, about ten years old, naively stares at the Jamaican woman while sipping a root beer float. Small tears stream down her face. "Daddy, why can't I be as pretty as her?" she asks her father.

"It doesn't matter if you're physically faithful to me," the Jamaican woman says to her husband. "Because with all these influences surrounding you, you're probably internalizing your deep desires for a genetically endowed female companion. And it kills me! Don't you understand?"

"Please honey... Are you ready to go home?" her husband replies softly. She hasn't taken a single bite of her brownie sundae and all of the ice cream has already melted. She sighs and stands up, weakly.

Three well-dressed white women in their late twenties talk cheerfully and sip Diet Cokes at a table near the door. They were all childhood friends at a local orphanage. When they were eventually placed in different foster homes, they lost contact with each other. This special reunion is their first time together in almost fifteen years.

"Did you see those three women by the door?" the Jamaican woman asks her husband as they walk to their car. "Wealthy white women like that don't even appreciate how easy their life has been."

12 LIES To Stop *Telling* Yourself

The worst lies are the ones we subconsciously tell ourselves. They've been ingrained in our minds by bad external influences and negative thinking. So the next time you decide to unclutter your life and clean up your space, start with your intellectual space by clearing out the old lies and negative self-talk you often recite to yourself.

Here are twelve such lies to stop telling yourself:

1 *I don't have enough yet to be happy.*

In every mistake and struggle there is a message. Some people miss the message because they're too busy berating themselves for the mistake, or fretting over the problem. To be upset about what you don't have is always a waste of what you do have. The happiest of people aren't the luckiest, and they usually don't have the best of everything; they just make the most of everything that comes their way. The reason so many people give up is because they tend to look at what's missing, and how far they still have to go, instead of what's present, and how far they have come.

2 *My dreams are impossible.*

Don't let someone who gave up on their dreams talk you out of going after yours. The best thing you can do in life is follow your heart. Take risks. Don't just make the safe and easy choices because you're afraid of what might happen. If you do, nothing will ever happen. If you keep doing what you're doing, you'll keep getting what you're getting. Let your dreams be bigger than your fears and your actions speak louder than your words. Do something every day that your future self will thank you for.

> *Lying to others is wrong,*
> *but lying to yourself is an absolute tragedy.*

I am stuck with people who hurt me.

Life is too short. Look out for yourself. If someone continuously mistreats you, have enough respect for yourself to leave them. It may hurt for a while, but it'll be OK. You'll be OK. Oftentimes walking away has nothing to do with weakness, and everything to do with strength. We walk away not because we want others to realize our worth, but because we finally realize our own worth.

My failed relationships were a waste of time.

There are certain people who aren't meant to fit into your life. But no relationship is ever a waste of time. If it doesn't bring you what you want, it teaches you what you DON'T want. We rarely lose friends, we just gradually figure out who our real ones are. Never force someone to make a space in their life for you, because if they know your worth, they will surely create one for you. And remember, when you're up, your 'friends' know who you are, when you're down, you know who your 'real friends' are. It just takes a little time to figure it all out.

5 Things will never get better.

There is no person in the world capable of flawlessly handling every punch thrown at them. That's not how we're made. In fact, we're made to get upset, sad, hurt, stumble and fall. Because that's part of living – to face problems, learn, adapt, and solve them over the course of time. This is what ultimately molds us into the person we become. When you find yourself cocooned in isolation and cannot find your way out of the darkness, remember that this is similar to the place where caterpillars go to grow their wings. Just because today is a terrible day doesn't mean tomorrow won't be the best day of your life. You just have to get there.

6 Failure is bad.

Sometimes you have to fail a thousand times to succeed. No matter how many mistakes you make or how slow you progress, you are still way ahead of everyone who isn't trying. Don't get so hung up on one failed attempt that you miss the opening for many more. All of your ideas that don't work are simply stepping stones on your way to the one idea that does. And remember, failure is not falling down; failure is staying down when you have the choice to get back up. Always get back up! Oftentimes good things fall apart so better things can fall together.

7 Great things will come to me effortlessly.

We are who we choose to be. Nobody's going to come and save you, you've got to save yourself. Nobody's going to give you anything, you've got to go out and earn it. Nobody knows what you want except for you. And nobody will be as sorry as you if you don't achieve it. Never leave your key to happiness in someone else's pocket, and don't wait on someone else to build your dream life for you. Be the architect and keeper of your own happiness. The more you take responsibility for your past and present, the more you are able to create the future you seek.

8 My past is 100% indicative of my future.

At some point, we've all made mistakes, been walked on, used and forgotten. We've let people take advantage of us, and we've accepted way less than we deserve. But we shouldn't regret one moment of it, because in those moments we've learned a lot from our bad choices. We've learned who we can trust and who we can't. We've learned the meaning of friendship. We've learned how to tell when people are lying and

when they're sincere. We've learned how to be ourselves, and appreciate the truly great people and things in our lives as they arrive. And even though there are some things we can never recover and people who will never be sorry, we now know better for next time.

9 I never need to meet anyone new.

It sounds harsh, but you cannot keep every friend you've ever made. People and priorities change. As some relationships fade, others will grow. Appreciate the possibility of new relationships as you naturally let go of old ones that no longer work. Trust your judgment. Embrace new relationships, knowing that you are entering into unfamiliar territory. Be ready to learn, be ready for a challenge, and be ready to meet someone that might just change your life forever.

10 I can't live without those who are gone.

If someone comes into your life and has a positive impact on you, but for some reason they can't stay, don't mourn for too long. Be thankful that your paths crossed and that they somehow made you happy, even if it was just for a short while. Life is change. People really do come and go. Some come back, some don't, and that's okay. And just because one person leaves, doesn't mean you should forget about everyone else who's still standing by your side. Continue to appreciate what you have, and smile about the memories.

11 *I'm not ready because I'm not good enough yet.*

Nobody ever feels 100% ready when an opportunity arises. Because most great opportunities in life force us to grow beyond our comfort zones, which means we won't feel totally comfortable at first. Stop berating yourself for being a work in progress. Start embracing it! Being a work in progress doesn't mean you're not good enough today; it means you want a better tomorrow, and you wish to love yourself completely, so you can live your life fully. It means you're determined to heal your heart, expand your mind and cultivate the gifts you know you're meant to share. You are ready. You just need to start.

12 *I have way too much to lose.*

In the end you will not regret the things you have done nearly as much as the things you have left undone. Trust me, you'd rather look back at your life and say, "I can't believe I did that!" instead of, "I wish I would have..." It's better to think "Oh well," than "what if." It's better to have a lifetime full of mistakes that you learned from, rather than a heart full of regrets and empty dreams.

10 THINGS to TELL Yourself Today

Count your blessings, not your troubles. Live one day at a time. Let the wrong things go. Give more than you take. Look for the good in people and situations. Make time for those who matter. Laugh when you can. Cry when you need to. Focus on your priorities. Make decisions, not excuses. And always stay true to your values.

Yes, today is the perfect day to stand up and say...

1 *I am fighting hard for the things I want most.*

The longer you have to wait for something, the more you will appreciate it when it finally arrives. The harder you have to fight for something, the more it will be worth to you once you achieve it. And the more pain you have to endure on your journey, the sweeter the arrival at your destination. Most great things don't come easy, but they are worth waiting for and fighting for.

2 *I am taking action now.*

Many great things can be done in a day if you don't always make that day tomorrow. Don't let your fear of making a mistake stop you. A life spent making mistakes is not only more enjoyable, but more useful than a life spent doing nothing.

3 *I am focusing on the next positive step.*

A situation can occur in life that stops us dead in our tracks, frozen with fear. We can either stay stuck in that place by continuing to give it our attention, or we can gently remove our attention from whatever is happening, and focus instead on our next step – on what is possible tomorrow. Remember, the future holds nothing but endless potential. There are far, far better things ahead than any we leave behind. We just have to get there.

4 I am proud to wear my truth.

How others see you is not important. How you see yourself means everything. To be beautiful means to live confidently in your own skin. Say it, and then say it again: "This is my life, my choices, my mistakes, and my lessons. Not yours."

5 I have a lot to smile about.

Happiness is not a result of getting something you don't have, but rather of recognizing and appreciating what you do have. You create happiness with your attitude, your behavior and your actions. It is all up to you.

6 I am making the best of it.

Everything you go through grows you. Sometimes you think doing something is a total waste of time, and then it ends up being one of the best things you ever did. Don't judge the day before it unfolds. Amazing things can and do happen when you least expect them. Let each day be a scavenger hunt in which you must find at least one of these things: a sincere laugh, an act of kindness, a realization, or a lesson that will lead you closer to your dreams.

7 I am letting go of yesterday's stress.

Sometimes the reason it's so hard for us to be happy is simply because we refuse to let go of the things that make us upset. As the sun sets on this day, let it go. Leave behind the stress, the drama and the worries. Lay this day to rest. Tomorrow is about hope, new possibilities, and the opportunity to make a better day.

8 There is enough time today to do something I love.

Where did you leave your happiness? With an old lover? In a city you once lived in? In a story you never finished writing? In a dream you gave up on? In a hope you got too weary to carry? Wherever you left it, go back and retrieve it. If you don't remember where you left it, dedicate a little time today to doing something you love to do, and you will find your happiness somewhere nearby.

9 I am priceless in someone's eyes.

Being with someone who overlooks your worth isn't loyalty, it's stupidity. Don't let the people who aren't worth it get to you. Focus on those who love and accept you for who you are, and shower them with the love and kindness they deserve. And above all, cherish the people who saw you when you were invisible to everyone else.

10 *It's not too late.*

No matter who you are, no matter what you did, no matter where you've come from, you can always change and become a better version of yourself. Peace, strength and direction will come to you when you manage to tune out the noisy judgments of others, in an effort to better hear the soft and steady hum of your own inner strength. And once you hear it, you will realize that it's not too late to be what you might have been.

17 DEADLIEST *Decisions* You Can Make

When the deepest part of you becomes engaged in what you are doing, when your activities and actions become gratifying and purposeful, when what you do serves both yourself and others, when you do not tire within because you are pursuing the sweet satisfaction of your life and your work, you are living life the way it is meant to be lived.

Sometimes it's the smallest decisions that can change your life forever. Here are some small, deadly decisions to avoid on your journey forward.

1 *Not loving what is.*

Love what you do, until you can do what you love. Love where you are, until you can be where you love. Love the people you are with, until you can be with the people you love most. This is the way we find happiness.

2 *Waiting and waiting and waiting.*

Good things don't come to those who wait. Good things come to those who pursue the goals and dreams they believe in. "Coulda, woulda, shoulda…" stop it! Don't blame your past for what you don't have. Blame your present. Ask yourself this: "What can I do NOW that will bring me closer to where I want be?"

3 *Changing who you are because others have changed.*

People change. Get used to it. Accept it. Wish them well anyway. Be happy anyway. If you're being true to yourself and it isn't enough for the people around you, change the people around you.

4 *Letting heartache define you.*

Don't allow your temporary wounds to permanently transform you into someone you aren't. A strong person is not the one who doesn't cry. A strong person is the one who cries for a moment openly, and then gets up and fights again for what they believe in.

5 Running away from problems.

Running away from your problems is a race you'll never win. You may not be proud of all the things you've done in the past, but right now is a new beginning. It's doesn't matter who you used to be; what matters is who you are today. What you do TODAY can improve all of your tomorrows. So don't run; instead do something that creates positive change.

6 Being ungrateful.

Even in the most peaceful surroundings, the ungrateful heart finds trouble. Even in the most troublesome surroundings, the grateful heart finds peace. Choose to see the world through grateful eyes; it will never look the same again.

7 Allowing long-term anger to occupy your heart.

The best medicine is a strong dose of love, laughter and letting go. Just like we would never allow even a tiny bit of poison to be in our food, let us not allow even a tiny bit of anger to live in our heart.

8 Believing that beauty looks a certain way.

We're taught to believe that miniature waists and perfect tans are beautiful. We're made to believe that blonde hair with blue eyes will win every time. But the truth is originality is beautiful. Big brown eyes, green eyes, blue eyes alike. Curves, and lots of them. Your natural skin tone is beautiful. Your hair color and your smile. Your voice, your laugh, and your personality. Every inch of you that shines with your unique essence. You're truly beautiful, just like the rest of us.

9 Letting your expectations run rampant.

Everyone has their own challenges, everyone has their own journey. It is meaningless to compare one with the other. Always love and accept the real people in front of you, not the fantasy of who you hope and wish these people could become.

10 Disrespecting others.

Treat people the way you want to be treated. Karma is only unkind if you are. No matter what happens in life, be good to the people around you. If you do, you'll leave a great legacy behind regardless of the dreams and ideals you choose to pursue.

11 Disrespecting yourself.

Being kind to yourself in thoughts, words and actions is just as important as being kind to others. The most painful thing is losing yourself in the process of loving others, and forgetting that you are special too.

12 Putting up with unfaithful friends and lovers.

The people who want to stay in your life will always find a way. Real friends and lovers stay faithful. You shouldn't have to fight for a spot in someone's life. Never force someone to make a space in their life for you, because if they truly care about you, they will create one for you.

13 Rushing love.

It's not hard to find someone who tells you they love you, it's hard to find someone who actually means it. But you will find them eventually. So don't rush love – don't settle. Find someone that isn't afraid to admit they miss you. Someone that knows you're not perfect, but treats you as you are. One who gives their heart completely. Someone who says, "I love you" and then shows it. Find someone who wouldn't mind waking up with you in the morning, seeing your wrinkles and grey hair, and then falls in love with you all over again.

14 Neglecting your most important relationships.

Relationships built on a foundation of love and respect can weather many storms and earthquakes. This foundation can be checked, maintained and kept healthy with generous doses of acceptance, forgiveness, listening, gratitude and considerate actions.

15 Trying to control every last detail about everything.

Sometimes it's better not to assume, not to wonder, not to imagine, and not to obsess. Just breathe, do what you can, and have faith that everything will work out for the best. When you least expect it, something great will come along – something better than you could have ever planned for.

16 Never taking risks.

Life is inherently risky. There is only one risk you should avoid at all costs, and that is the risk of doing nothing. Get out there and make something happen, even if it's just a small step in the right direction. Strive for progress, not perfection.

17 Giving up on YOU.

Sometimes life doesn't give you what you want; not because you don't deserve it, but because you deserve better. No matter how many times you break down, there should always be a little voice inside you that says, "NO, you're not done yet! Get back up!" That's the voice of passion and

courage. Life is a journey, often difficult
and sometimes incredibly cruel; but you
are well equipped for it as long as you tap
into your talents and gifts, and allow them
to flourish.

12 CHOICES ⇐⇒
Your **FUTURE** Self Will *Thank You* For

When life pushes you over, stand up and push back even harder. Where there is a fork in the road and choices to make, make the ones your future self will thank you for.

Today, start...

1 *Choosing YOU.*

Wearing a mask wears you out. Faking it is fatiguing. The most exhausting activity is pretending to be who you know you aren't. No matter how loud their opinions are, they do not choose who YOU are. Choose YOU even if nobody else is choosing you.

2 *Appreciating what you have.*

Sometimes, when you make the most out of what you have, it turns out being a lot more than you ever imagined. A beautiful day begins with a beautiful mindset. When you wake up, take a second to think about what a privilege it is to simply be alive and healthy. The moment you start acting like life is a blessing, I assure you that it will start to feel like one. Time spent living is time worth appreciating.

3 *Believing in yourself and your dreams.*

The most difficult phase of life is not when no one understands you; it's when you don't understand yourself. Believe in YOU. Listen to your soul. Trust your instincts. Acknowledge your own strengths. Dream it and dare it. Do what you are afraid of, and capable of. Follow your vision. Know that anything is possible. Know you CAN.

4 *Being positive.*

You can't live a positive life with a negative attitude. Heaven on Earth is a choice we must make, not a place we must find. Let every day be a dream you can touch. Let every day be a love you can feel. Let every day be a reason to live. Life is too short to be anything but positive.

5 *Taking action.*

The happiest and most successful people are usually those who have broken the chains of procrastination, who find satisfaction in doing the job at hand. They're full of eagerness, passion, and productivity. You can be too. Remember, success in real estate is about location, location, location. Success in life is about action, action, action.

6 *Letting go.*

The only thing that makes it a big part of your life is that you keep thinking about it. The biggest step in changing the world around you is to change the world within you. Don't cry over the past, it's gone. Don't stress about the future, it hasn't arrived. Just live in the present, concentrate on the things you can control, and take one small step at a time.

7 *Picking yourself back up.*

Where you are in life is temporary; where you end up in life is permanent; how you get from here to there is entirely up to you. So don't give up. Sometimes when things go wrong it's because they would have turned out worse if they had gone right.

8 *Ignoring negative people.*

You are not a rug; some people may try to walk all over you, but you don't have to lie there and take it. There are seven billion people in the world; don't waste your time by letting one of them ruin your happiness. You are good enough, smart enough, beautiful enough, and strong enough. Somewhere someone is looking for exactly what you have to offer.

9 *Staying in touch with close friends and family.*

Having somewhere to go is what we call 'home.' Having someone to love, who loves us in return, is what we call 'family.' Having both is a blessing. There comes a time in life when you'll have to leave everything behind for awhile and start something new, but never forget the people who stood by your side, especially your close friends and family who never gave up on you.

10 *Making time for fun.*

Fun is way underrated. With all of life's responsibilities, fun will sometimes seem like an indulgence. It shouldn't be. It should be a requirement. It's a happy talent to know how to let loose and play. People who make it a point play around and have fun are twenty times more likely to feel happy in the long run.

11   *Spreading love and kindness.*

The amazing thing about life is that you choose what you allow into it and out of it – you choose how things affect you, and how you affect the world. The happiness surrounding you is greatly affected by the choices you make every day. So choose to spread love and kindness to a least one person a day. Imagine the amount of happiness you would create in a lifetime if you did.

12   *Being the change you want to see in the world.*

Don't tell others how to live; LIVE and let them watch you. Practice what you preach or don't preach at all. Walk the talk. The people who look up to you will likely emulate your actions and strive to become who you are; so BE who you want them to be.

JUST THE **WAY** **YOU** ARE

What is uttered from the heart alone,
Will win the hearts of others to your own.

\- Johann Wolfgang von Goethe

This morning I was writing a blog entry at a local beach-side coffee shop here in San Diego when a young woman approached me. "You're Marc, right?" she asked.

I looked up at her. She had piercing eyes, a pierced nose, an elegant smile... but nothing that rang a bell. "I'm sorry. Do I know you?" I inquired politely.

"No," she replied. "But I know you." She swiftly walked back to the table where she'd been sitting, picked up her laptop, and carried it over to me. On the screen was Marc and Angel Hack Life. "You look just like your photo," she said in a chipper tone.

I smiled. "So you're one of the seven people who read it."

She blushed. "What I like about your writing is that it's so real."

I cleared my throat. "Real?" I asked.

"I mean... you don't hide anything. You say it just like it is. And that gives me hope!"

"How do you know that I don't hide anything?" I asked.

She paused, tilted her head slightly and squinted her eyes as if, maybe, to look for something inside me that she had missed before. "Well, your words seem so, so... honest."

Her compliment was appreciated, but it didn't feel fair. Perhaps because I'm not very good at accepting compliments, or perhaps because I've been thinking about honesty lately... and I've decided that I don't like the word and its connotations.

The Ruse

"There are some things you should probably know," I said. "If I know a picture is being taken of me, I usually make a crooked half smile because I think it's sexy. If an attractive girl touches my arm, I flex a little bit because I think she prefers harder muscles. And if I know people are coming over to my condo, I run around like a mad man and make it spotless before they arrive, because I'd like them to think that I'm clean and organized all of the time."

"But…"

"And that's just the beginning," I continued. "When I write a blog entry, I'm typically only writing about the people and experiences that inspire a single sentence that moves me. For instance, in today's post that sentence is: "Honesty is a matter of perception and intention." The rest is just my attempt to bring that sentence to life – to show why it's meaningful to me."

"But can't you see…"

"And when I want to impress someone I've just met for the first time, I pretend that I'm overly outgoing and fearless. And I try to say funny or profound things like, "Better to understand a little than to misunderstand a lot." But it usually doesn't come out right because I don't really want to be funny or fearless or profound. Not right then. I just want to break the ice and introduce myself. And I want to do it without stumbling over my words…"

"Marc, this is exactly the kind of honesty that inspires me!"

"You're missing the point. These are revelations… and they're revealing the ruse. The sexy crooked smiles aren't the smiles you see most often. And the blog posts rarely include the sentences that inspire them. And the folks I introduce myself to don't see the real me, and they don't realize that I'm nervous because I'm trying to impress them… because I want them to like me… and because…"

You're The Guy

"Who are you trying to impress?" she asked.

"That's not the point," I said.

"But I want to know," she insisted.

"This is what I mean…" I continued. "An honest person would just tell it to you straight. But I write stories about a guy who wishes he was his cat, and nights of dancing naked, and Jamaican women in ice cream parlors… and who the heck knows what will come next."

"But you're the guy who wishes he was his cat, right?" she asked.

I grinned. "Shhh… don't tell anyone."

"But won't the new people you want to impress and all of the important people in your life know how you feel... now?" she asked.

"No," I replied. "I don't think they read this blog."

Revelation

We shared a long silence during which her gaze locked directly into the depths of my eyes. Finally, she said, "I think I understand better why you give me hope."

"Why?" I asked.

"Because at some point the world forgot – or perhaps never knew – that honesty isn't about whether we make sexy smiles for the camera, mask autobiographical blog posts about our desires to be a cat, or try not to show our apprehension before meeting someone new. Rather, honesty – revelation – is a matter of perception and intention. And somebody recognizes that. And it gives me hope and makes me think."

I smiled. "And one other thing," she said.

"What?" I asked.

"I'm pretty sure that whoever you want to impress will appreciate you just the way you are. I know I do."

10 to WRITE a *Life Story* Worth Living
WAYS

When writing the story of your life, don't let someone else hold the pen. Make conscious choices every day that align your actions with your values and dreams. Because the way you live each day is a sentence in the story of your life. Each day you make a choice as to whether the sentence ends with a period, a question mark, or an exclamation point.

How are you writing your life's story?

Here are ten ideas for writing a life story worth living:

1 Find a passion that makes you come alive.

Each new day is a blank page in the story of your life. The secret is in turning that blank page into the best chapter you possibly can. Don't ask what the world needs. Ask what makes you come alive, and go do it. Because what the world needs, and what every great story has, are characters who have come alive in the pursuit of something that inspires them.

2 Work hard on that passion.

The best dreams happen when you're wide awake and working hard on something you're passionate about. A dream is your creative vision for your life in the future. You must break out of your current comfort zone and become comfortable with the new and unfamiliar. So dream big, pursue your passion, and give yourself permission to work toward a future you know you are capable of creating.

3 Live happily in your own way.

You are not in this world to live up to the expectations of others, nor should you feel that others are here to live up to yours. Pave your own unique path. What success means to each of us is totally different. Success to some may mean fancy cars and homes. Success to others may mean being a good parent, spouse, or friend. For others, it may mean to simply be happy. Or it can be all of the above. Remember, success is ultimately about spending your life happily in your own way.

4 *Change your path when you must, but keep moving forward.*

There are thousands of possible paths one could take up the mountain of life. You get to choose which one you take, and you can jump from one path to another if you run into a hazardous road block. All of these paths are unique, but lead in a similar general direction, so it really doesn't matter which path you start off on. The only mistake you can make is by wasting time running around at the base of the mountain, telling everyone that your life path is wrong.

5 *When the going gets tough, keep fighting.*

The wisest, most loving, well rounded people you have met are likely those who have known failure, known defeat, known suffering, and have found their way out of the depths of their own despair. These people have experienced many ups and downs, and have gained an appreciation, a sensitivity, and an understanding of life that fills them with compassion,

understanding, and a deep loving concern. People like this aren't born; they develop slowly over the course of a lifetime.

6 *Let go of the past and live consciously in the present.*

Life can only be understood backwards; but it must be lived forwards. The past is a good place to visit on occasion, but not a great place to stay. Don't sit around trying to relive or change your past when you have priceless moments unfolding in front of you and your entire future to look forward to.

7 *Embrace new ideas, lessons, and challenges.*

Sometimes growing up means growing apart from old habits, relationships, and situations, and finding something new that truly moves you. There is nothing more wonderful than seeing life as an adventure. You should try things that you're afraid of. You should look very clearly into the unknown and enjoy it. Because when you come in contact with things that you don't know, that's when you're learning, growing, and truly living.

8 *Appreciate the little things in life that mean a lot.*

What if you woke up tomorrow with only the things you were thankful for today?

Think of all the beauty that remains around you, and be happy. Be thankful for all the small things in your life, because when you put them all together you will see just how significant they are. Remember, it's not happiness that makes us grateful, but gratefulness that makes us happy.

9 *Live honorably through kindness.*

If you live honorably, no matter how old you get, you'll never lose your beauty; it will just gradually shift from your face to your heart. And remember, there is no better exercise for the heart than reaching out and holding the hand of someone in need.

10 *Spend quality time with people you love.*

Lost time is never found again. People don't live forever. Appreciate what you have, who loves you and who cares for you. You'll never know how much they mean to you until the day they are no longer beside you. Spend lots of quality time with the people you love. Someday you will either regret not doing so, or you will say, "I'm glad I did."

11 THINGS You **FORGET** You're Doing *Wrong*

Don't forget, when you stop doing the wrong things, the right things eventually catch you.

So make sure you're not...

Making blind judgments.

1 Don't always judge a person by what they show you. What you've seen is oftentimes only what that person has chosen to show you, or what they were driven to show based on their inner stress and pain. Too often we jump to conclusions, only to cause ourselves and others unnecessary worry, hurt, and anger. So exercise restraint, be kind, and save the jumping for joy.

2 *Expecting people to be perfect.*

When you open up to love, you must be open up to getting hurt as well. If you expect to love someone, and not have disappointment every now and then, then you don't want love, you want something perfect that doesn't exist. When you stop expecting people to be perfect, you can start appreciating them for who they truly are.

3 *Focusing on everything and everyone except YOU.*

Make the world a better place one person at a time, and start with YOU. If you're looking out into the world to find where your purpose resides, stop, and look inside instead. Look at who you already are, the lifestyle you choose to live, and what makes you come alive. Then nurture these things and let them grow until your current life can no longer contain them. And finally, as you're being forced to grow, follow them into the world with courage, trusting that where they will take you will be where your purpose finds its home.

4 Holding on to the wrong things for too long.

To let go isn't to forget. Letting go involves cherishing the memories, overcoming the obstacles, and moving on. To let go is to be thankful for the experiences that made you laugh, made you cry, and helped you learn and grow. It's the acceptance of everything you have, everything you once had, and the possibilities that lie ahead. It's all about finding the strength to embrace life's changes and continue taking positive steps forward.

5 Denying your mistakes.

Mistakes are almost always forgivable if you have the courage to admit them. You have to be courageous and wise enough to know that if what you are doing isn't producing the desired results, you must take different actions. Sometimes falling flat on your face is exactly what's needed to help you see things from a totally different perspective, and get back on track.

6 Avoiding your fears.

Go to your fears, sit with them, and stare at them. Your fears are your friend; their only job is to show you undeveloped parts of yourself that you need to cultivate to live a happy life. The more you do the things you're most afraid of doing, the more life opens up. Embrace your fears and your fears will embrace you.

7 Accepting less than you know you deserve.

Do not sacrifice your heart or your dignity. Love yourself enough to never lower your standards for the wrong reasons. Do not get so anxious for something that you'll accept anything. Hold to your standards and be willing to walk away, with your head held high.

8 Storing mental clutter.

Just as you don't move from one home to another without first sorting through what you've gathered over the years, throwing away what is broken and no longer useful, so too should you do the same with what you've mentally gathered, before you move on. Do some sorting, throw away regrets and old pains, and take only the treasures worth keeping: The lessons, the love, and the best of what you've lived.

9 Worrying about things that can't be changed.

One of the happiest moments is when you feel the courage to let go of what you can't change. Refuse to ruin a perfectly good today by thinking about a bad yesterday. The past cannot be changed, forgotten, or erased. However, the lessons learned can prepare you for a brighter tomorrow.

10 *Letting hope gradually slip away.*

Every mistake, breakup, and setback in life
is an opportunity to do it better next time.
So keep your head held high. We can live
without a lot of things, but hope isn't one
of them. Cultivate hope by latching onto
stories of triumph, and words that inspire.
But most of all, listen to the quiet whisper
of your inner strength when it tells you that
this is only temporary, and that you will get
through this stronger than you were before.

11 *Thinking it's too late.*

Whether you know it or not the rest of your
life is being shaped right now. You can
choose to blame your circumstances on fate
or bad luck or bad choices, or you can fight
back. Things aren't always going to be fair
in the real world; that's just the way it is.
But for the most part you get what you give.
The rest of your life is being shaped by the
goals you chase, the choices you make, and
the actions you take. The rest of your life is
a long time, and it starts right now.

14 RULES for Being *You*

Be yourself. Trying to be anyone else is a waste of the person you are. Embrace that individual inside you that has ideas, strengths and beauty like no one else. Be the person you know yourself to be – the best version of you – on your terms. And above all, be true to YOU – if you cannot put your heart in it, take yourself out of it.

Starting today...

1 Get your priorities straight.

Twenty years from now it won't really matter what shoes you wore today, how your hair looked, or what brand of jeans you bought. What will matter is how you loved, what you learned and how you applied this knowledge.

2 Take full responsibility for your goals.

If you really want good things in your life to happen, you have to make them happen yourself. You can't sit around and hope that somebody else will help you; you have to make your own future and not think that your destiny is tied to the actions and choices of others.

3 Know your worth.

When someone treats you like you're just one of many options, help them narrow their choice by removing yourself from the equation. Sometimes you have to try not to care, no matter how much you do. Because sometimes you can mean almost nothing to someone who means so much to you. It's not pride – it's self-respect. Don't expect to see positive changes in your life if you surround yourself with negative people. Don't give part-time people a full-time position in your life. Know your value and what you have to offer, and never settle for anything less than what you deserve.

4 Choose the right perspective.

Perspective is everything. When faced with long check-out lines, traffic jams, or waiting an hour past your appointment time, you have two choices: You can get frustrated and enraged, or you can view it as life's way of giving you a guilt-free breather from rushing, and spend that time daydreaming, conversing, or watching the clouds. The first choice will raise your blood pressure. The second choice will raise your consciousness.

5 Don't let your old problems punish your dreams.

Learn to let go of things you can't control. The next time you're tempted to rant about a situation that you think ended unfairly, remind yourself of this: You'll never kill off your anger by beating the story to death. So close your mouth, unclench your fists, and redirect your thoughts. When left untended, the anger will slowly wither, and you'll be left to live in peace as you grow toward a better future.

6 Choose the things that truly matter.

Some things just don't matter much – like the kind of car you drive. How big of a deal is that in the grand scheme of life? Not a big at all. But lifting a person's heart?

Now, that matters. The whole problem with most people is, they KNOW what matters, but they don't CHOOSE it. They get distracted. They don't put first things first. The hardest and smartest way to live is choosing what truly matters, and pursuing it passionately.

7 Love YOU.

Let someone love you just the way you are – as flawed as you might be, as unattractive as you sometimes feel, and as unaccomplished as you think you are. Yes, let someone love you despite all of this; and let that someone be YOU.

8 Accept your strengths and weaknesses.

Be confident being YOU. We often waste too much time comparing ourselves to others, and wishing to be something we're not. Everybody has their own strengths and weaknesses, and it is only when we accept everything we are, and everything we aren't, that we are able to become who we are capable of being.

9 Stand up for YOU.

You were born to be real, not to be perfect. You're here to be YOU, not to be what someone else wants you to be. Stand up for yourself, look them in the eye, and say, "Don't judge me until you know me, don't underestimate me until you challenge me, and don't talk about me until you've talked to me."

0 *Learn from others, and move on when you must.*

You can't expect to change people. Either you accept who they are, or you start living your life without them. And just because something ends, doesn't mean it never should have been. You lived, you learned, you grew, and you moved on. Some people come into your life as blessings; others come into your life as lessons.

11 *Be honest in your relationships.*

Don't cheat! If you're not happy, be honest, and move on if you must. When you're truly in love, being faithful isn't a sacrifice, it's a joy.

12 *Get comfortable with being uncomfortable.*

Life as we know it can change in a blink of an eye. Unlikely friendships can blossom, important careers can be tossed aside and a long lost hope can be rekindled. It might feel a little uncomfortable at times, but know that life begins at the end of your comfort zone. So if you're feeling uncomfortable right now, know that the change taking place in your life is not an ending, but a new beginning.

13 *Be who you were born to be.*

Don't get to the end of your life and find that you lived only the length of it; live the width of it as well. When it comes to living as a passionate, inspired human being, the only challenge greater than learning to walk a mile in someone else's shoes, is learning to walk a lifetime comfortably in your own. Follow your heart, and take your brain with you. When you are truly comfortable in your own skin, not everyone will like you, but you won't care about it one bit.

14 *Never give up on YOU.*

This is your life; shape it, or someone else will. Strength shows not only in the ability to hold on, but in the ability to start over when you must. It is never too late to become what you might have been. Keep learning, adapting, and growing. You may not be there yet, but you are closer than you were yesterday.

11 WAYS to Become the PERSON You *Love*

You are powerful when you believe in yourself – when you know that you are capable of anything you put your mind to. You are beautiful when your strength and determination shines as you follow your own path – when you aren't disheveled by the obstacles along the way. You are unstoppable when you let your mistakes educate you, as your confidence builds from experiences – when you know you can fall down, pick yourself up, and move forward.

Here are 11 ways to become the person you love.

1 *Stop judging, and appreciate the beauty within you.*

Judging yourself is not the same as being honest with yourself. When it comes to living as a compassionate, non-judgmental human being, the only challenge greater than learning to walk a mile in someone else's shoes, is learning to walk a lifetime comfortably in your own. In every smile there is beauty. In every heart there is love. In every mind there is wisdom. In every human being there is a soul, there is life, there is worth, and there is the ability to see all these things in everyone, including one's self.

2 *Treat yourself the way you want others to treat you.*

Accept yourself! Insecurity is what's ugly, not you. Be you, just the way you are, in the beautiful way only you know how. The way you treat yourself sets the standard for others. You must love who you are or no one else will either. And when you are truly comfortable in your own skin, not everyone will like you, but you won't care about it one bit.

Care less about who you are to others.

Don't lose YOU in your search for acceptance by others. Be aware that you will always appear to be a little less than some people prefer you to be, but that most people are unaware that you are so much more then what they see. You are good enough just the way you are. You have nothing to prove to anyone else. Care less about who you are to others and more about who you are to yourself.

Know your worth.

We often accept the love we think we deserve. It makes no sense to be second in someone's life, when you know you're good enough to be first in someone else's.

5 Don't rush intimate relationships.

Love is not about sex, going on fancy dates, or showing off. It's about being with a person who makes you happy in a way nobody else can. You don't need a perfect one, you just need someone who you can trust – who shows you that you're the only one. If you haven't found true love yet, don't settle. There is someone out there who will love you unconditionally, even if it's not the person you were initially hoping for.

6 Let go of those who aren't really there.

There are certain people who aren't meant to fit into your life no matter how much you want them to. And the only ones truly worthy of your love are the ones who stand with you through the hard times and laugh with you after the hard times pass. Maybe a happy ending doesn't include anyone else right now. Maybe it's just you, on your own, picking up the pieces and starting over, freeing yourself for something better in the future. Maybe the happy ending is simply letting go.

7 Forgive yourself and others.

Of all the things that can be stolen from you – your possessions, your youth, your health, your words, your rights – what no one can ever take from you is your freedom to choose what you will believe in, and who and what your heart will love going forward. Life begins where your fear and resentment ends. Just because someone hurt you yesterday, doesn't mean you should hate the world, or start living life today in constant fear of being hurt tomorrow. When you forgive yourself and others, and stop the inner imprisonment, you're creating the love of your life.

8 *Focus on the positive.*

Do not let the pain make you hopeless. Do not let the negativity wear off on you. Do not let the bitterness steal your sweetness. Even though others may disagree with you, take pride in the fact that you still know the world is a beautiful place. Change your thoughts and you change your reality. Our thoughts are the makers of our moods, the inventors of our dreams, and the creators of our will. That is why we must sort through them carefully, and choose to respond only to those that will help us build the life we want, and the outlook we want to hold as we're living it.

9 *Believe in the person you are capable of being.*

The real purpose of your life is to evolve and grow into the whole person you are capable of being. Have a mind that is open to everything and attached to nothing. Change really is always possible – there is no ability that can't be developed with experience. Don't ever let your negative beliefs stand in the way of your own improvement.

10 *Work on goals you believe in.*

Never put off or give up on a goal that's important to you. Not because you still have tomorrow to start or try again, but because you may not have tomorrow at all. Life is shorter than it sometimes seems. Follow your heart today.

11 *Keep looking and moving straight forward.*

Moving on doesn't mean you have forgotten; it means you have accepted what happened in the past and choose to continue living in the present. Moving on doesn't mean you're giving up; it means you're giving yourself another chance by making a choice to be happy rather than hurt. Through all the problems you have faced, the burdens weighing down on your shoulders, the pain in your heart, you have only one thing to say, "I survived and I now know better for next time."

In the end, loving yourself is about enjoying your life, trusting your own feelings, taking chances, losing and finding happiness, cherishing the memories, and learning from the past. Sometimes you have to stop worrying, wondering, and doubting. Have faith that things will work out, maybe not exactly how you planned, but just how it's meant to be.

WHY **WE** ARE
WEIRD

Somewhere Else

During my competitive cross-country running days it wasn't uncommon for me to run five miles at 5AM and another ten miles at 10PM, six days a week. I was competitive. I wanted to win races. And I was smart enough to know that if I dedicated myself to extra training, while my opponents were sleeping or socializing, I would be one step ahead of them when we crossed the finish line.

When I first started these early morning and late night runs, the experience was rather brutal. My body didn't want to cooperate. It ached and cramped up. And I found out that the only way to endure the extra training was to disassociate my mind from my body, putting my mind somewhere else while my body ran.

Can't Relate

Over time, I became quite proficient at doing this. I got so good at it, in fact, that I actually looked forward to running. Because when I ran, my mind was clear and at peace with the world – especially when nobody else was around. In the midst of what seemed to be a strenuous workout, my mind was in a soothingly relaxed state... similar to that of a deep meditation.

I don't compete in races anymore, but I still run almost every day. Even though I no longer have to, I typically still run in the wee hours of the morning or very late at night. And since my friends know that I have a flexible work schedule, most of them think I'm a bit weird for running at such 'odd' hours. I've tried to explain to them why I do it, and how it soothes my mind. But they can't relate. So I'm still a weirdo in their eyes.

She Was Right

Last night, I went running on the Pacific Beach boardwalk at 11PM. It was calm and quiet out – just the way I like it. I was about three miles into my run when a peculiar looking woman sitting on the boardwalk's barrier wall shouted, "Hey, you!" and then waved me down. My first inclination was to just ignore her and continue running. But my curiosity got the best of me. So I stopped.

The woman had long blonde dreadlocks, several piercings in her ears and nose, tattoos on both arms, and a Grateful Dead t-shirt on. She was strumming an acoustic guitar and had a thick, white joint burning in a small ashtray beside her.

She stopped strumming her guitar and began to chuckle as soon as she saw me looking down at the joint. "Don't worry," she said. "I'm legit. I have a medical prescription for it."

"It's none of my business," I quickly replied.

"Anyway," she continued. "Perhaps you don't realize this, but it's pretty late to be out exercising. I've seen you out here a few times before, running after midnight."

"So, what's your point?" I asked.

"Well thousands of people run on this boardwalk every single day, but you seem to be the only runner I see in the middle of the night. And it strikes me as being kind of weird. So what's your deal?"

I told her about my love for a quite landscape, and the way in which

running soothes my mind. "...like a deep mediation," I told her.

She smiled, strummed once on her guitar, and took a drag of her joint. "Well then, I'm doing the same thing as you right now," she replied. "Only in my own way – a way that works for me. Can you dig that?"

I stared at her for a second and then laughed, because I knew she was right. "Yeah, I can dig that," I said. She winked and started strumming her guitar again. I winked back and started running again.

Conclusion

Some of us run in the middle of the night. Some of us strum acoustic guitars and smoke joints. And others go to church. Or sip expensive wine. Or surf on dangerous waves. Or jump out of perfectly good airplanes. When we try to understand people by personally relating to the things that they do, we usually can't make any sense of it. Because it's easier to see weirdness in a sea of normality, than it is to decode the logical methods behind one's madness.

But when we look just a little deeper, by making a noble effort to understand people by truly listening to why they do the things that they do, they never seem quite as weird. Actually, they begin to seem...

Almost normal.

LESSONS LIFE TAUGHT US

THINK ABOUT ALL THE THINGS YOU WOULD LOVE TO TELL YOURSELF IF YOU COULD TRAVEL BACK IN TIME TO GIVE YOUR YOUNGER SELF SOME ADVICE ABOUT LIFE.

SPEND MORE TIME WITH THOSE WHO MAKE YOU SMILE AND LESS TIME WITH THOSE WHO YOU FEEL PRESSURED TO IMPRESS.

LAUGH AT STUPID JOKES. APOLO-GIZE. TELL SOMEONE HOW MUCH THEY MEAN TO YOU. IT'S THE SMALL MOMENTS THAT MAKE LIFE GRAND.

LIFE IS WAY MORE ENJOYABLE WHEN YOU STOP TRYING TO BE COOL AND SIMPLY FOCUS ON BEING YOURSELF.

COMPLAINING IS LIKE SLAPPING YOURSELF FOR SLAPPING YOURSELF. IT DOESN'T SOLVE THE PROBLEM, IT JUST HURTS YOU MORE.

LEARN TO ADJUST THE SAILS OF YOUR LIFE TO UNPREDICTABLE WINDS, WHILE KEEPING YOUR FO-CUS CLEAR ON YOUR DESTINATION. AND KEEP SAILING UNTIL YOU GET THERE.

FREEDOM IS THE GREATEST GIFT. SELF-SUFFICIENCY IS THE GREAT-EST FREEDOM.

IF YOU WANT SOMETHING IN YOUR LIFE YOU'VE NEVER HAD, YOU'LL HAVE TO DO SOMETHING YOU'VE NEVER DONE.

YOUR HEALTH IS YOUR LIFE, KEEP UP WITH IT. GET AN ANNUAL PHYSI-CAL CHECK-UP.

LIVING A LIFE OF HONESTY CREATES PEACE OF MIND, AND PEACE OF MIND IS PRICELESS. PERIOD. DON'T BE DISHONEST AND DON'T PUT UP WITH PEOPLE WHO ARE.

FORGIVING YOURSELF IS FAR MORE IMPORTANT (AND DIFFICULT) THAN GETTING OTHERS TO FORGIVE YOU.

THERE ARE FEW JOYS IN LIFE THAT EQUAL A GOOD CONVERSATION, A GOOD READ, A GOOD WALK, A GOOD HUG, A GOOD SMILE, OR A GOOD FRIEND.

LAUGHTER IS THE BEST MEDICINE FOR STRESS. LAUGH AT YOURSELF OFTEN. FIND THE HUMOR IN WHAT-EVER SITUATION YOU'RE IN.

EVERYTHING THAT HAPPENS IN LIFE IS NEITHER GOOD NOR BAD. IT JUST DEPENDS ON YOUR PERSPECTIVE.

YOU'RE NOT ALONE. EVERYONE HAS PROBLEMS. SOME PEOPLE ARE JUST BETTER AT HIDING THEM THAN OTHERS.

Self Love
QUESTIONS
to Make You *think*

If you had a friend who spoke to you in the same way that you sometimes speak to yourself, how **LONG** would you allow that person to be your *friend*?

What has the little **VOICE** inside your head been *saying* lately?

Why are **YOU,** *you*?

What makes you **FEEL** *incomplete*?

In one sentence, what do you **WISH** for your *future* self?

What's something **NEW** you recently learned about *yourself*?

What's something you have that **EVERYONE** *wants*?

What would you do **DIFFERENTLY** if you knew nobody would *judge* you?

What's something **NOBODY** could ever *steal* from you?

What **PROMISE** to yourself do you still need to *fulfill*?

Part Five
Passion and Growth

Be true to YOU.
If you cannot put your heart in it,
take yourself out of it.

I WOULD **RATHER** SOUND **STUPID**

Magic Happens

I've always believed in the beauty of a great journey – discovering new places, seeking life experiences, fostering relationships and pursuing my dreams. In fact, it's all I've ever really wanted to do. I just want to believe in something that's worth believing in and then pursue it with every facet of my being.

Such journeys, I've found, are best when we share them with others who, like me, are 'crazy' enough to assume that our wildest dreams are just a brief distance away from reality. These are the folks who realize that 'impossible' is simply a mindset – something we get when we haven't trained our minds and our hearts to see past the systems that currently exist to ones that don't yet exist. Because when our minds and our hearts and our hands work together, magic happens.

Fear

And only one thing has ever prevented me from making this magic happen more often. Fear. Being afraid of what others might think. Afraid of the repercussions of putting my crazy ideas out there for the world to see and judge. Afraid to let go of my comfort zone and just go for it. Because... What if I fail? What if... What if...

Now, in most situations, fear no longer stands in my way. But that doesn't mean it doesn't exist. It most certainly does. I've just learned to curb my fears and adapt to change a bit more proficiently than I used to. But I still feel the nerves of fear sneak up on me. And the more important something or someone is to me, the more nervous I get, the more I stumble over my words, and the more I sound like an incoherent fool.

A few years ago when I began talking to my friends and family about my goal to write and start the blog that would eventually become Marc and Angel Hack Life, I mostly got half smiles, nods, and quizzical facial reactions. And when I tried to say anything meaningful to Angel when we first met back in September of 2000, she would often laugh at me because she literally found herself trying to decode my jumbled, shaky sentences.

Clarity

One of the most remarkable things about our lives is that clarity and progression occur with enduring love, passion, and patience. This blog is now an easy topic for me to talk about... and now, it's even easy for others to talk about, including my friends and family. And although it may take her a second or two, Angel now gets the gist of my jumbled, shaky sentences almost immediately.

And that makes me smile. Because I want to continue to evolve and grow with the people and dreams that inspire me. After all, I only have one shot – like we all do – to make this life meaningful. And I know for sure, after coping with my fears on numerous journeys, that I would rather sound stupid...

Than be stupid and take no action at all.

18 THINGS My DAD Was ✔ Right About

Fifteen years ago, when I was a freshman in high school, my English teacher gave my class a homework assignment entitled, "Advice for a Younger Generation." The concept of the assignment was simple: Each student had to interview a person who was over the age of 25, gather enough information to write a basic biography of their life and find out what their top tips are for a younger generation. I chose to interview my dad. He was 53 at the time and he gave me 18 pieces of advice.

I had completely forgotten about all this until last week when I was visiting my parents. My mom had me clean out a few old boxes she had stored in the attic. In one of these boxes I found the original "Advice for a Younger Generation" assignment dated April 22nd, 1996. I read through it and was totally blown away.

Even though my dad's advice is relevant to a person of any age, my 29-year-old self can relate to it in a way my 14-year-old self didn't quite grasp at the time. In fact, the first thought that went through my head was, "My dad was right."

Here are his 18 pieces of advice for a younger generation, transcribed with his permission.

1 *Your 30's, 40's and 50's won't feel like your 30's, 40's and 50's.*

Adults are just older children. When you get older you won't feel as old as you imagine you will. For the most part, you still feel exactly the way you feel right now, just a little wiser and more confident. You've had time to establish your place in the world and figure out what's important to you. Don't fear growing up. Look forward to it. It's awesome.

2 *Bad things will happen to you and your friends.*

Part of living and growing up is experiencing unexpected troubles in life.

People lose jobs, get in car accidents and sometimes die. When you are younger, and things are going pretty well, this harsh reality can be hard to visualize. The smartest, and oftentimes hardest, thing we can do in these kinds of situations is to be tempered in our reactions. To want to scream obscenities, but to be wiser and more disciplined than that. To remember that emotional rage only makes matters worse. And to remember that tragedies are rarely as bad as they seem, and even when they are, they give us an opportunity to grow stronger.

3 Everyone can make a huge difference.

Making one person smile can change the world. Maybe not the whole world, but their world. So start small and start now.

4 First impressions aren't all they're cracked up to be.

Everyone and everything seems normal from a distance, or at a glance. The 10th, 20th, or even the 50th impression is when you start to truly understand someone else for who they truly are.

5 Big results come when you narrow your focus.

Concentrate your efforts on smaller and smaller areas. When your efforts are diffused over a wide area they won't have much of an impact. So focus on smaller areas and your efforts will be felt more fully. It could take time for change to happen, but keep that focus narrow.

6 Love yourself. Become your own priority.

Strive to be the 'you' you want to be. Nourish your mind and body. Educate yourself every day until you die.

7 Sometimes you just have to go for it.

Put your uncertainty and fears aside for a second and ask yourself this: "If I try and I don't get it right the first time, what will I have lost and what will I have gained?" The answer is: You will have lost nothing but a little bit of your time while gaining an important lesson that will help you get it right the second or third time. People rarely get it right the first time. In fact, usually the only people who ever get it right are those who continue going for it even when they've come up short numerous times before.

8 In order to get, you have to give.

Supporting, guiding and making contributions to other people is one of life's greatest rewards. Everything you do comes back around.

9 Not much is worth fighting about.

If you can avoid it, don't fight with loved ones. Don't let a single poisonous moment of misunderstanding make you forget about the countless lovable moments you've spent together. If you're angry at someone you love, hug them and mean it. You may not want to hug them, which is all the more reason to do so. It's hard to stay angry when someone shows that they love you, and that's precisely what happens when we hug each other.

10 Don't try to impress everyone.

Purposely impressing people is an act that brings nothing but a momentary ego boost. Be real with people instead. Connect with fewer people on a level that is deeper and more profound.

11 Keep having fun.

Fun is way underrated. With all of life's responsibilities, fun will sometimes seem like an indulgence. It shouldn't be. It should be a requirement. Make time for fun.

12 Keep it simple.

There is a world of magnificence hidden in simplicity. Pick the five most important things in your life now and focus on those things. Let the other stuff go. Stop the busyness and really enjoy what's important to you.

13 Little things stick with you.

So pay attention to them. Like watching your child sleep. Preparing a meal with your family. Sharing a great laugh with an old friend. This is the real stuff life is made of.

14 Less advice is often the best advice.

People don't need lots of advice, they need to live. I've seen young, rocky relationships develop into wonderful marriages and fleeting inspirations ignite a lifetime of passion and happiness. Our life stories, like the answers we give to long essay questions, are uniquely ours. What people want to know is already somewhere inside of them. We all just need time to think, be and breathe, and continue to explore the undirected journeys that will eventually help us find our direction.

15 *Manage your time.*

Your situation and environment is ever changing, so be careful not to confuse things that are urgent with things that are important.

16 *Manage your money.*

Don't buy stuff you don't need. Don't spend more than you make. Don't let your money manage you.

17 *What you learn in school does matter.*

While you may not use the specifics of every classroom lesson, every lesson does expand the core thought process of your mind. Over time you will develop problem solving skills that are universally applicable. No single classroom lesson can teach this, and no single classroom lesson is more important.

18 *Dreams will remain dreams forever if you don't take action.*

Don't dream about it anymore. Start doing it. In 40 years from now what is it that you will regret not having accomplished, appreciated or attempted? Do it, appreciate it and attempt it NOW!

10 THINGS

To STOP *Caring* About Today

Every day is a new beginning. But in life, sometimes you have to stop before you can truly begin. So starting today...

1 *Stop caring about everyone's opinion of you.*

For the most part, what other people think and say about you doesn't matter. When I was younger I let the opinions of my high school and early college peers influence my decisions. And at times they steered me away from ideas and goals I strongly believed in. I realize now, many years later, that this was a foolish way to live, especially when I consider that nearly all of these people whose opinions I cared so much about are no longer a part of my life.

Unless you're trying to make a great first impression (job interview, first date, etc.), don't let the opinions of others stand in your way. What they think and say about you isn't important. What is important is how you feel about yourself.

2 *Stop caring about being politically correct.*

I had a discussion with a friend yesterday about censorship and how speaking a certain way simply to please others contributes to the loss of one's true inner voice. During the discussion I watched him closely, and I could actually pinpoint the heated moment when he was about to give me a piece of his mind, but stopped himself. It was so obvious! So I called him out on it. "You just censored yourself, didn't you?" He laughed and nodded.

Everyone has this little watchdog inside their head. It's always there watching you. It was born and raised by your family, friends, coworkers, bosses and society at large, and its sole purpose is to watch you and make sure you stay in line. And once you become accustomed to the watchdog's presence, you begin to think his opinion of what's acceptable and unacceptable are absolute truths. But the watchdog's views are not truths, they're just opinions – forceful opinions that have the potential to completely brainwash you of your own opinions if you aren't careful.

Remember, the watchdog is just a watchdog, he just watches. He can't actually control you. He can't do anything about it if you decide to rise up and go against the grain.

No, you should not start randomly cussing and acting like a fool. But you must say what you need to say when you need to say it. If it isn't politically correct, so what.

Don't censor yourself. Speak the truth. Your truth.

3 Stop caring about looking a certain way.

There is no right way to dress or right way to wear your hair. No, I'm not saying you should dress like a clown simply to rebel either. Everyone who purposely tries to look different ends up looking the same.

Be you, just the way you are, in the unique way only you know how. Wear clothes and styles you feel comfortable wearing. Dress the way YOU dress.

You're one of a kind. Trying to look like someone else is a waste of your own

beauty. In this crazy world that's trying to make you like everyone else, find the courage to keep being your awesome self.

4 Stop caring about what everyone else wants for you.

The minute you stop overwhelming your mind with caring about what everyone

else thinks, and start doing what you feel in your heart is right, is the minute you will finally feel freedom. In fact, you can end half your troubles immediately by no longer permitting people to tell you what you want. You have to put your life in your own hands. Others may be able stop you temporarily, but only you can do it permanently.

Some people will kill you over time if you let them; and how they'll kill you is with tiny, harmless phrases like, "be realistic." When this happens, close your ears and listen to your inner voice instead. Remember that real success in life isn't what others see, but how you feel. It's living your truth and doing what makes you feel alive.

5 Stop caring about the boundaries others set up.

No matter how much progress you make there will always be the people who insist that whatever you're trying to do is impossible. Or they may incessantly suggest that the idea or dream as a whole is utterly ridiculous because nobody really cares. When you come across these people, don't try to reason with them. Instead, forget that they exist. They will only waste your time and energy.

Try what you want to try. Go where you want to go. Follow your own intuition. Don't accept false choices. Don't let others put a cage around you. Definitely don't listen to the watchdog.

6 Stop caring about what everyone else has.

Whenever somebody discredits you and tells you that you can't do something, keep in mind that they are speaking from within the boundaries of their own limitations. Ignore them and press on.

When you catch yourself comparing yourself to a colleague, neighbor, friend, or someone famous, stop! Realize that you are different, with different strengths – strengths those other people don't possess. Take a moment to reflect on all the awesome abilities you have and to be grateful for all the good things in your life.

The problem with many of us is that we think we'll be happy when we reach a certain level in life — a level we see others operating at – your boss with her corner office, that friend of a friend who owns a

mansion on the beach, etc. Unfortunately, it takes awhile before you get there, and when you get there you might have a new destination in mind.

Instead, appreciate where you are and what you have right now. Try comparing yourself to those who have less, those who are dealing with tragedy, and those who are struggling to survive. Hopefully it opens your eyes to all the things you should be grateful for.

7 Stop caring about the imaginary state of perfect.

Perfect is the enemy of good.

Many of us are perfectionists in our own right. I know I am at times. We set high bars for ourselves and put our best foot forward. We dedicate copious amounts of time and attention to our work to maintain our high personal standards. Our passion for excellence drives us to run the extra mile, never stopping, never relenting. And this dedication towards perfection undoubtedly helps us to achieve results... So long as we don't get carried away.

But what happens when we do get carried away with perfectionism?

We become disgruntled and discouraged when we fail to meet the (impossibly high) standards we set for ourselves, making us reluctant to take on new challenges or even finish tasks we've already started. Our insistence on dotting every 'I' and crossing every 'T' breeds inefficiency, causing major delays, stress overload and subpar results.

True perfectionists have a hard time starting things and an even harder time finishing them... always. I have a friend who has wanted to start a graphic design business for several years. But she hasn't yet. Why? When you sift through her extensive list of excuses it comes down to one simple problem: She is a perfectionist. Which means she doesn't, and never will, think she's good enough at graphic design to own and operate her own graphic design business.

Remember, the real world doesn't reward perfectionists. It rewards people who get things done. And the only way to get things done is to be imperfect 99% of the time. Only by wading through years of practice and imperfection can we begin to achieve momentary glimpses of the perfection.

So make a decision. Take action. Learn from the outcome. And repeat this method over and over and over again in all walks of life.

8   *Stop caring about being right all the time.*

We all dance to the beat of a different drum. There are few absolute 'rights' and 'wrongs' in the world. What's right for you may be wrong for me, and vise versa.

People need to live their lives their way – the way that's right for them.

When it comes to life choices and opinions, not much is worth fighting about. Step back from arguments with your spouse, family members or neighbors. When you feel anger surging up and you want to yell that vulgar remark on the tip of your tongue, just close your mouth and walk away. Let the mind calm down. You don't have to be right or win an argument.

Instead, open your mind to new ideas and opinions. Don't just concentrate on what others are doing, spend time figuring out why they are doing what they're doing.

9   *Stop caring about mistakes.*

If you can avoid it, don't fight with loved ones. Don't let a single poisonous moment of misunderstanding make you forget about the countless lovable moments you've spent together. If you're angry at someone you love, hug them and mean it. You may not want to hug them, which is all the more reason to do so. It's hard to stay angry when someone shows that they love you, and that's precisely what happens when we hug each other.

10 *Stop caring about things you can't control.*

Some forces are out of your control. Accept this fact of life. Wasting your time, talent and emotional energy on things that are beyond your control is a recipe for frustration, misery and stagnation.

The smartest thing you can do to compensate for the things you can't control is adjusting your attitude. Your attitude has a profound effect on your overall potential. Consuming yourself with the negative aspects of a circumstance gets nothing productive accomplished. But if you instead look at the circumstance productively and positively, coming from the standpoint of "What's my next best move?" you put yourself back in the driver's seat.

Bottom line: As Maria Robinson once said, "Nobody can go back and start a new beginning, but anyone can start today and make a new ending." You can't change what happened, but you can change how you react to it. If you awake every morning with the thought that something wonderful will happen in your life today, and you pay close attention, you'll often find that you're right. The opposite is also true. The choice is yours to make.

12 THINGS To START Caring About Today

Life is all about taking chances. It's about doing something you initially thought you could never do. It's about being a little crazy, following your heart, and not worrying about every detail of what everyone else thinks. And above all, it's about learning to love who you are and what you have.

Here are twelve things to start caring about on your journey forward.

1 Start caring about your own happiness.

It's important to make people happy, but you have to start with yourself. Your needs matter. Sometimes we get lost trying to live our lives for someone else, trying to meet their expectations, or trying to do things just to impress others. But you've got to live, do and love so that YOU are happy. Because when it comes down to it, relationships can end in an instant, but you will live with yourself for the rest of your life. Remember, it is possible to take care of your own needs while simultaneously caring for those around you. And once your needs are met, you will likely be far more capable of helping those who need you most.

2 Start caring about your goals and dreams.

If you want to know where your heart is, look where your mind goes when it wanders. Don't ignore these ideas, act on them. Give your dreams a chance. This isn't the wrong time and place, because you can make it the right time and place. Today is the first day of a new beginning – the conception of a new life. The next nine months are all yours. You can do with them as you please. Make them count. Because a new person is born in nine months. The only question is: Who do you want that person to be?

3 Start caring about how you invest your time every day.

There might not be a tomorrow, not for everyone. Right now, someone on Earth is planning something for tomorrow without realizing they're going to die today. This is sad but true. So spend your time wisely and pause long enough to appreciate it. Remember, what you do every day matters more than what you do every once in awhile. Use a time management system to control events, rather than have events controlling you. It may take a little time to get where you want to be, but if you think for a moment, you will realize that you are no longer where you once were. Do not stop – keep going. You're getting closer every day.

4 Start caring about how you think and what you think about.

In your quiet moments, what do you think about? How far you've come, or how far you have to go? Your strengths, or your weaknesses? The best that might happen, or the worst that might come to be? In your quiet moments, pay attention to your self-talk. Because maybe, just maybe, the only thing that needs to shift in order for you to experience more happiness, more love, and more vitality, is your way of thinking.

5 Start caring about how you treat yourself.

Your relationship with yourself is the closest and most important relationship you will ever have. When was the last time someone told you that they loved you just the way you are, and that what you think and how you feel matters? When was the last time someone told you that you did a good job, or took you someplace, simply because they know you feel happy when you're there? When was the last time that 'someone' was YOU? The way you treat yourself sets the standard for others. You must love who you are or no one else will either. And when you are truly comfortable in your own skin, not everyone will like you, but you won't care about it one bit.

6 Start caring about how you treat others.

Live so that when the people around you think of fairness, caring and integrity, they think of you. Start noticing what you like about others and tell them. Having an appreciation for how amazing the people around you are leads to good places – productive, fulfilling, peaceful places. So be happy for those who are making progress. Cheer for their victories. Be thankful for their blessings, openly. What goes around comes around, and sooner or later the people you're cheering for will start cheering for you.

7. *Start caring about how others treat you.*

Choose your relationships wisely. Being alone will never cause as much loneliness as the wrong relationship. If you don't value yourself, look out for yourself, and stick up for yourself, you're sabotaging yourself. Life is too short to spend time with people who suck the happiness out of you. Love the people who treat you right, and distance yourself from the ones who don't.

Start caring about your health.

Exercise to be fit, not skinny. Eat to nourish your body. And always ignore the haters, doubters and unhealthy examples that were once feeding you. To truly be your best, you must give your body the fuel it needs. Toss the junk and fill your kitchen with fresh, whole foods. Run, swim, bike, walk... just move! Good health is essential for having the energy, stamina and outlook to tackle your goals and dreams. Bottom line: Your health is your life. Don't let it go. Eat right, exercise and get an annual physical check-up.

9. *Start caring about your education and personal growth.*

Achieving higher consciousness comes from your commitment to personal growth. You're a totally different person compared to who you were at this time last year; next year will be no different. How much you grow and who you become is up to you. But remember, the acquisition of knowledge doesn't mean you're growing. Growing happens when what you know changes how you live.

10. *Start caring about doing the best YOU can.*

Don't worry about what others are doing better than you. Concentrate on beating your own records every day. Success is a battle between YOU and YOURSELF only. And whatever you do, refuse to lower your standards to accommodate those who refuse to raise theirs.

11. *Start caring about all the wonderful things you have right now.*

Learn to appreciate the things you have before time forces you to appreciate the things you once had. No matter how good or bad you have it, wake up each day thankful for your life. Someone somewhere else is desperately fighting for theirs. Instead of thinking about what you're missing, try thinking about what you have that everyone else is missing.

12 *Start caring about this moment we call 'life.'*

When I watched the Grammy Awards recently, I realized that many of the speeches musicians make when they accept an award go something like this: "This means so much to me. My whole life has been leading up to this moment." But the truth is, our whole lives have been leading up to every moment. Think about that for a second. Every single thing you've gone through in life, every high, every low, and everything in between, it has led you to this moment right now. This moment is priceless, and it's the only moment guaranteed to you. This moment is your 'life.' Don't miss it.

10 LIES You Will HEAR Before You Pursue Your *Dreams*

Unfortunately, just before you take your first step on the righteous journey to pursue your dreams, people around you, even the ones who deeply care for you, will give you awful advice. It's not because they have evil intentions. It's because they don't understand the big picture – what your dreams, passions, and life goals mean to you. They don't understand that, to you, the reward is worth the risk.

So they try to protect you by shielding you from the possibility of failure, which, in effect, also shields you from the possibility of making your dreams a reality.

As our friend Steve Jobs says:

> *"Your time is limited, so don't waste it living someone else's life. Don't be trapped by dogma, which is living with the results of other people's thinking. Don't let the noise of others' opinions drown out your own inner voice, heart and intuition. They somehow already know what you truly want to become. Everything else is secondary."*

Here are 10 ill-advised tips (lies) people will likely tell you when you decide to pursue your dreams, and why they are dreadfully mistaken.

1 *You can follow your dreams someday, but right now you need to buckle down and be responsible.*

Someday? When is 'someday?' Someday is not a day at all. It's a foggy generalization of a time that will likely never come. Today is the only day guaranteed to you. Today is the only day you can begin to make a difference in your life. And pursuing your dreams is what life is all about. So don't be irresponsible. Don't wait until 'someday.' Make today the first day of the rest of your new life.

2   *You're totally screwed if it doesn't work out.*

Wrong! This is a giant, lame load of BS. You're not even close to being screwed. In fact, the worst case scenario is that things don't work out and you have to go back to doing exactly what you are doing right now.

3   *It's safer to stay at your day job.*

Sure, I suppose. But you know what's even safer than that? Going home, locking yourself in your bedroom, and never, ever coming out. And just like that you will have flushed your entire life and your dreams down the toilet. Remember, safer doesn't always mean better.

That's impossible!

It's only impossible if you never do anything about it. The reason certain things seem impossible is simply because nobody has achieved them yet. But this doesn't mean that with your help these things won't become possible in the future. If you truly dedicate yourself to an end result, almost anything is possible. You just have to want it bad enough.

Only a lucky few "make it."

That's because those lucky few got off their rear ends and did something about

it! They had the drive, determination, and willpower that you have right now. You can be one of them. It's up to you, and only you.

6   *You might fail. And failing is bad.*

Failures are simply stepping stones to success. No matter how it turns out, it always ends up just the way it should be. Either you succeed or you learn something. Win-Win. The biggest mistake you can make is doing nothing because you're too scared to make a mistake. If you can't handle failure, then you can't handle success either.

7   *You will sacrifice too much for too little.*

When it comes to working hard to achieve a dream – earning a degree, building a business, or any other personal achievement that takes time and commitment – one thing you have to ask yourself is: "Am I willing to live a few years of my life like many people won't, so I can spend the rest of my life like many people can't?"

8 *You need more money saved before you can take the first step.*

You don't need more money. You need a plan. You need a budget. Eliminate ALL the nonessential costs in your life. If pursuing your dream requires you to leave your day job, figure out the absolute minimum amount of income that you require to realistically live. Studying those who have succeeded with similar ventures also helps. But above all, take baby steps. Don't be foolish and assume that you must have a certain amount of money saved right now, or that you must quit your day job today in order to pursue your dreams. Instead, ask yourself, "What actions can I take right now with the money and resources I have right now that will bring me closer to my desired goal?"

9 *You don't need any help. It's smarter to go after it alone.*

Surrounding yourself with positive people will increase your effectiveness and your chances for success. So spend time with people who support your goals, because you are the average of the people you spend the most time with. In other words, who you spend your time with has a great impact on the person you eventually become. If you are around cynical and negative people all the time, you will become cynical and negative. Does who you are and who you want to be reflect in the company you keep?

10 *That sounds like a lot of hard work.*

You're darn right it does! But that doesn't mean it's not worth it. I think success in life hinges on one key point: Finding hard work you love doing. As long as you remain true to yourself and follow your own interests, values and dreams, you can find success through passion. Perhaps most importantly, you won't wake up a few years from now working in a career field you despise, wondering "How the heck am I going to do this for the next 30 years?" So if you catch yourself working hard and loving every minute of it, don't stop. You're on to something big. Because hard work isn't hard when you concentrate on your passions and dreams.

Disregard these misguided bits of nonsense and you'll be well on your way to fulfilling your dreams.

Now get out there and make a splash!

WHAT **LIFE** IS ALL **ABOUT**

Once upon a time, there was a girl who could do anything in the world she wanted. All she had to do was choose something and focus. So one day she sat down in front of a blank canvas and began to paint. Every stroke was more perfect than the next, slowly and gracefully converging to build a flawless masterpiece. And when she eventually finished painting, she stared proudly at her work and smiled.

It was obvious to the clouds and the stars, who were always watching over her, that she had a gift. She was an artist. And she knew it too. She felt it in every fiber of her being. But a few moments after she finished painting, she got anxious and quickly stood up. Because she realized that while she had the ability to do anything in the world she wanted to do, she was simply spending her time moving paint around on a piece of canvas.

She felt like there was so much more in the world to see and do – so many options. And if she ultimately decided to do something else with her life, then all the time she spent painting would be a waste. So she glanced at her masterpiece one last time, and walked out the door into the moonlight. And as she walked, she thought, and then she walked some more.

While she was walking, she didn't notice the clouds and the stars in the sky who were trying to signal her, because she was preoccupied with an important decision she had to make. She had to choose one thing to do out of all the possibilities in the world. Should she practice medicine? Or design buildings? Or teach children? She was utterly stumped.

Twenty-five years later, the girl began to cry. Because she realized she had been walking for so long, and that over the years she had become so enamored by everything that she could do – the endless array of possibilities – that she hadn't done anything meaningful at all. And she learned, at last, that life isn't about possibility – anything is possible. Life is about making a decision – deciding to do something that moves you.

So the girl, who was no longer a girl, purchased some canvas and paint from a local craft store, drove to a nearby park, and began to paint. One stroke gracefully led into the next just as it had so many moons ago. And as she smiled, she continued painting through the day and into the night. Because she had finally made a decision. And there was still some time left to revel in the magic that life is all about.

20 WAYS

To CREATE *Million Dollar* I.D.E.A.S

Big companies like Apple, super successful websites like Facebook, and bestselling books like The 4-Hour Workweek all have one thing in common: They began with a million dollar idea.

The big question is: How did their creators come up with these ideas? Did they sit around waiting for an inspirational flash or a mystic spell of luck?

The answer is: Spontaneity and luck had little to do with it.

In this article, we'll take a brief look at 20 tried and true techniques that some of the brightest and most successful entrepreneurs have used to generate million dollar ideas.

1 *Generate lots of ideas.*

The more ideas you create, the more likely you are to create an idea worth a million bucks.

2 *Fail a lot.*

All of the ideas that don't work are simply stepping stones on your way to the one idea that does. Sometimes you have to fail a thousand times to succeed. No matter how many mistakes you make or how slow you progress, you are still way ahead of everyone who isn't trying.

3 *Consume information consciously.*

Some of my friends think it's wasteful that I spend so much time reading books and blogs. It's not. It's what gives me an edge. I feel engulfed with new ideas and information. And I've actually used what I've learned to launch a few successful websites. When you read things and interact with people, take off your consumer cap and put on your creator cap. There are million dollar ideas (or at least some really good ideas) all around you waiting for discovery.

> *You don't need to have a 100-person company*
> *to develop and execute a good idea.*
> – Larry Page (Google)

Focus on topics and ideas with large markets.

A million dollars is not a lot of money in the grand scheme of things, but it certainly is if you're trying to earn it in a small market with limited opportunities. Even if you put Steve Jobs in the role of CEO for a new venture with a maximum market size of 100 people he wouldn't make more than a few cents. 'Big bucks' result from high demand in a substantial market.

Make sure there's money in your market.

Bank robbers rob banks because that's where the money is. Before you become emotionally attached to an idea, do a little market research. Make sure the idea you're pursuing is where the money is. Who are the clients and consumers? How much disposable income do they have? Etc.

6 Keep your eyes, ears and mind wide open.

Oftentimes one idea's failure will open a door to a new idea. Don't get so hung up on one failed attempt that you miss the opening for many more.

7 Test variations of the same idea.

Think about the iPhone and the iPad for a second. One is just a variation of the other. Both are multi-million dollar ideas.

8 Figure out what works well in one market and tailor it to another.

Find an idea that's already proven and think about how it could be applied in a different context. Take a formula that works in one niche and apply it to a new niche. Or take the best aspects of one product and combine it with another product.

9 Put the pieces together.

YouTube's creators didn't invent Flash. They didn't invent modern digital cameras that can record computer-ready mpeg video. And they didn't invent broadband Internet connections, cheap web hosting, embedded website content, or one-click website uploading technologies either. What they invented is a technology that takes all of these existing pieces and combines them into an online video sharing portal.

10 Spin a new twist on a previous breakthrough.

A new twist on an old idea can still be a million dollar idea. Take Facebook for instance, it wasn't the first big social networking site, but Mark Zuckerberg and company added twists and features the others did not grasp. How can you take an existing million dollar idea, or even a common idea, and give it a new twist, a new direction and journey?

11 Systematize a popular service into a reproducible product.

A service is productized when its ownership can be exchanged. Think about Alienware and Dell back in their infancy. Both companies simply systematized the service of building IBM compatible PCs and then sold them as a packaged product. If you can convert a high demand service into a scalable, systematized, efficient process and sell it as a packaged deal, the million appears.

12 Play with opposites.

When something becomes extremely popular, the opposite often also becomes popular as people turn away from the mainstream. When Wordpress, Blogger and Movable Type exploded in popularity by giving anyone with an Internet connection the ability to share long, detailed blog posts with the world, Twitter and Tumblr came along and started the micro-blogging revolution – for people grasping to share extremely short content snippets. There are hundreds of other examples. Just remember, the opposite of a million dollar idea can paradoxically give birth to another million dollar idea.

13 Look for problems and solve them.

There are many real problems in this world. Like a business owner wondering why his profits are sinking. Like a golfer worrying about his slice. Like a young man who is growing bald at 26. Like a mom whose child is suffering with allergies. Like a new dog owner who's unsure what to do about her puppy barking all night. Solving problems like these can make millions.

14 Design new products that support other successful products.

How much money do you think iPod, iPhone and iPad case manufacturers are making? Millions? Billions? What about companies that jumped into the market of manufacturing LCD and Plasma TV mounting brackets eight years ago? You get the idea.

15 Keep it simple.

Don't over complicate a good idea. Business marketing studies have shown that the more product choices offered, the less products consumers typically buy. After all, narrowing down the best product from a pool of three choices is certainly easier than narrowing down the best product from a pool of three hundred choices. If the purchasing decision is tough to make, most people will just give up. So if you're designing a product line, keep it simple.

16 Use the tools and skills you already have.

It's not as much about acquiring the right tools and skills as it is about using the ones you already have. Don't let what you can't do stop you from what you can do. No more excuses, no more wasting precious time. This moment is as good a time as any to begin doing what matters most. Start exactly where you are right now. Do what you can with what you have right now. Stop over-thinking and start DOING!

17 Surround yourself with other thinkers.

You are the sum of the people you spend the most time with. If you hang with the wrong people, they will affect you negatively. But if you hang with the right people, you will be more capable and powerful than you ever could have been alone. Find your tribe and collaborate to make a difference in all your lives. Bounce ideas off each other, etc.

18 Be enthusiastic about what you're doing.

Enthusiasm is the lifeblood of creativity. Big ideas blossom when you're passionate and enthusiastic about what you're doing. It's nearly impossible to pioneer ground breaking solutions in a domain where there is not passionate intensity. But when your mind is stimulated by a fundamental curiosity and interest in the subject matter, your creativity will run rampant and your motivation will skyrocket.

19 Accept constructive criticism, but ignore naysayers.

When someone spews negativity about your idea or product, remember, it doesn't matter how many people don't get it, it matters how many do. No matter how much progress you make there will always be the people who insist that whatever you're trying to do is impossible. Or they may jealously suggest that the idea or concept as a whole is utterly ridiculous because nobody really cares. When you come across these people, don't try to reason with them. Instead, forget that they exist. They will only waste your time and energy.

20 *Actually do something with your ideas!*

A million dollar idea is simply a good idea given the chance to grow. On paper, Google and Facebook sprung from fairly ordinary ideas: 'a search engine that's accurate' and 'a website where friends connect with each other.' Remember, neither of these companies were the first ones in their market. Their ideas weren't groundbreaking at the time. Many people had the same ideas even before Google and Facebook existed. But Google's and Facebook's creators did something with their ideas. They worked hard and one-upped the competition. Their initial success was in their execution. Remember, it's not the ideas themselves that count, it's what you do with them. With the right execution, a simple idea can evolve into a million dollar idea.

8 REASONS to **STOP** Waiting for APPROVAL

One of the greatest freedoms is simply not caring what everyone else thinks of you. Sometimes you need to step outside, get some air, and remind yourself of who you are and what you want to be. The best thing you can do is follow your heart. Take risks. Don't just accept the safe and easy choices because you're afraid of what others will think, or afraid of what might happen. If you do, nothing will ever happen. Don't let small minds convince you that your dreams are too big. They aren't.

Starting today, stop waiting for approval. Here's why:

1 *You only get one life to pursue the dreams that make you come alive.*

It is better to be failing (and learning) at doing something you love, rather than succeeding at doing something you hate. So take chances on behalf of what you believe in. Fail until you succeed. Make sacrifices and step out beyond the safety of your comfort zone over and over again. Face your fears with courage and passion. Keep your word and hold true to your vision until it comes to life.

2 *Someone else's approval is just another opinion.*

Someone else's approval is just another opinion. – Never let someone's opinion become your reality. Never sacrifice who you are, or who you aspire to be, because someone else has a problem with it. Love who you are inside and out, and keep pushing forward. No one else has the power to make you feel small unless you give them that power. You are the only one who can create your dreams and happiness.

The only opinion of you that really matters is your own.

In life, the thing that is really hard and really amazing is giving up on the desire to be perfect in the eyes of others, and beginning the journey of becoming your true self. So let your love flow freely. Because what you love determines your dreams, your dreams determine your actions, and your actions determine your destiny.

Some people will never give you their approval anyway.

Do not let the negative opinions of others destroy your inner peace. There are two kinds of people – those who are a drain on your energy and creative force, and those who give you energy and support your creativity, even with the simplest gesture, like a smile. Avoid the first kind. Be happy. Be who you want to be. If others don't like it, let them be. Happiness is a choice – YOUR choice. Life isn't about pleasing everyone.

5 Everyone's journey and perspective on life is totally different.

Who you are is what makes you extraordinary. Do not change your unique foundation for anyone. What lies ahead will always be a bit of a mystery. Do not be afraid to explore, learn and grow. Why some things happen will never be certain. Take it in stride and move forward. When life pushes you over, stand up and push back even harder. Where there is a fork in the road and choices to make, make the one your future self will thank you for.

6 Firsthand experience is often necessary for personal growth.

Some life lessons can only be understood by going through them on your own. Doing so allows you to form your own conclusions based on firsthand experience, rather than someone else's subjective opinion. This experience gives you the ability to think more logically and take educated steps in a positive direction.

7 Your intuition requires no approval.

When it comes to exercising your inner genius, you must try what you want to try, go where you want to go, and follow your own intuition. Don't accept false choices. Don't let others put a cage around your ideas. If it feels right, take a chance. Because you never know how absolutely perfect it could turn out to be.

8 | *Life is too short to wait any longer.*

If you knew for certain you had a terminal illness – if you had a very limited time left to live – you wouldn't waste a minute of it. Well wake up! You do have a terminal illness; it's called 'life.' In the grand scheme of things, you don't have much time left – no one does. So look around at this gift you've been given, as its miracles unfold before your eyes. And choose to be happy, without approval – or you will never be happy at all.

10 THINGS to DO Even if They Judge You

What would you do differently if you knew nobody would judge you?

Truth be told, no one has the right to judge you. People may have heard your stories, but they can't feel what you are going through; they aren't living YOUR life. So forget what they say about you. Focus on how you feel about yourself, and do what you know in your heart is right.

Here are ten things to do even if others judge you for it:

1 Take care of yourself.

Your relationship with yourself is the closest and most important relationship you will ever have. If you don't take good care of yourself, then you can't take good care of others either; which is why taking care of yourself is the best selfish thing you can do.

2 Do what you know is right, for YOU.

Don't be scared to walk alone, and don't be scared to like it. Don't let anyone's ignorance, drama, or negativity stop you from being the best you can be. Keep doing what you know in your heart is right, for

you. Because when you are totally at peace within yourself, nothing can shake you.

3 Follow your own unique path.

Every new day is a chance to change your life. Work on making life all that you want it to be. Work hard for what you believe, and keep your dreams big and your worries small. You never need to carry more than you can hold; just take it one day at a time. And while you're out there making decisions instead of excuses, learning new things, and getting closer and closer to your goals, know that there are others out there, like me, who admire your efforts and are striving for greatness too.

Lock yourself away from the world and work on your goals.

Dream big dreams, but realize that short term, realistic goals are the key to success. Success is directly connected with daily action. The way we spend our time defines who we are. Successful people keep moving, by doing small things every day that bring them a couple steps closer to their dream. They make mistakes along the way, but they don't quit – they learn and press on.

Adjust your goals and dreams as life changes.

A great deal of pain in life comes from having a specific dream that you've fallen in love with, and when it doesn't work out exactly as planned, you become angry that you now have to pursue a different path. If you want to tame your inner demons and make the most of life, you must not become rigidly attached to just one specific dream, and remain open to there being an even better, equally as happy path ahead. Life is unpredictable, but it provides plenty of opportunities to make dreams come true. Just don't forget that sometimes taking a positive step forward requires you to slightly adjust your dreams, or plan new ones – it's OK to change your mind or have more than one dream.

6 Forgive those who have wronged you.

Forgiveness is a gift you give yourself. Forgiveness is an attribute of the strong and wise. Forgiveness allows you to focus on the future without combating the past. To understand the potential of everything going forward is to forgive everything already behind you. Without forgiveness, wounds can never be healed, and moving on can never be accomplished. What happened in the past is just one chapter. Don't close the book, just turn the page.

7 Show everyone your love and kindness.

If you are reserving your love only for those who you have decided are worthy of it – all strangers excluded – it may come as a surprise to learn that this is not love at all, it is called judgment. Judgment is selective, love is all embracing. Just as the sunlight and the wind do not discriminate, true love does not make any such distinctions either. Love and kindness is a way of living. Where there is love, there is no judgment. Where there is judgment, there is no love.

Stand up for others, even if it's the unpopular thing to do.

Sometimes you will say something really small and simple, but it will fit right into an empty space in someone's heart. Dare to reach into the darkness, to pull someone else into the light. Remember, strong people stand up for themselves, but stronger people stand up for others too, and lend a hand when they're able.

Fight through your failures.

When you are feeling down or dealing with failure, don't be ashamed. There's nothing to be ashamed of. You are going through a difficult time, and you are still pushing forward. That's something to be proud of – that you are fighting through it and slowly rising above it. Let everyone know that today you are a lot stronger than you were yesterday, and you will be.

Keep your head held high and keep on smiling.

Every day of your life is a page of your history. The only time you run out of chances is when you stop taking them. Don't cry over the past, cry to get over the past. Don't smile to hide the pain, smile to heal the pain. Don't think of all the sadness in the world, think of all the beauty that still remains around you.

15 WAYS to LIVE, and Not Merely *Exist*

As Jack London once said, "The proper function of man is to live, not to exist." Far too often we travel through life on autopilot, going through the motions, accepting what is, and having every day pass like the one before it. Everything seems relatively normal and comfortable, except that constant twitch in the back of your mind that's saying, "It's time to make some changes."

Here are 15 simple suggestions for those who want to break free from the mold and truly live more of their life – to experience it and enjoy it to the fullest, instead of settling for a mere existence.

1 Appreciate the great people and things in your life.

Sometimes we don't notice the things others do for us until they stop doing them. Don't be like that. Be grateful for what you have, who loves you, and who cares for you. You'll never know how much they mean to you until the day they're no longer beside you. Truly appreciate those around you, and you'll soon find many others around you. Truly appreciate life, and you'll find that you have more of it to live.

2 Ignore other people's negativity.

If you allow people to make more withdrawals than deposits in your life, you will be out of balance and in the negative before you know it. Ignore unconstructive, hurtful commentary. No one has the right to judge you. They may have heard your stories, but they didn't feel what you were going through. You do not have control over what others say; but you do have control over whether or not you allow them to say these things to you. You alone can deny their poisonous words from invading your heart and mind.

3 Forgive those who have hurt you.

I forgive people, but that doesn't mean I trust them. I just don't have time to hate people who hurt me, because I'm too busy loving people who love me. The first to apologize is the bravest. The first to forgive is the strongest. The first to move forward is the happiest. Be brave. Be strong. Be happy. Be free.

4 Be who you really are.

If you're lucky enough to have something that makes you different from everybody else, don't change. Uniqueness is priceless. In this crazy world that's trying to make you like everyone else, find the courage to keep being your awesome self. And when they laugh at you for being different, laugh back at them for being the same. It takes a lot of courage to stand alone, but it's worth it. Being YOU is worth it!

5 Choose to listen to your inner voice.

Life is a courageous journey or nothing at all. We cannot become who we want to be by continuing to do exactly what we've been doing. Choose to listen to your inner voice, not the jumbled opinions of everyone else. Do what you know in your heart is right for YOU. It's your road, and yours alone. Others may walk it with you, but no one can walk it for you. And be sure

to appreciate every day of your life. Good days give you happiness, bad days give you experience, and the worst days give you the best lessons.

6 Embrace change and enjoy your life as it unfolds.

The hardest part about growing is letting go of what you were used to, and moving on with something you're not. Sometimes you have to stop worrying, wondering, and doubting, and have faith that things will work out. Laugh at the confusion, live consciously in the moment, and enjoy your life as it unfolds. You might not end up exactly where you intended to go, but eventually you will arrive precisely where you need to be.

7 Choose your relationships wisely.

The best relationships are not just about the good times you share, they're also about the obstacles you go through together, and the fact that you still say "I love you" in the end. And loving someone isn't just about saying it every day, it's showing it every day in every way. Relationships must be chosen wisely. Don't rush love. Wait until you truly find it. Don't let loneliness drive you back into the arms of someone you know you don't belong with. Fall in love when you're ready, not when you're lonely. A great relationship is worth waiting for.

8 Recognize those who love you.

The most memorable people in your life will be the ones who loved you when you weren't very loveable. Pay attention to who these people are in your life, and love them back, even when they aren't acting loveable.

9 Love yourself too.

If you can love children, in spite of the messes they make; your mother, in spite of her tendency to nag; your father, even though he's too opinionated; your sibling, even though she's always late; your friend, even though he often forgets to return what he borrows, then you know how to love imperfect people, and can surely love yourself.

10 Do things your future self will thank you for.

What you do every day matters more than what you do every once in a while. What you do today is important because you are exchanging a day of your life for it. Make sure it's worthwhile.

11 Be thankful for all the troubles you don't have.

There are two ways of being rich: One is to have all you want, the other is to be satisfied with what you have. Accept and appreciate things now, and you'll find more happiness in every moment you live. Happiness comes when we stop complaining about the troubles we have and offer thanks for all the troubles we don't have. And remember, you have to fight through some bad days to earn the best days of your life.

12 Leave enough time for fun.

Sometimes you need to take a few steps back to see things clearly. Never let your life become so filled with work, your mind become so crammed with worry, or your heart become so jammed with old hurts or anger, that there's no room left in them for fun, for awe, or for joy.

13 Enjoy the little things in life.

The best things in life are free. There is absolute joy and wonder to be had in the simplest of moments. Watching the sunset over the horizon or spending time with a family member. Enjoy the little things, because one day you may look back and discover they were the big things.

Accept the fact that the past is not today.

Don't let the past steal your present and future from you. You might not be proud of all the things you've done in the past, but that's okay. The past is not today. The past cannot be changed, forgotten, or erased. It can only be accepted. We all make mistakes, have struggles, and even regret things in our past. But you are not your mistakes, you are not your struggles, and you are here NOW with the power to shape your day and your future.

Let go when you must.

It's not always about trying to fix something that's broken. Some relationships and situations just can't be fixed. If you try to force them back together, things will only get worse. Sometimes it's about starting over and creating something better. Strength shows not only in the ability to persist, but in the ability to start over again with a smile on your face and passion in your heart.

THE **ART** OF BEING **NAKED**

The Girl

She has dirty blond hair, a seductive smile, and the most engaging set of hazel green eyes I've ever seen. It's the kind of engaging I can't ignore... the kind that makes me want to engage too. Because she's mysterious. And I'm curious. And I need to know more.

Yet, I do my best to avoid making eye contact. So I stare down at the pool table and pretend to study my opponent's next move. But only long enough for her to look the other way, so I can once again catch a glimpse of magnificence.

I do this, not because she intimidates me, but because I think she may be the girl Chad met last night. A wild night that, he said, "involved two bottles of port wine, chocolate cake, and sweaty bed sheets."

Then, just as her eyes unexpectedly meet mine, my opponent groans, "It's been your turn for like five minutes. Ya planning on going sometime today?" And she walks gracefully away.

So I continue to wonder... "Is she the port wine and chocolate cake girl? Gosh, she doesn't look like that kind of girl." But I don't wonder too long because Chad enters the room and says, "Marc, there's someone I want you to meet." So I follow him into the kitchen and we bump right into her. "Oh, Angel," Chad says. "This is my buddy, Marc."

And I smile ear to ear and chuckle...

Because she's not the port wine and chocolate cake girl. But also because I spent the last twenty minutes thinking about the port wine, and the chocolate cake, and the sweaty bed sheets.

The Dance

Hours later, the party begins winding down. But the band is still playing, the two painters who have been painting a wall mural all evening are still painting, and Angel and I are still dancing.

"Are you tired?" I ask.

"No," Angel says. "Dancing is my outlet. When I dance, I transcend myself and the doubts that sometimes prevent me from being me. This evening has been enchanting, just dancing with you and being me."

So I twirl her around. And the drummer keeps drumming. The guitarist keeps strumming. The singer keeps singing. The painters keep painting. And now we're the only ones dancing.

As we continue to dance, she says, "I feel as if we're naked. And not just you and me, but the drummer, the guitarist, the singer, and the painters too. Everyone left in this room is naked... naked and free."

I smile and tell her that I agree. "We are naked. We are free."

As I know we don't have to take our clothes off to be naked. Because moments of passion flow into each other like port wine flows into chocolate cake. And if we let them, these moments can expose us completely, and continuously. And create climaxes that don't even require sex.

Because a true climax has little to do with orgasm, and everything to do with passion, love, and devotion. In the same way, nakedness has little to do with how much clothing one wears, and everything to do with one's awareness in a given moment of time... An unfettered awareness that frees their mind and allows them to truly live the moment for all it's worth.

The Climax

After a few more songs, Angel asks if I'd like to join her out on the front porch where it's quieter. "Just so we can talk about life," she says.

I give her a little wink. "I love life in this crazy world! It is crazy, isn't it?"

She smiles. "Yeah, a world in which we can be naked with our clothes on and experience continuous climax without intercourse."

"Because instead we can achieve both with music, or paint, or dance, or any form of avid self-expression," I add.

"You got it. Even the sincerity in this conversation is beginning to work for me," she says as we step out the front door and into the moonlight.

When passion and skill work together, the end result is a masterpiece.

Your work is to discover your work and then, with all your heart, to give yourself to it.

If you are passionate about it, pursue it, no matter what anyone else thinks. That's how dreams are achieved.

The heart of human excellence often begins to beat when you discover a pursuit that absorbs you, frees you, challenges you, and gives you a sense of meaning, joy and passion.

A writer writes. If you want to be a writer, write. This concept can be universally applied.

It's not how much money you make that ultimately makes you happy. It's whether or not your work fulfills you.

No matter how many times you break down, there should always be a little voice inside you that says, "NO, you're not done yet! Get back up!" That's the voice of passion and courage.

Only passions, great passions, can elevate the soul to great things.

Find what makes you come alive, whatever it is. Become it and let it become you, and great things happen FOR you, TO you and BECAUSE of you.

Continue to work hard at what you love no matter what the odds are. Eventually, someone will praise and appreciate what you do.

Purpose is the reason you journey. Passion is the fire that lights your way.

If you cannot put your heart in it, take yourself out of it.

It's not about getting a chance, it's about taking a chance. You'll rarely be 100% sure it will work, but you can always be 100% sure doing nothing won't work. Sometimes you just have to go for it.

Quotes to help you FOLLOW your PASSION

Passion
QUESTIONS
to Make You *think*

What will you
NEVER
give up
on?

Are you doing what you
BELIEVE in,
or are you
settling for
what you are doing?

What activities make you
LOSE track
of *time*?

What **ONE** thing
have you not done that
you really want to do?
What's
holding
you back?

What
FASCINATES
you?

What is something
you would **HATE**
to go *without*
for a day?

What's
SOMETHING
you would do
every day
if you could?

Would you rather have
LESS work to do, or
more work you
actually enjoy doing?

At what time in your
recent past have you felt
most
PASSIONATE
and *alive*?

What would you
do **DIFFERENTLY** if you knew
nobody would
judge you?

Part Six
Productivity

No matter how many
mistakes you make or how slow
you progress, you are still way
ahead of everyone
who isn't trying.

THE **ADVICE**
THAT SAVED MY **LIFE**

Six years ago he walked into my dorm room on the verge of tears.

"I can't take it anymore!" he groaned. "I'm just running in place! I aim. I sprint. I leap. I fall. I get nowhere. Nowhere!"

His desperate eyes stared into mine, hoping... searching for an answer.

His Story

He has dreamed of pursuing a career in software engineering since he was a kid. "Businesses worldwide will rely on my code someday," he used to tell his computer programming teacher in high school. Now, as a junior enrolled in computer science at a reputable university, he finally has a clear shot at making his dream a reality.

He wakes up every morning filled with excitement and positive intentions. Studying is actually the first thing that crosses his mind. "I've got to get that chapter read," he tells himself. But first he needs to grab some Starbucks and a muffin. "Okay, now I'm ready."

He sits down at his desk and cracks open the book Agile Software Development. The phone rings. It's Jen, a good friend he met in his sophomore English class. "Lunch today? Yeah, I could do that. How's noon sound? Perfect. See you then." Before he sits back down to read, he remembers that he skipped his workout yesterday. "A quick workout will only take forty-five minutes and it will energize my mind for a few hours of diligent studying," he thinks to himself. He puts his sneakers on, grabs his iPod and heads over to the campus gym.

When he returns from the gym, he takes a shower and is once again ready to read. "Chapter 1: Welcome to the power of agile software development. This book is divided into..." "Ah, crap! I forgot to email my mother those photos I promised her. Heck, it will only take a second." He quickly fires-up his laptop and logs into Gmail. Before he has time to send the email, he gets an IM from an old high school buddy, Danny, whom he hasn't spoken to in six months. After a forty minute chat session, he sends the email to his mother and returns to the book.

He glances up at the wall clock and realizes he has to leave in thirty minutes to meet Jen for lunch. "Gosh, it's pointless to get into the groove of a focused study session for just thirty measly minutes," he says aloud. He convinces himself that it's in his best interest to save the reading for after lunch. So he logs into Facebook, replies to a few messages from his friends and then heads off to meet Jen. Once he returns from lunch an hour and a half later, he feels exhausted. The post-meal grogginess is kicking in hard. "All I need is another round of Starbucks and I'll be ready." He hustles out to grab it.

As he sits down at his desk with a fresh cup of coffee he repeats the word "focus" over and over as a mantra in his mind. He cracks the book back open. "Chapter 1: Welcome to the power of agile software development. This book is divided into..." But then his neighbor knocks on his door. "Turn on the Local 6 news channel! The college apartment complex down the street is on fire!" his neighbor chants. He thinks about it for a second, puts the book down and clicks on the television. "This should only take a second..."

And another day comes closer to an end.

Her Story

She gets up early every morning, grabs her soccer ball, and heads outside before she even washes her face, or eats, or pees. She juggles the ball between her feet nonstop until she achieves a continuous count of fifty. An old high school coach once told her that Mia Hamm (the greatest female soccer player ever) used to do this. When she's done, she gears-up for the day, grabs a glass of milk and a protein bar, and heads off to soccer practice.

Sometimes she catches up with me after practice, just before our 9 A.M. Economics class. I love it when she does, because her positive attitude is contagious. Her eyes always radiate with contentment and verve. In the few minutes before class we usually philosophize about our lives, our ambitions, and our relationships. For instance, today she said, "It's all about balance. We've got to somehow mesh our long-term goals with our momentary pleasures." She always explains herself clearly until she's confident that I understand her point of view.

Once class starts, she's silent, entirely focused on the professor's lecture. Her notes are more diligent than most. And although she rarely raises her hand, when she does, her question or comment usually brings a respectful smile to the professor's face.

Outside of class, I seldom see her during the day. She locks herself away in her dorm room, or in the library, or on the soccer field. She reads, writes, learns, and practices. She conditions her mind and her body with perpetual vigor.

Once or twice a week, when she actually takes a break, she'll call me at lunchtime. She usually goes off on a short tangent about something she's recently learned or experienced that excites her. And she always finishes by saying, "I'll fill you in on the details later." Because she knows I'm interested in hearing them. Because she mindfully extracts interesting details from data sources... details that most of us miss.

After a little nourishment, she gets back to work. Pages turn. Notes are taken. Keys on her laptop click repeatedly. And she carries forth until her vision blurs. When it does, she gets up, juggles her soccer ball to a count of twenty, and refocuses herself on her work. Again she forges ahead for another couple of hours until her brain has trouble focusing and her belly aches with hunger. Then she swings by my dorm room.

It's pretty late now, and both of us are done with whatever we've been working on. So we head out for a bite to eat. She fills me in on her day and speaks enthusiastically about the things that move her. Sometimes it's something new she learned. Sometimes it's an entrepreneurial idea. Sometimes it's

soccer. Or someone she met on campus. Or a song she heard on the radio that inspires her.

When we finish eating, she walks back to her dorm room. She thinks, or reads poetry, or listens to music, or works on the novel she's been leisurely writing for the last few months. When her eyes finally get heavy, she snuggles into her bed and falls blissfully asleep in an instant.

Satisfied with today. Eager for tomorrow.

The Advice

When he walked into my dorm room that day, I told him about her, and how she lives her life.

And although we don't talk as much as we used to, I received an email from him last night. It was a cheerful email about the software company he started last year. As it turns out, he just landed his first six-figure contract.

In the P.S. section of the email, he wrote: "Do you remember that story you told me in college about the girl who played soccer? Thank you. That advice saved my life."

10 WAYS

Successful People START Their Mornings

The day may have 24 hours of equivalent length but every hour is not created equal. Beginning the day with a purpose and a plan increases your chances of success.

In her book What the Most Successful People Do Before Breakfast, Laura Vanderkam writes, "Seizing your mornings is the equivalent of that sound financial advice to pay yourself first. If you wait until the end of the month to save what you have left, there will be nothing left over. Likewise, if you wait until the end of the day to do meaningful but not urgent things like exercise, pray, read, ponder how to advance your career or grow your organization, or truly give your family your best, it probably won't happen."

Here are 10 smart ways to start your day. I would suggest that the most successful people do the majority of these things during the first couple hours of their morning as part of their daily routine.

1 Get an early start.

This extra time will help you avoid speeding tickets, tardiness and other unnecessary headaches. In addition, most markets and businesses open by 9 A.M. Whether you work from home or commute to an office, the more time you've had to digest the day's news and obstacles ahead, the greater advantage you'll have over your competition.

2 Review your Focus list.

What is your number one goal right now? What's most important to you? What makes you happy? Design your time around these things. Remember, time is your greatest limited resource, because no matter how hard you try you can't work 25/8.

3 Prune any nonessential commitments for the day.

The mark of a successful person is the ability to set aside the 'somewhat important' things in order to accomplish the vital ones first. When you're crystal clear about your priorities, you can painlessly arrange them in the right order and discard the activities and commitments that do not support the ones at the top of your list.

4 Exercise.

Other than the obvious health benefits, movement increases brain function and decreases stress levels. Developing a consistent habit of exercising is a discipline which will carry over into your business day – Apple CEO, Tim Cook, is in the gym by 5 A.M. every morning. If you can, go outside for a walk, or jump on the treadmill and start out slow. This will jump-start your metabolism and your day.

5 Eat a healthy breakfast.

Your brain and body speed are a function of what you intake. Bagels, muffins and sugars have the tendency to slow you down. Fruits, proteins and grains help provide a consistent stream of energy without the sudden drop-off. Try a mixture of orange, apple and lemon juice with a spinach omelet one morning and let me know how much better you feel.

6 Kiss your partner goodbye.

It sounds cheesy, but most truly successful people have a great home life. Acknowledging your partner (and kids) mentally relaxes you, allowing you to focus on the day ahead. Don't lose sight of the fact that you're striving to be successful so they may benefit as well.

7 Practice 15 minutes of positive visualization.

In his program Get the Edge, Tony Robbins explains the importance of gratitude visualization first thing every morning. In a nutshell, spend roughly 15 minutes thinking of everything you're grateful for: in yourself, among your family and friends, in your career, and the like. After that, visualize everything you want in your life as if you had it today. The effect? Elevated certainty in everything you do, and always being in peak state. Despite how 'new age' it sounds, it's had incredible effects on associating success into my every-day life.

8 Eat that frog.

Brian Tracy's classic time-management book Eat That Frog gets its title from a Mark Twain quote that says, if you eat a live frog first thing in the morning, you've got it behind you for the rest of the day, and nothing else will be more difficult. In others words, get the tough stuff done first.

9 Connect with the right people.

Relationships are the basis of business – communication is the basis of relationships. Successful people associate with people who are likeminded, focused, and supportive. These people create energy when they enter the room, versus those who create energy when they leave. Connecting with these positive people in the morning can set you up for a positive day.

10 Stay informed.

Whether you prefer National Public Radio or the Wall Street Journal, spend a few minutes each morning learning about what is going on in the world. Not only will it educate you, it may change your perspective or inspire your actions for the day.

20 BAD Habits Holding *Good* People Back

A change in bad habits leads to a good change in life...

Here are twenty bad habits many of us repeatedly struggle with:

1 *Expecting life to be easy.*

Nothing starts easy; everything begins at some level of difficulty. Even waking up in the morning sometimes requires notable effort. But one beautiful thing about life is the fact that the most difficult challenges are often the most rewarding and satisfying.

2 *Overlooking your true path and purpose.*

What really matters in life is not what we buy, but what we build; not what we have, but what we share with the world; not our capability but our character; and not our success but our true significance. Live a life that makes you proud – one that matters and makes a difference. Live a life filled with passion and love.

3 *Chasing after those who don't want to be caught.*

Do not chase people. Be you, do your own thing and work hard on your passions. The right people who belong in your life will eventually come to you, and stay.

4 *Not asking for help when you know you need it.*

No matter how far you've gone down the wrong road, you can always turn back. Be STRONG enough to stand alone, SMART enough to know when you need help, and BRAVE enough to ask for it.

5 *Letting one dark cloud cover the entire sky.*

Take a deep breath. It's just a bad moment, or a bad day, not a bad life. Everyone has troubles. Everyone makes mistakes. The secret of happiness is to count your blessings while others are adding up their troubles.

6 Holding on to things you need to let go of.

Letting go doesn't mean giving up, but rather accepting that there are things in life that should not be. Sometimes letting go is what makes us stronger, happier and more successful in the long run.

7 Spending time with people who make you unhappy.

People can be cruel, and sometimes they will be. People can hurt you and break your heart, and sometimes they will. But only YOU can allow them to continuously hurt you. Value yourself enough to choose to spend time with people who treat you the way you treat them. Know your worth. Know when you have had enough. And move on from the people who keep chipping away at your happiness.

8 Not making time for those who matter most.

When we take things for granted, these things eventually get taken away. Too often we don't realize what we have until it's gone. Too often we are too stubborn to say, "I'm sorry, I was wrong." Too often it seems we hurt the ones closest to us by letting insignificant issues tear us apart.

Appreciate what you have, who loves you and who cares for you. You'll never know how much they mean to you until the day they are no longer beside you.

9 Denying personal responsibility.

You're getting almost everything you're getting right now based on the decisions you have made; and you will continue to receive the same things until you choose differently. You always have some element of control. There are always other options. The choices might not be easy, but they are available. You will not get a different result until you exercise a choice that forces you to grow by habit, by action, and by change.

10 Letting everyone else make decisions for you.

Never allow someone or something that adds very little to your life, control so much of it. You've got to stop caring about what everyone else wants for you, and start actually living for yourself. Let go of the people and things that continuously hold you back and no longer serve you, because you only get one shot at life.

11 Giving up who YOU are.

Remove yourself from any situation that requires you to give up any one of these three things: 1) Who you are. 2) What you stand for. 3) The goals you aspire to achieve.

12 *Quitting as soon as things get slightly difficult.*

An arrow can only be shot by pulling it backward; and such is life. When life is pulling you back with difficulties, it means it's going to eventually launch you forward in a positive direction. So keep focusing, and keep aiming!

13 *Doing too much and pushing too hard, without pausing.*

Plenty of people miss their share of happiness, not because they never find it, but because they never stop long enough to enjoy it. Sometimes we are so focused on what we want that we miss the things we need most.

14 *Discrediting yourself for everything you aren't.*

STOP discrediting yourself for everything you aren't. START giving yourself credit for everything that you are.

15 *Running from current problems and fears.*

Trust me, if everyone threw their problems in a pile for you to see, you would grab yours back. Tackle your problems and fears swiftly, don't run away from them. The best solution is to face them head on no matter how powerful they may seem. Either you own your problems and fears, or they will ultimately own you.

16 *Constantly mulling over past hardships.*

You'll never see the great things ahead of you if you keep looking at the bad things behind you. To reach up for the new, you must let go of the old. You are exactly where you need to be to reach your goals. Everything you've been through was preparation for where you are right now and where you can be tomorrow.

17 *Denying your mistakes.*

Remember that the most honorable people of all are not those who never make mistakes, but those who admit to them when they do. And then go on to do their best to make the wrong things right.

18 *Expecting your significant other to be perfect.*

Remember that you will never find a PERFECT partner to love you in the exact way you had envisioned, only a person who is willing to love you with all that they are. Someone who will accept you for who you can and cannot be. And although they will never be PERFECT, finding a partner like this is even BETTER.

9 *Focusing on the negative.*

Positive thinking isn't about expecting the best thing to happen every time, it's about accepting that whatever happens is good for this moment, and then making the best of it. So stay positive, and hold on to what's truly important. Let your worries go. No matter how you look at it, some outcomes just don't make sense right away. Choosing to carry on with your goals through this uncertainty is what matters.

Never allowing things to be good enough.

We are human. We are not perfect. We are alive. We try things. We make mistakes. We stumble. We fall. We get hurt. We rise again. We try again. We keep learning. We keep growing. And we are thankful for this priceless opportunity called life.

12 CHOICES Winners Make Every Day

Follow in the footsteps of a winner. Don't wake up at seventy-five years of age, sighing over what you should have tried. Just do it, and be willing to fail and learn along the way. At least you will know you gave it your best shot.

At the end of the day, whether you choose to go with it, flow with it, resist it, change it, or hide from it, life goes on. If what you did today didn't turn out as you hoped, tomorrow is a new opportunity to do it differently, or to do nothing at all. What's important is to realize that you have a choice.

Here are 12 choices winners make every day:

1 They don't give up on the things they believe in.

If J.K. Rowling stopped after being turned down by multiple publishers for years, there would be no Harry Potter. If Howard Schultz gave up after being turned down by banks 200+ times, there would be no Starbucks. If Walt Disney quit too soon after his theme park concept was trashed by 300+ investors, there would be no Disney. One thing for sure: If you give up on your dreams too soon, you will miss out on seeing them become a reality.

2 They work with, and spend time with, the right people.

A day spent with the right people is always a day spent well. Sometimes the most ordinary ideas and projects can be made extraordinary, simply by discussing them and doing them with the right people.

3 They concentrate on the present.

Remember, you can't reach what's in front of you until you let go of what's behind you. Today is a new day. Don't let your history interfere with your destiny. It doesn't matter what you did or where you were;

> *You were born to win, but to be a winner, you must plan to win, prepare to win, and expect to win.*
>
> -Zig Ziglar

it matters where you are and what you're doing now. Never give up on yourself, and never abandon your values and dreams. As long as you feel pain, you're still alive. As long as you make mistakes, you're still human. And as long as you keep trying, there's still hope.

4 They maintain a positive attitude.

Only you can change your life, no one can do it for you. Happiness always comes from within, and it's found in the present moment by making peace with the past and looking forward to the future. Each morning when you open your eyes, think only three things first: Thank you, thank you, and thank you. Then set out to make the best use of the gift of this day that you can.

5 They endure the pain.

Maybe there's something you're afraid to say, or someone you're afraid to love, or somewhere you're afraid to go. Maybe it's going to hurt. Maybe it's going to hurt because it matters, and because it expands your horizons. Remember, pain isn't always a bad thing; sometimes it's just another step toward personal growth.

6 They ignore the naysayers.

Unless someone has walked in your shoes on the same path that you have traveled, and lived through all of your ups and downs alongside you, they have no right to judge you. Unless they can look into the core of your heart and see the degree of your passion, or look into the depths of your soul and see the extent of your will, then they have no business telling you who you are or what you can or can't achieve. Everyone has a story. Everyone has unique gifts. Unless that someone is YOU, their opinion of you means nothing in the long run.

7 They live through love.

Every human thought, word, or deed is based on fear or love. Fear is the energy which contracts, closes down, draws in, hides, hoards, and harms. Love is the energy which expands, opens up, sends out, reveals, shares, and heals. The only question is: What choice will you make today?

They accept 100% responsibility for their current situation.

The next five years can be the best five years of your life, or just another five years. The decision is yours. The best part of your life will start on the day you decide your life is your own – no one to lean on, rely on, or blame. It takes courage and strength, but you need to say it: "The gift of life is mine, it is an amazing journey, and I alone am responsible for the quality of it."

They take action and plant the right seeds.

Many great things can be done in a day if you don't always make that day tomorrow. Take positive action and plant the right seeds in your life right now. Nature herself does not distinguish between what seeds she receives. She grows whatever seeds are planted; this is the way life works. Be mindful of the seeds you plant today, as they will become the crop you harvest in the future.

10 They don't lose themselves in the commotion.

There are two things you shouldn't waste your time on: things that don't matter and people who don't think you matter. Remember, sometimes in the midst of all the commotion and negativity swirling around, life will force you to make a choice between losing yourself and losing someone or something else. Regardless of the situation, don't lose yourself. Stay true to your path and keep moving forward.

11 They appreciate what they have.

Sometimes people throw away something good for something better, only to find out later that good was actually good enough and better never even came close. Stop long enough to appreciate things. When you appreciate what you have, what you have appreciates in value. When you truly appreciate your life, you'll find that you have more of it to live.

12 They make a positive difference.

Let a person's character be their currency and you will sadly find that a lot of rich people are actually bankrupt. Being the richest man or woman in the cemetery doesn't matter; going to bed every night knowing that you're making a positive deference in the world is what matters.

10 TO☠IC *Personalities*
Living Inside You

Unfortunately we all have unhealthy personalities buried deep within us that have the potential to negatively impact our lives. Although we are all human and have our own 'personality issues,' some 'issues' are, quite frankly, toxic. They are toxic to our happiness. They are toxic to our relationships. They are toxic to our self-esteem. And they are toxic to our dreams.

Here are 10 such personalities to look for in yourself, and avoid.

1 *The negativity committee.*

You can never fail in life or love; you just produce results. It's up to you how you interpret those results. Positive thinking is the ability to feel negative when you have to and still maintain enough hope to keep on going. You cannot tailor-make the situations in life, but you can tailor-make the attitudes to fit those situations. You must view your life through a positive lens. Instead of slapping your forehead and asking, "What was I thinking?" you must breathe and ask the more encouraging question, "What was I learning?"

2 *The hoarder of pain and loss.*

One of the hardest lessons in life is letting go - whether it's guilt, anger, love or loss. Change is never easy – you fight to hold on, and you fight to let go. But oftentimes letting go is the healthiest path forward. You've got to emotionally free yourself from the things that once meant a lot to you, so you can move beyond the past and the pain it brings you.

3 *The jealous competitor.*

Don't be jealous of others. Jealousy is the art of counting someone else's blessings instead of your own. Stop comparing your journey with everyone else's. Your journey is YOUR journey, NOT a competition. You are in competition with one person and one person only – yourself. You are competing to be the best you can be. If you want to measure your progress, compare yourself to who you were yesterday.

The mask.

No matter what age, race, sex, or sexuality you are, underneath all your external decorations you are a pure, beautiful being – each and every one of us are. We each have light to shine, and missions to accomplish. Celebrate being different, off the beaten path, a little on the weird side, your own special creation. If you find yourself feeling like a fish out of water, by all means find a new river to swim in. But DO NOT change who you are; BE who you are.

The superficial judge.

Don't always judge a person by what they show you. Remember, what you've seen is oftentimes only what that person has chosen to show you, or what they were driven to show based on their inner stress and pain. Alas, when another person tries to make you suffer, it is usually because they suffer deep within themselves. Their suffering is simply spilling over. They do not need punishment or ridicule, they need help.

6 The busy body.

It is extremely healthy to spend time in solitude. You need to be alone sometimes, to think and relax in a peaceful environment where you are not defined by anyone else. Today, take some time out to take care of yourself.

7 The perfectionist.

As human beings, we often chase hypothetical, static states of perfection. We do so when we are searching for the perfect house, job, friend, or lover. The problem, of course, is that perfection doesn't exist in a static state. Because life is a continual journey, constantly evolving and changing. What is here today is not exactly the same tomorrow – that perfect house, job, friend, or lover will eventually fade to a state of imperfection. But with a little patience and an open mind, over time, that imperfect house evolves into a comfortable home. That imperfect job evolves into a rewarding career. That imperfect friend evolves into a steady shoulder to lean on. And that imperfect lover evolves into a reliable lifelong companion.

8 The cheater.

Cheating is a choice, not a mistake, and not an excuse! If you decide to cheat, and you succeed in cheating someone out of something, don't think that this person is a fool. Realize that this person trusted you much more than you ever deserved. Be bigger than that. Don't do immoral things simply because you can. Don't cheat. Be honest with yourself and everyone else. Do the right thing. Integrity is the essence of everything successful.

9 *The victim.*

Don't let your dreams waste away on another person's promise. Stop giving opportunities to people who make you feel inferior and let you down as soon as it's convenient for them. Saying "no" to the 'wrong' people gives you the time and resources required to say "yes" to 'right' people and the 'right' opportunities. Stand up for yourself and take charge of your life.

10 *The procrastinator.*

You don't have to see the whole staircase, you just have to take the first step; and the first step to living the life you want is slowly leaving the life you don't want. Taking this first step is always the hardest. But then each subsequent step gets easier and easier. And with each step you get closer and closer to the life you seek. Until eventually, what had once been invisible, starts to become visible. And what had once felt unattainable, becomes a reality.

THE **TOOLS**
OF THE **MIGHTY**

*We shape our **tools** and afterwards our **tools** shape us.*

\- Marshall McLuhan

Last weekend Angel and I attended a show at a local comedy club. During the last skit of the night, the comedian on stage delivered a fairly humorous rant on the age-old dispute of whether the pen is mightier than the sword. "Some people think too much," he said as he pulled out an imaginary sword from an imaginary holster. "If you're really dumb enough to think the pen is mightier than the sword, go ahead and arm yourself with a pen and I'll take my chances with this sword... then we'll see who's left standing in ten seconds."

His antics were hilarious, so naturally I chuckled. All of a sudden, he pointed directly at me in the third row and said, "Hey son, do you think I'm a funny man? You look like a pen-pushing, desk jockey! Get out your pen! Wanna fight?"

I was a bit startled. This was the first time I'd ever been called out and put on the spot in front of a large audience at a comedy club. The audience laughed and then silence swept over the auditorium. Everyone waited for me to either cower in my chair or stand up to the challenge. I stood up and spotlight shined down on me.

"Actually funny man, yes I do have a pen," I said, pulling a fountain pen from my jeans pocket and holding it up for all to see. "However, I don't intend to physically fight you with this pen. Instead, I'll use the pen to sign a fat check that entitles me to a bazooka which I'll use to blow your funny rear end right off that stage."

The audience roared. The comedian groaned and said, "You little punk, I'll use my sword and my cat-like reflexes to cut you, your check, and that pretty girl next to you in half before you can even blink an eye!" He looked at Angel who was sitting next to me and gave her a dirty wink.

The audience laughed again. I smirked and waved my empty hand around in the air noting that the comedian was, in fact, waving an imaginary sword at me. "I feel quite certain that your sword is incapable of doing any damage to anyone or anything," I said.

Another short round of laughter escaped from the audience and I sat back down. The comedian made a few more foolish comments and moved on with the remainder of his routine. But I don't really recall anything else he said or did. I started thinking about the ease with which so many people use rhetoric to mislead and deceive each other.

The Right Tool for the Job

In the hands of a poetic pioneer laying the groundwork for positive change, the pen is mightier than the sword because it can be used to create literary masterpieces capable of motivating an army of fellow citizens to join the revolution. In the hands of a foot soldier at the forefront of a battlefield, the sword is mightier than the pen because the soldier can use the sword to defend himself from imminent, physical danger.

Different people in different situations require different tools. Any object can be mightier than another if it is used as a tool in the proper context. A ply of soft tissue is mightier than a sword when you have a runny noise. A glass of water and an apple are mightier than a pen when what's needed is hydration and nourishment.

"The mighty," I believe, are those people who know when to use the sword, and when to use the tissue. They drink water when they're thirsty and eat apples when they're hungry. They use a pen and paper (or a computer) when then want to inspire others. And, I suppose, they invoke powerful, imaginary bazookas when they get called out and put on the spot in comedy clubs.

40 POSI+IVE Effects of a *TV Free* Week

"What could you accomplish if you stopped watching TV? What would you do with all the extra time?" My wife asked me these questions two weeks ago. After a short discussion, we decided to find out for ourselves. We completely eliminated television from our lives last week. It turned out to be an incredibly rewarding experience. We now have a plan to drastically reduce our future viewing habits.

Here are 40 positive effects from our week without television.

1 *Wrote 4 blog posts.*

I usually only have time to write 2 articles a week.

2 *Made it to the gym 5 times.*

I went Monday through Friday for about 45 minutes, hitting every major muscle group.

3 *Increased household communication.*

TV kills the flow of household communication. We both noticed that we had a lot more time to talk.

4 *Read a novel cover to cover.*

I read the short novel "Siddhartha" by Herman Hesse. It's a powerful story about the importance of life experiences as they relate to approaching an understanding of reality and attaining enlightenment. I highly recommend it.

5 *Caught up on current events twice as fast.*

I typically waste a good hour everyday watching CNN. This week I grabbed my news off the web. It took me significantly less time to scan CNN.com.

6 Enhanced focus on everything.

TV is a huge distraction, even when you hear it from the other room. It's so much easier to concentrate when you don't have a TV yapping at you. I had no idea how much if affected my ability to concentrate until it was gone.

7 Learned a few new skills.

I took my own advice and learned how to change the oil in my truck... pretty darn easy.

8 Spent more time with friends and family.

We invited Angel's sister and some friends over for a mid-week dinner party.

9 Cleaned the house.

Something Angel and I habitually evade by watching TV instead.

10 Learned new recipes and prepared 5 home cooked meals.

We cooked large portions so we could have leftovers for lunch every day.

11 Spent more time enjoying simple pleasures.

Deep conversations, long walks, telling jokes, etc.

12 Finally trimmed the hedges in our front yard.

I always put this off because I am tired after mowing the lawn. This time, however, I did it on a totally separate evening. It only took me 30 minutes.

13 Cleaned out the garage and sold 2 old dehumidifiers on eBay.

We setup a 5-day eBay auction and got $65 for each one of them!

14 Took 2 evening strolls around a local park.

We hadn't been to this park in years... there's only 1 reason why.

15 Saved money on our electric bill.

Our power company's website allows you to check your daily usage. Sure enough, less TV equals less electricity usage.

16 Burned more calories.

We were off the couch moving around.

7 Backed-up critical files on both of our laptops.

Transferred them all over to our Iomega 500 GB external drive.

8 I played my guitar.

...for the first time in a year. I'm hooked again!

19 Found 2 new bands I like.

I used online music comparison services to find 2 awesome bands with similar music styles to my favorite band, Counting Crows.

20 Listened to more music.

In addition to finding new bands, I had more time to listen to my favorite music.

21 We stargazed in our backyard.

...for the first time since Angel and I first started dating. It was blissful.

22 Caught up on times with an old friend.

I hadn't spoken to my buddy Jon since my wedding a year and a half ago. We had a pleasant 30 minute conversation on the phone.

23 Handled basic household maintenance.

Replaced the AC filter, applied pest control spray, replaced fire alarm batteries, etc.

24 Took Angel out on a romantic date.

I took her to one of our favorite Italian restaurants and then out to a local pub where we slow danced to a live music.

25 Finished up a little DIY project.

I've been stalling on staining, sanding and hanging a certain wooden shelf for nearly 6 months.

26 Updated the photo frames throughout the house.

Sometimes it's nice to mix things up. We spent some time sorting through our digital photos and replaced a few photos in various photo frames throughout the house.

27 Played racquetball.

Great 2-person sport!

Organized my monthly planner.

Entered all my known commitments into my planner and did a little time planning each night.

29 Reviewed our long-term goals.

Angel and I had an open discussion last Tuesday night about our goals for the next 3 – 5 years.

Setup recurring automatic payments for most of our bills.

Now our electricity, phone, insurance and cable bills are automatically withdrawn from our account each month. This basically buys me 30 additional minutes of free time every month.

31 Updated my resume.

It only took me 45 minutes.

32 Quiet relaxation.

Instead of clicking on the TV, I spent some quiet time gathering my thoughts each day when I returned home from work.

33 Intelligent conversations at suppertime.

Quite frequently we eat supper in front of the TV. Since there was no TV watching this week, Angel and I had some really interesting conversations instead.

34 Hit it off with our new neighbors.

We spent more time outside and ended up running into our new neighbors. They seem like pretty cool people. There's certainly the potential for friendship here.

35 Exchanged back massages.

It sure beats canned laughter.

36 There was more time for "quality time".

You know... just me and her and some classical music in the background.

37 More real life experiences.

Because we were off of the couch, actually doing something.

38 Watched 1 quality movie.

Instead of watching whatever was on, we went to Blockbuster and selected 1 quality movie to rent.

39 *Ironed my clothes each weeknight before bedtime.*

...since I had more free time in the evenings. It made my mornings less stressful.

40 *We got more done.*

Because we had so much more time to do it all.

I strongly recommend a week without television to everyone. You'll be amazed...

50 THINGS

You NEED To *Give Up* Today

When you stop chasing the wrong things, you give the right things a chance to catch you.

So starting today...

1 Give up trying to be perfect.

The real world doesn't reward perfectionists, it rewards people who get things done.

2 Give up comparing yourself to others.

The only person you are competing against is yourself.

3 Give up dwelling on the past or worrying too much about the future.

Right now is the only moment guaranteed to you. Right now is life. Don't miss it.

4 Give up complaining.

Do something about it.

5 Give up holding grudges.

Grudges are a waste of perfect happiness.

6 Give up waiting.

What we don't start today won't be finished by tomorrow. Knowledge and intelligence are both useless without action.

7 Give up lying.

In the long-run the truth always reveals itself. Either you own up to your actions or your actions will ultimately own you.

8 Give up trying to avoid mistakes.

The only mistake that can truly hurt you is choosing to do nothing simply because you're too scared to make a mistake.

Give up saying, "I can't."

As Henry Ford put it, "Whether you think you can or you think you can't, you are right."

10 Give up trying to be everything to everyone.

Making one person smile can change the world. Maybe not the whole world, but their world. Start small. Start now.

Give up thinking you're not ready.

Nobody ever feels 100% ready when an opportunity arises. Because most great opportunities in life force us to grow beyond our comfort zones, which means we won't feel totally comfortable at first.

12 Give up setting small goals for yourself.

Many people set small goals because they're afraid to fail. Ironically, setting these small goals is what makes them fail.

13 Give up trying to do everything by yourself.

You are the sum of the people you spend the most time with. If you work together, you will be far more capable and powerful than you ever could have been alone.

14 Give up buying things you don't need.

Manage your money wisely so your money does not manage you. Do not spend to impress others. Do not live life trying to fool yourself into thinking wealth is measured in material objects.

15 Give up blaming others for your troubles.

The extent to which you can live your dream life depends on the extent to which you take responsibility for your life. When you blame others for what you're going through, you deny responsibility – you give others power over that part of your life.

16 Give up making mountains out of molehills.

One way to check if something is worth mulling over is to ask yourself this question: "Will this matter in one year's time? Three years? Five years? If not, then it's not worth worrying about.

17 Give up trying to live up to the expectations of others.

Work on it for real and exceed your own expectations. Everything else will fall into place.

18 Give up the 'easy street' mentality.

There is too much emphasis on finding a 'quick fix' in today's society. For example taking diet pills to lose weight instead of exercising and eating well. No amount of magic fairy dust replaces diligent, focused, hard work.

19 Give up making promises you can't keep.

Don't over-promise. Over-deliver on everything you do.

20 Give up letting your thoughts and feelings bottle up inside.

People are not mind readers. They will never know how you feel unless you tell them.

21 Give up beating around the bush.

Say what you mean and mean what you say. Communicate effectively.

22 Give up avoiding change.

However good or bad a situation is now, it will change. That's the one thing you can count on. So embrace change and realize that change happens for a reason. It won't always be easy or obvious at first, but in the end it will be worth it.

23 Give up your sense of entitlement.

Nobody is entitled to anything in this world. We are all equal. We breathe the same air. We get what we give. We get what we earn.

24 Give up waiting until the last minute.

Those who fail to plan, plan to fail.

25 Give up being dramatic.

Stay out of other people's drama and don't needlessly create your own.

26 Give up being anti-athletic.

Get your body moving! Simply take a long, relaxing walk or commit 30 minutes to an at-home exercise program.

27 Give up junk food.

You are what you eat.

28 Give up eating as a means of entertainment.

Don't eat when you're bored. Eat when you're hungry.

Give up foolish habits that you know are foolish.

Don't text and drive. Don't drink and drive. Don't smoke. Etc.

Give up relationships with people who bring you down.

Saying "no" to right people gives you the time and resources required to say "yes" to right opportunities. Spend time with nice people who are smart, driven and likeminded.

Give up being shy.

Network with people. Meet new people. Ask questions. Introduce yourself.

Give up worrying about what others think of you.

Unless you're trying to make a great first impression (job interview, first date, etc.), don't let the opinions of others stand in your way. What they think and say about you isn't important. What is important is how you feel about yourself.

Give up trying to control everything.

Life is an unpredictable phenomenon. No matter how good or bad things seem right now, we can never be 100% certain what will happen next. So do you best with what's in front of you and leave the rest to the powers above you.

34 Give up doing the same thing over and over again.

In order to grow, you must expand your horizons and break free of your comfort zone. If you keep doing what you're doing, you'll keep getting what you're getting.

35 Give up following the path of least resistance.

Life is not easy, especially when you plan on achieving something worthwhile. Don't find the easy way out. Do something extraordinary.

35 Give up persistent multi-tasking.

Do one thing at a time and do it right.

37 Give up thinking others are luckier than you.

The harder you work, the luckier you will become.

38 **Give up filling every waking moment with commitments and activities.**

It's okay to be alone. It's okay to do nothing sometimes. Think. Relax. Breathe. Be.

39 **Give up making emotional decisions.**

Don't let your emotions trump your intelligence. Slow down and think things through before you make any life-changing decisions.

40 **Give up doing the wrong things just because you can get away with it.**

Just because you can get away with something doesn't mean you should do it. Think bigger. Keep the end in mind. Do what you know in your heart is right.

41 **Give up focusing on what you don't want to happen.**

Focus on what you do want to happen. Positive thinking is at the forefront of every great success story. If you awake every morning with the thought that something wonderful will happen in your life today, and you pay close attention, you'll often find that you're right.

42 **Give up taking yourself so seriously.**

Few others do anyway. So enjoy yourself and have a little fun while you can.

43 **Give up spending your life working in a career field you're not passionate about.**

Life is too short for such nonsense. The right career choice is based on one key point: Finding hard work you love doing. So if you catch yourself working hard and loving every minute of it, don't stop. You're on to something big. Because hard work isn't hard when you concentrate on your passions.

44 **Give up thinking about the things you don't have.**

Appreciate everything you do have. Many people aren't so lucky.

45 **Give up doubting others.**

People who are determined do remarkable things. Remember, the one who says it can't be done should never interrupt the one doing it.

46 *Give up fussing with every beauty product on the market.*

Good looks attracts the eyes. Personality attracts the heart. Be proud to be you. That's when you're beautiful.

47 *Give up trying to fit in.*

Don't mold yourself into someone you're not. Be yourself. Oftentimes, the only reason they want you to fit in is that once you do they can ignore you and go about their business.

48 *Give up trying to be different for the sake of being different.*

Nonconformity for the sake of nonconformity is conformity. When people try too hard to be different, they usually end up being just like everyone else who is trying to be different. Once again, be yourself.

49 *Give up trying to avoid risk.*

There's no such thing as 'risk free.' Everything you do or don't do has an inherent risk.

50 *Give up putting your own needs on the back burner.*

Yes, help others, but help yourself too. If there was ever a moment to follow your passion and do something that matters to you, that moment is now.

And remember, mistakes make us human, failures help us grow, hope keeps us going and love is the reason we're alive. So keep learning, loving and living. Never give up on yourself.

12 HABITS Standing Between You & What You Want

Close the door to the habits that have been holding you back, change the record, clean the house, and get rid of the dust and dirt. Stop denying yourself a fair chance. Stop being who you were, and become who you really are.

Starting today, stop...

1 *Playing it safe.*

Have you ever tucked something of value "in a safe place" out of fear that someone might ruin it or steal it from you? And then one day woke to the realization that you had hid it so well that even YOU couldn't find it? If so, then you understand the wisdom of leaving your heart and your dreams in the wide open. To reach for what can be, even when we're doubtful. To let go of what is lost, even when it's painful. To live as though we're brave, even when we're fearful. These are the trials we face and the choices we make along the path to happiness and success.

2 *Letting everyone else decide for you.*

When you feel out of control, it can be tempting to look for someone willing to take charge of your life for you. But before

you do, consider this: If you put a collar around your own neck and hand the leash to someone else, you'll have little or no say about where they lead you. Set your own boundaries and run freely within them.

3 *Doubting your own dreams.*

It doesn't matter if your hope is to write a book, find lasting love, start a business, achieve forgiveness, heal your body, learn to play a musical instrument, find inner peace, or something else. The first step – and often the longest, most arduous one – is to believe that your dream in possible.

4 *Tolerating the influence of negative people.*

Sometimes we forgive people simply because we want them in our life, and sometimes we let go of them simply because we have had enough. Saying goodbye is one of the most painful ways to solve a problem, but from time to time it's necessary.

5 *Letting failed relationships haunt new relationships.*

There's a purpose to every failed relationship. The purpose is not to lower your expectations, but to raise your standards. Remember, you don't want someone who chooses you solely for what's good about you. You need someone who sees the bad too, and still appreciates you just the way you are.

6 *Expecting constant bliss.*

True happiness is not found just within positivity, it is found within reality, which means accepting the fact that both positivity and negativity coexist. Trying to be 100% positive all the time is wanting to be an ocean in which waves only rise up and never come crashing down. However, when we recognize that the rising and crashing waves are part of the same one ocean, we are able to let go and be at peace with the way things are, which leads us to happier, more productive places in the long-term.

7 *Dwelling on the things you've lost.*

In life, there are some people and things you're going to have to lose in order to find your best self. So be grateful for what you have right now, try not to dwell on the things you've lost, strive for what you want most, and keep marching forward.

8 *Overlooking the lesson.*

Everything happens for a reason – a reason you can learn and grow from. People change so you can learn how to let go. Things go wrong so you learn to appreciate things when they go right. You believe lies at first so you eventually learn who you can truly trust. And sometimes good things fall apart so better things can fall together.

9 *Holding on to resentment.*

No matter what resentment tells you, to forgive is always in your favor. Leave no residue of hostility in your heart. Release the bitter thoughts you have towards yourself and others. Only then can you satisfy your craving for happiness.

10 *Being overly critical of yourself.*

If you feel like everyone is judging you all the time, realize that we often feel this way when we are too busy judging ourselves.

11 *Letting pessimism feed your procrastination.*

We have two choices when we wake up in the morning: either we go back to sleep and dream, or we wake up and chase that dream. We often spend way too much time wondering why we're not good enough, and discrediting ourselves, instead of giving ourselves credit. We waste too much time with our heads down and hearts closed, never giving ourselves a chance to look up from the ground to see that the sun is shining bright, and that today is another perfect opportunity to take action and pursue our dreams.

12 *Giving up too soon.*

From time to time people ask me how I hold my head up so high after all I've been through, and I always tell them the same thing: "It's because no matter what, I am a survivor, not a victim." Never let go of hope. Remember what you deserve and keep pushing forward. Someday all the pieces will come together. Unimaginably good things will transpire in your life, even if everything doesn't turn out exactly the way you had anticipated. And you will look back at the times that have passed, smile, and ask yourself, "How did I get through all of that?"

12 HIGHLY *Productive*

THINGS   People Do Differently

Being highly productive is not an innate talent; it's simply a matter of organizing your life so that you can efficiently get the right things done.

So, what behaviors define highly productive people? What habits and strategies make them consistently more productive than others? And what can you do to increase your own productivity?

Here are some ideas to get you started...

1 *Create and observe a TO-DON'T list.*

A 'TO-DON'T list' is a list of things not to do. It might seem amusing, but it's an incredibly useful tool for keeping track of unproductive habits, like checking Facebook and Twitter, randomly browsing news websites, etc. Create one and post it up in your workspace where you can see it.

2 *Organize your space and data.*

Highly productive people have systems in place to help them find what they need when they need it – they can quickly locate the information required to support their activities. When you're disorganized,

that extra time spent looking for a phone number, email address or a certain file forces you to drop your focus. Once it's gone, it takes a while to get it back – and that's where the real time is wasted. Keeping both your living and working spaces organized is crucial.

3 *Ruthlessly eliminate distractions while you work.*

Eliminating all distractions for a set time while you work is one of the most effective ways to get things done. So, lock your door, put a sign up, turn off your phone, close your email application, disconnect your internet connection, etc. You can't remain in hiding forever, but you can be twice as productive while you are. Do whatever it takes to create a quiet, distraction free environment where you can focus on your work.

4 Set and pursue S.M.A.R.T. goals.

These goals must be Specific, Measurable, Attainable, Relevant, and Timely.

5 Break down goals into realistic, high impact tasks.

Take your primary goal and divide it into smaller and smaller chunks until you have a list of realistic tasks, each of which can be accomplished in a few hours or less. Then work on the next unfinished, available task that will have the greatest impact at the current time. For example, if you want to change careers, that goal may be driven by several smaller goals like going back to school, improving your networking skills, updating your resume or getting a new certification. And each of these smaller goals is supported by even more granular sub-goals and associated daily tasks. And it is these small daily tasks that, over time, drive larger achievement.

6 Work when your mind is fresh, and put first things first.

Highly productive people recognize that not all hours are created equal, and they strategically account for this when planning their day. For most of us, our minds operate at peak performance in the morning hours when we're well rested. So obviously it would be foolish to use this time for a trivial task like reading emails. These peak performance hours should be 100% dedicated to working on the tasks that bring you closer to your goals.

7 Focus on being productive, not being busy.

Don't just get things done; get the right things done. Results are always more important than the time it takes to achieve them. Stop and ask yourself if what you're working on is worth the effort. Is it bringing you in the same direction as your goals? Don't get caught up in odd jobs, even those that seem urgent, unless they are also important.

8 Commit your undivided attention to one thing at a time.

Stop multi-tasking, and start getting the important things done properly. Single-tasking helps you focus more intently on one task so you can finish it properly, rather than having many tasks started and nothing finished. Quickly switching from task to task makes the mind less efficient. Studies have shown that changing tasks more than 10 times during an 8-hour segment of work drops a person's IQ by an average of 10-15 points.

9   *Work in 90 minute intervals.*

In an interview with The Globe and Mail, Tony Schwartz, author of the NY Times bestseller The Way We're Working Isn't Working, makes the case for working in no more than 90 consecutive minutes before a short break. Schwartz says, "There is a rhythm in our bodies that operates in 90-minute intervals. That rhythm is the ultradian rhythm, which moves between high arousal and fatigue. If you're working over a period of 90 minutes, there are all kinds of indicators in your physiology of fatigue; so what your body is really saying to you is, 'Give me a break! Refuel me!'"

10   *Reply to emails, voicemails, and texts at a set times.*

This directly ties into the ideas of single-tasking and distraction-avoidance. Set specific time slots 2-3 times a day to deal with incoming communication (e.g. once at 8AM, once at 11AM, once at 3PM), and

set a reasonable max duration for each time slot. Unless an emergency arises, be militant about sticking to this practice.

11   *Invest a little time to save a lot of time.*

How can you spend a little time right now in order to save a lot of time in the future? Think about the tasks you perform over and over throughout a work week. Is there a more efficient way? Is there a shortcut you can learn? Is there a way to automate or delegate it? Perhaps you can complete a particular task in 20 minutes, and it would take two hours to put in place a more efficient method. If that 20 minute task must be completed every day, and a two-hour fix would cut it to 5 minutes or less each time, it's a fix well worth implementing. A simple way of doing this is to use technology to automate tasks (email filters, automatic bill payments, etc.). Also, teaching someone to help you and delegating work is another option. Bottom line: The more you automate and delegate, the more you can get done with the same level of effort.

12   *Narrow the number of ventures you're involved in.*

In other words, say "no" when you should. The commitment to be productive is not always the biggest challenge, narrowing the number of ventures to be productive in is. Even when you have the knowledge and ability to access highly productive states, you get to a point where being simultaneously productive on too many fronts at once causes all activities to slow down, stand still, and sometimes even slide backwards.

LESS THAN **PERFECT** IS A **PERFECT START**

Her First Subscriber

"How did you do it?" she asked. "In a sea of blogs that never make it, how did you start a personal blog that attracted the attention of 10,000 subscribers?"

I chuckled. "You know, I've been trying to wrap my mind around that one myself."

"Come on, Marc," she insisted. "I'm being serious here. I'm getting ready to start my own blog and I'm nervous about failing. I want to cross all my T's and dot all my I's – I don't want to start it until I know how to do it right."

I stared at her for a moment. "Well, one Sunday evening a few years ago, I made a decision to write an article about something that inspired me, and then I published it on my blog. And every Sunday evening since, I've made a similar decision."

"That's it?" she asked. "No launch plan? No design tweaks? No marketing?"

"No, at least not initially," I replied. "I did a little tweaking later on down the road, but by then my blog already had a catalog of articles up online. And most of the tweaks were based on reader feedback and analyzing visitor stats to see which articles were attracting the most attention."

"So you think I simply need to start writing, right now... about the things that inspire me?"

"Yeah," I replied. "The only way you can fail is by not writing – by waiting around until you have the perfect plan before you start. Because 'perfect' doesn't exist. It isn't human. It isn't you.

She smiled and said, "Thank you."

Later that afternoon, she emailed me a link to her first published blog article. And I became her first subscriber.

What's the core purpose?

The hardest part, I have found, of creating something new – a website, a product, a technology – is simply the act of starting. We let our creative minds get so caught up in planning and designing idealistic requirements and prerequisites for our new creation, that we drastically hinder the actual process of creating it.

What stops most people from starting with a less than perfect plan or product is the fear of failure. There's a common misconception that if you don't get it done exactly right the first time, your creation will fail and all efforts will be lost. That without this feature or that tweak, there's no point at all. Nonsense.

The truth is that every successful creation or innovation has a foundational core purpose – a tiny essence that justifies its existence. Any tweak or feature above and beyond the scope of this core purpose is optional. When my friend decided she wanted to start a blog, she spent all of her energy trying to map out the perfect plan and design, instead of simply writing her first few blog articles – which is the core purpose of a blog.

So the next time you decide to create something new, back yourself into a corner, cut out the fluff, and release your core creation into the wild ASAP for others to experience and tinker with. Less than perfect is a perfect start. The need for intelligent tweaks and adjustments will arise naturally as time rolls on.

If you really want to do something, you'll find a way. If you don't, you'll find an excuse.

No matter how many mistakes you make or how slow you progress, you are still way ahead of everyone who isn't trying.

You will never become who you want to be if you keep blaming everyone else for who you are now.

You cannot change what you refuse to confront.

You can learn great things from your mistakes when you aren't busy denying them.

Life is 10% of what happens to you and 90% of how you react to it.

In life, if you don't risk anything, you risk everything.

When you stop chasing the wrong things you give the right things a chance to catch you.

Quotes that Will CHANGE the Way You THINK

It's better to know and be disappointed than to never know and always wonder.

It's better to know and be disappointed than to never know and always wonder.

You don't drown by falling in the water. You drown by staying there.

Productivity
QUESTIONS
to Make You *think*

What should you **AVOID** to *improve* your productivity**?**

So far, what has been the primary **FOCUS** of your *life***?**

What is **WORSE,** *failing* or *never trying***?**

What do you **DO** when you feel like *giving up* **?**

When it's all **SAID** and **DONE,** will you have *said more* than you've *done***?**

What are you one step **CLOSER** to *today* than you were yesterday**?**

If you haven't **ACHIEVED** it yet, what do you have to *lose***?**

What **PEOPLE** and **ACTIVITES** *energize* you**?**

If not **NOW,** then *when***?**

What are you **GLAD** you *quit* **?**

Part Seven
Goals and Success

In the end, you're going to
succeed because you're crazy
enough to think
you can.

HOW TO **WALK** ON **WATER**

This past Sunday I was relaxing at the water's edge of a local beach when a young boy ran full speed right by me and into the shallow surf. He continuously hopped up and down as he was running forward, kicking his little legs in the air and across the surface of the water before inevitably falling face-first into the waves. He got back up and repeated this act several times, each time with more determination than the previous attempt. It became obvious that he was trying to run across the surface of the water. I couldn't help but to laugh. His combined levels of determination and exertion were priceless.

After several attempts, he noticed my laughter and walked over to me. "What's so funny?" he asked.

"You remind me of me, and it makes me smile." I said.

"Do you know how to walk on water?" he asked. "Like a superhero?"

"Well, I think I can help you out." I said. "Let me give you a few pointers."

Curious, the boy sat down on the sand next to me. His mother scurried over, worried... but I reassured her that her son wasn't bothering me. Relieved, perhaps, to have her son sitting safely on the sand instead of flying face-first through the air, she went back to her beach chair 20 feet away and continued a conversation with another lady.

"So, you want to walk on water, eh?" I asked. He nodded his head anxiously.

A Rough Summary of What I Told Him

1. Make sure you were born to walk on water.

You must follow your heart, and be who you were born to be. Some of us were born to be musicians... to communicate intricate thoughts and rousing feelings with the strings of a guitar. Some of us were born to be poets... to touch people's hearts with exquisite prose. Some of us were born to be entrepreneurs... to create growth and opportunity where others saw rubbish. And still, some of us were born to walk on water... to invent the capability of doing so. If you're going to walk on water, you better feel it in every fiber of your being. You better be born to do it!

2. Decide that nothing can stop you.

Being born to walk on water isn't enough by itself. We must each decide to accept our calling. Unfortunately, most of us make excuses instead. "But I might drown trying," we say. Or, "But I have a family to think about first." Walking on water, or doing anything that hasn't been done before, requires absolute, unconditional dedication. The only person who can control your level of dedication is you. If you're serious about walking on water, you must decide that nothing... not gravity, not a group of naysayers, NOTHING... can stop you!

3. Work on it for real.

While many of us decide at some point during the course of our lives that we want to answer our calling... to accomplish our own version of walking on water, only an astute few of us actually work on it. By "working on it", I mean truly devoting oneself to the end result. The rest of us never act on our decision. Or, at best, we pretend to act on it by putting forth

an uninspired, half-ass effort. But to truly walk on water, you'll have to study physics, rheology, hydrophobic substances, etc... and then you'll have to define and redefine next-generation theories and complex hypotheses, which must be tested relentlessly. When the tests fail, you must be ready to edit your theories and test them again. This kind of work, the real kind, is precisely what enables us to make the impossible possible.

4. Let the whole world know what you're up to.

When you're trying to walk on water, or do anything that nobody else has done before, life can get lonely pretty quickly. To keep your motivation thriving, it's important to let others know that you're attempting to defeat the formerly impossible. Don't be shy! Let the whole world know that you're trying to walk on water. No doubt, it'll place a bit of extra pressure on your back, and you'll almost certainly hear some laughter in the crowd. But this kind of pressure fuels motivation, which is exactly what you'll need to accomplish such a colossal undertaking. And when you finally do succeed, the last bit of laughter heard will be your own.

5. Value the people who value your ambitions.

When most people hear about your "mission impossible" aspirations, their natural reaction may be to roll their eyes, call you crazy, and tell you to quit being foolish. But fortunately, the world is also inhabited by pioneers and believers who see the value in your dreams. These people understand that achieving the formerly impossible is one of the greatest gifts human beings possess. They'll likely give you tips, bits of assistance, and the extra push you need to succeed. These are extraordinary people, and you'll want to surround yourself with them, because they will ultimately assist you over the hurdles and across the surface of the water. Think of them as an influential, personal support team. Without them, walking on water will be a far more difficult feat, if not completely impossible.

6. Ignore the negative naysayers.

No matter how much progress you make, there will always be the people who insist that walking on water is impossible, simply because it hasn't been done before. Or they may incessantly suggest that the idea as a whole is utterly ridiculous because nobody really cares about walking on water anyways. When you come across these people, don't try to reason with them. Instead, forget that they exist. They will only waste your time and energy.

7. Prepare yourself for the pain.

Even though you're no longer mindlessly running face-first into the oncoming ocean surf, but instead forming complex theories based on the studies of rheology and fluid viscosity, it doesn't mean you won't experience your fair share of pain. You're in the business of walking on water, of doing something that has never been done before. You'll likely get a waterlogged lung on a regular basis. But the pain will seem like a small price to pay when you become the first person to jog across the rapids of the Mississippi River.

8. Enjoy the pain of your greatest challenge.

Superheroes aren't real. In real life nobody has ever walked on water. But lots of people have achieved formerly impossible feats, and continue to enjoy the possibilities of new challenges. These people will all tell you there's nothing more gratifying than the thrill of your greatest challenge. The inherent pains along the way are simply mile markers on your trip to the finish line. When you finally do finish, you may actually find yourself missing the daily grind. Ultimately, you'll realize that pleasure and pain can be one and the same.

9. Never give up! Never quit!

The reason nobody has walked on water isn't because people haven't tried. Remember, you just tried several times in a row, and I'm sure many others have too. The reason nobody has succeeded is, simply, that within the scope of modern science and physics, it's currently impossible. But this doesn't mean that with your help it won't become possible in the future. If you were born to do it and truly dedicate yourself to the end result, anything, including walking on water, is entirely possible!

Just a Chance

When we were done talking, the young boy got up and ran back over to his mother. He pointed over to me and I smiled and waved back. Then he said to her, "Mommy, mommy! That guy just taught me how to walk on water!"

A few moments later she walked over to scold me for supposedly giving out reckless advice. She told me I was giving her son a false sense of hope. I told her all I was giving him was a chance.

10 of ENEMIES Personal *Greatness*

Beware! These ten inner enemies can quickly erode your grandest plans and your noblest intentions. They can drain your life of passion and potential, and fill your spirit with lifelong regret.

1 *Always taking the path of least resistance.*

Just because you are struggling does NOT mean you are failing. Every great success requires some kind of struggle to get there. Good things don't come to those who wait. Good things come to those who work hard and struggle to pursue the goals and dreams they believe in.

2 *Comparing yourself to everyone else.*

You will never fully believe in yourself if you keep comparing yourself to everyone else. Being true to yourself in thoughts, words and actions is as important as being kind and true to others.

3 *Worrying too much about what others think of you.*

As long as you are worried about what others think of you, you are owned by them. Only when you require no approval from outside yourself can you own yourself. If you're being true to yourself and it isn't enough for the people around you, change the people around you.

4 *Ignoring your gut instincts.*

There's a difference between being agreeable and agreeing to everything. Give yourself permission to immediately walk away from anything that gives you bad vibes. There is no need to explain or make sense of it. Just trust the little inner voice when it's telling you, "This is a bad idea."

5 Holding on when you need to move on.

Moving on doesn't mean forgetting, it means you choose happiness over hurt. Sometimes you have to love people from a distance and give them the space and time to get their minds right before you let them back into your life.

6 Living in the past.

If you don't leave your past in the past, it will destroy your future. Live for what today has to offer, not for what yesterday has taken away. Life is a journey that is only traveled once. Today's moments quickly become tomorrow's memories. So appreciate every moment for what it is, because the greatest gift of life is life itself.

7 Doing the wrong things just because others are too.

Wrong is wrong, even if everyone is doing it. Right is right, even if you are the only one doing it. Always do what you know in your heart is right, for you.

8 Allowing small problems to overwhelm you.

Everything is going to be alright; maybe not today but eventually. When you're upset, ask yourself, "Will this matter to me in a year's time?" Most of the time it won't.

Remember, sometimes bad things in life open up your eyes to the good things you weren't paying attention to before.

9 Surrendering to the draw of comfort.

The most common and harmful addiction in the world is the draw of comfort. Why pursue greatness when you've already got 324 channels and a recliner? Just pass the chip dip and forget about your grand plans. NO! The truth is growth begins at the end of your comfort zone. Stepping outside of your comfort zone will put things into perspective from an angle you can't grasp now, and open doors of opportunity that would otherwise not exist.

10 NOT believing that you CAN.

If we don't know that greatness is possible, we won't bother attempting it. All too often, we literally do not know any better than good enough. Sometimes you have to try to do what you think you can't do, so you realize that you actually CAN. And sometimes it takes more than one attempt. If 'Plan A' doesn't work out, don't fret; the alphabet has another 25 letters that would be happy to give you a chance to get it right. The wrong choices usually bring us to the right places, eventually. But you must believe in your own potential to get there.

12 THINGS

SUCCESSFUL *People* Do Differently

I've always been fascinated by people who are consistently successful at what they do; especially those who experience repeated success in many areas of their life throughout their lifetime. In entertainment, I think of Clint Eastwood and Oprah Winfrey. In business, I think of Steve Jobs and Warren Buffett. We all have our own examples of super successful people like these who we admire. But how do they do it?

Over the years I've studied the lives of numerous successful people. I've read their books, watched their interviews, researched them online, etc. And I've learned that most of them were not born into success; they simply did, and continue to do, things that help them realize their full potential. Here are twelve things they do differently that the rest of us can easily emulate.

1 They create and pursue S.M.A.R.T. goals.

Successful people are objective. They have realistic targets in mind. They know what they are looking for and why they are fighting for it. Successful people create and pursue S.M.A.R.T. goals.

S.M.A.R.T. goals are Specific, Measurable, Attainable, Relevant, and Timely. Let's briefly review each:

Specific – A general goal would be, "Get in shape." But a related specific goal would be, "Join a health club and workout 3 days a week for the next 52 weeks." A specific goal has a far greater chance of being accomplished because it has defined parameters and constraints.

Measurable – There must be a logical system for measuring the progress of a goal. To determine if your goal is measurable, ask yourself questions like: How much time? How many total? How will I know when the goal is accomplished? etc. When you measure your progress, you stay on track, reach your target dates, and experience the exhilaration of achievement that spurs you on to continued efforts required to reach your goal.

Attainable – To be attainable, a goal must represent an objective toward which you are both willing and able to work. In other words, the goal must be realistic. The big question here is: How can the goal be accomplished?

Relevant – Relevance stresses the importance of choosing goals that matter. For example, an internet entrepreneur's goal to "Make 75 tuna sandwiches by 2:00PM." may be Specific, Measurable, Attainable, and Timely, but lacks Relevance to an entrepreneurs overarching objective of building a profitable online business.

Timely – A goal must be grounded within a time frame, giving the goal a target date. A commitment to a deadline helps you focus your efforts on the completion of the goal on or before the due date. This part of the S.M.A.R.T. goal criteria is intended to prevent goals from being overtaken by daily distractions.

When you identify S.M.A.R.T. goals that are truly important to you, you become motivated to figure out ways to attain them. You develop the necessary attitude, abilities, and skills. You can achieve almost any goal you set if you plan your steps wisely and establish a time frame that allows you to carry out those steps. Goals that once seemed far away and out of

reach eventually move closer and become attainable, not because your goals shrink, but because you grow and expand to match them.

2 They take decisive and immediate action.

Sadly, very few people ever live to become the success story they dream about. And there's one simple reason why:

They never take action!

The acquisition of knowledge doesn't mean you're growing. Growing happens when what you know changes how you live. So many people live in a complete daze. Actually, they don't 'live.' They simply 'get by' because they never take the necessary action to make things happen – to seek their dreams.

It doesn't matter if you have a genius IQ and a PhD in Quantum Physics, you can't change anything or make any sort of real-world progress without taking action. There's a huge difference between knowing how to do something and actually doing it. Knowledge and intelligence are both useless without action. It's as simple as that.

Success hinges on the simple act of making a decision to live – to absorb yourself in the process of going after your dreams and goals. So make that decision. And take action.

3 They focus on being productive, not being busy.

In his book, The 4-Hour Workweek, Tim Ferris says, "Slow down and remember this: Most things make no difference. Being busy is often a form of mental laziness – lazy thinking and indiscriminate action." This is Ferris' way of saying "work smarter, not harder," which happens to be one of the most prevalent modern day personal development clichés. But like most clichés, there's a great deal of truth to it, and few people actually adhere to it.

Just take a quick look around. The busy outnumber the productive by a wide margin.

Busy people are rushing all over the place, and running late half of the time. They're heading to work, conferences, meetings, social engagements, etc. They barely have enough free time for family get-togethers and they rarely get enough sleep. Yet, business emails are shooting out of their smart phones like machine gun bullets, and their daily planner is jammed to the brim with obligations.

Their busy schedule gives them an elevated sense of importance. But it's all an illusion. They're like hamsters running on a wheel.

The solution: Slow down. Breathe. Review your commitments and goals. Put first things first. Do one thing at a time.

Start now. Take a short break in two hours. Repeat.

And always remember, results are more important than the time it takes to achieve them.

4 They make logical, informed decisions.

Sometimes we do things that are permanently foolish simply because we are temporarily upset or excited.

Although emotional 'gut instincts' are effective in certain fleeting situations, when it comes to generating long-term, sustained growth in any area of life, emotional decisions often lead a person astray. Decisions driven by heavy emotion typically contain minimal amounts of conscious thought, and are primarily based on momentary feelings instead of mindful awareness.

The best advice here is simple: Don't let your emotions trump your intelligence. Slow down and think things through before you make any life-changing decisions.

5 They avoid the trap of trying to make things perfect.

Many of us are perfectionists in our own right. I know I am at times. We set high bars for ourselves and put our best foot forward. We dedicate copious amounts of time and attention to our work to maintain our high personal standards. Our passion for excellence drives us to run the extra mile, never stopping, never relenting. And this dedication towards perfection undoubtedly helps us achieve results... So long as we don't get carried away.

But what happens when we do get carried away with perfectionism?

We become disgruntled and discouraged when we fail to meet the (impossibly high) standards we set for ourselves, making us reluctant to take on new challenges or even finish tasks we've already started. Our insistence on dotting every 'I' and crossing every 'T' breeds inefficiency, causing major delays, stress overload and subpar results.

True perfectionists have a hard time starting things and an even harder time finishing them, always. I have a friend who has wanted to start a graphic design business for several years. But she hasn't yet. Why? When you sift through her extensive list of excuses it comes down to one simple problem: She is a perfectionist. Which means she doesn't, and never will, think she's good enough at graphic design to own and operate her own graphic design business.

Remember, the real world doesn't reward perfectionists. It rewards people who get things done. And the only way to get things done is to be imperfect 99% of the time. Only by wading through years of practice and imperfection can we begin to achieve momentary glimpses of the perfection. So make a decision. Take action, learn from the outcome, and repeat this method over and over again in all walks of life.

6 They work outside of their comfort zone.

The number one thing I persistently see holding smart people back is their own reluctance to accept an opportunity simply because they don't think they're ready. In other words, they feel uncomfortable and believe they require additional knowledge, skill, experience, etc. before they can aptly partake in the opportunity. Sadly, this is the kind of thinking that stifles personal growth and success.

The truth is nobody ever feels 100% ready when an opportunity arises. Because most great opportunities in life force us to grow emotionally and intellectually. They force us to stretch ourselves and our comfort zones, which means we won't feel totally comfortable at first. And when we don't feel comfortable, we don't feel ready.

Significant moments of opportunity for personal growth and success will come and go throughout your lifetime. If you are looking to make positive changes and new breakthroughs in your life, you will need to embrace these moments of opportunity even though you will never feel 100% ready for them.

7 They keep things simple.

Leonardo da Vinci once said, "Simplicity is the ultimate sophistication." Nothing could be closer to the truth. Here in the 21st century, where information moves at the speed of light and opportunities for innovation seem endless, we have an abundant array of choices when it comes to designing our lives and careers. But sadly, an abundance of choice often leads to complication, confusion and inaction.

Several business and marketing studies have shown that the more product choices a consumer is faced with, the less products they typically buy. After all, narrowing down the best product from a pool of three choices is certainly a lot easier than narrowing down the best product from a pool of three hundred choices. If the purchasing decision is tough to make, most people will just give up. Likewise, if you complicate your life by inundating yourself with too many choices, your subconscious mind will give up.

The solution is to simplify. If you're selling a product line, keep it simple. And if you're trying to make a decision about something in your life, don't waste all your time evaluating every last detail of every possible option. Choose something that you think will work and give it a shot. If it doesn't work out, learn what you can from the experience, choose something else and keep pressing forward.

8 They focus on making small, continuous improvements.

Henry Ford once said, "Nothing is particularly hard if you divide it into small pieces." The same concept configured as a question: How do you eat an elephant? Answer: One bite at a time. This philosophy holds true for achieving your biggest goals. Making small, positive changes – eating a little healthier, exercising a little, creating some small productive habits, for example – is an amazing way to get excited about life and slowly reach the level of success you aspire to.

And if you start small, you don't need a lot of motivation to get started either. The simple act of getting started and doing something will give you the momentum you need, and soon you'll find yourself in a positive spiral of changes – one building on the other. When I started doing this in my life, I was so excited I had to start this blog to share it with the world.

Start with just one activity, and make a plan for how you will deal with troubles when they arise. For instance, if you're trying to lose weight, come up with a list of healthy snacks you can eat when you get the craving for snacks. It will be hard in the beginning, but it will get easier. And that's the whole point. As your strength grows, you can take on bigger challenges.

9 They measure and track their progress.

Successful people are not only working in their job/business, they are also working on it. They step back and assess their progress regularly. They track themselves against their goals and clearly know what needs to be done to excel and accelerate.

You can't control what you don't properly measure. If you track the wrong things you'll be completely blind to potential opportunities as they appear over the horizon. Imagine if, while running a small business, you made it a point to keep track of how many pencils and paperclips you used. Would that make any sense? No! Because pencils and paperclips are not a measure of what's important for a business. Pencils and paperclips have no bearing on income, customer satisfaction, market growth, etc.

The proper approach is to figure out what your number one goal is and then track the things that directly relate to achieving that goal. I recommend that you take some time right now to identify your number one goal, identify the most important things for you to keep track of, and then begin tracking them immediately. On a weekly basis, plug the numbers into a spreadsheet and use the data to create weekly or monthly trend graphs so you can visualize your progress. Then fine-tune your actions to get those trends to grow in your favor.

10 They maintain a positive outlook as they learn from their mistakes.

Successful people concentrate on the positives – they look for the silver lining in every situation. They know that it is their positivity that will take them to greatness. If you want to be successful, you need to have a positive outlook toward life. Life will test you again and again. If you give in to internal negativity, you will never be able to achieve the marks you have targeted.

Remember, every mistake you make is progress. Mistakes teach you important lessons. Every time you make one, you're one step closer to your goal. The only mistake that can truly hurt you is choosing to do nothing simply because you're too scared to make a mistake.

So don't hesitate – don't doubt yourself! Don't let your own negativity sabotage you. Learn what you can and press forward.

11 They spend time with the right people.

Successful people associate with people who are likeminded, focused, and supportive. They socialize with people who create energy when they enter the room versus those who create energy when they leave. They reach out to connected, influential individuals who are right for their dreams and goals.

You are the sum of the people you spend the most time with. If you hang with the wrong people, they will negatively affect you. But if you hang with the right people, you will become far more capable and successful than you ever could have been alone. Find your tribe and work together to make a difference in all of your lives.

12 *They maintain balance in their life.*

If you ask most people to summarize what they want out of life they'll shout out a list of things like: 'fall in love,' 'make money,' 'spend time with family,' 'find happiness,' 'achieve goals,' etc. But sadly, a lot of people don't balance their life properly to achieve these things. Typically they'll achieve one or two of them while completely neglecting the rest. Let me give you two examples:

I know an extremely savvy businesswoman who made almost a million dollars online last year. Based on the success of her business, every entrepreneur I know looks up to her. But guess what? A few days ago, out of the blue, she told me that she's depressed. Why? "I'm burnt out and lonely. I just haven't taken enough time for myself lately, and I feel like something is missing in my life," she said. "Wow!" I thought. "One of the most successful people I know doesn't feel successful because she isn't happy with how she has balanced her life."

I also know a surfer who surfs all day, every day on the beach in front of our condo complex in San Diego. He's one of the most lighthearted, optimistic guys I've ever met – usually smiling from ear to ear. But he sleeps in a rusty van he co-owns with another surfer, and they both frequently panhandle tourists for money. He has admitted to me that the stress of making enough money to eat often keeps him up at night. So while I can't deny that this man seems happy most of the time, I wouldn't classify his life as a success story.

These are just two simple examples of imbalanced lifestyles that are holding people back from their full potential. When you let your work life (or social life, family life, etc.) consume you, and all your energy is focused in that area, it's extremely easy to lose your balance. While drive and focus are important, if you're going to get things done right, and be truly successful, you need to balance the various dimensions of your life. Completely neglecting one dimension for another only leads to long-term frustration and stress.

30 THINGS to STOP Doing to *Yourself*

As Maria Robinson once said, "Nobody can go back and start a new beginning, but anyone can start today and make a new ending." Nothing could be closer to the truth. But before you can begin this process of transformation you have to stop doing the things that have been holding you back.

Here are some ideas to get you started:

1 *Stop spending time with the wrong people.*

Life is too short to spend time with people who suck the happiness out of you. If someone wants you in their life, they'll make room for you. You shouldn't have to fight for a spot. Never, ever insist yourself to someone who continuously overlooks your worth. And remember, it's not the people that stand by your side when you're at your best, but the ones who stand beside you when you're at your worst that are your true friends.

2 *Stop running from your problems.*

Face them head on. No, it won't be easy. There is no person in the world capable of

flawlessly handling every punch thrown at them. We aren't supposed to be able to instantly solve problems. That's not how we're made. In fact, we're made to get upset, sad, hurt, stumble and fall. Because that's the whole purpose of living – to face problems, learn, adapt, and solve them over the course of time. This is what ultimately molds us into the person we become.

3 *Stop lying to yourself.*

You can lie to anyone else in the world, but you can't lie to yourself. Our lives improve only when we take chances, and the first and most difficult chance we can take is to be honest with ourselves.

! Stop putting your own needs on the back burner.

The most painful thing is losing yourself in the process of loving someone too much, and forgetting that you are special too. Yes, help others; but help yourself too. If there was ever a moment to follow your passion and do something that matters to you, that moment is now.

! Stop trying to be someone you're not.

One of the greatest challenges in life is being yourself in a world that's trying to make you like everyone else. Someone will always be prettier, someone will always be smarter, someone will always be younger, but they will never be you. Don't change so people will like you. Be yourself and the right people will love the real you.

! Stop trying to hold onto the past.

You can't start the next chapter of your life if you keep re-reading your last one.

7 Stop being scared to make a mistake.

Doing something and getting it wrong is at least ten times more productive than doing nothing. Every success has a trail of failures behind it, and every failure is leading towards success. You end up regretting the things you did NOT do far more than the things you did.

8 Stop berating yourself for old mistakes.

We may love the wrong person and cry about the wrong things, but no matter how things go wrong, one thing is for sure, mistakes help us find the person and things that are right for us. We all make mistakes, have struggles, and even regret things in our past. But you are not your mistakes, you are not your struggles, and you are here NOW with the power to shape your day and your future. Every single thing that has ever happened in your life is preparing you for a moment that is yet to come.

9 Stop trying to buy happiness.

Many of the things we desire are expensive. But the truth is, the things that really satisfy us are totally free – love, laughter and working on our passions.

10 Stop exclusively looking to others for happiness.

If you're not happy with who you are on the inside, you won't be happy in a long-term relationship with anyone else either. You have to create stability in your own life first before you can share it with someone else.

11 *Stop being idle.*

Don't think too much or you'll create a problem that wasn't even there in the first place. Evaluate situations and take decisive action. You cannot change what you refuse to confront. Making progress involves risk. Period! You can't make it to second base with your foot on first.

12 *Stop thinking you're not ready.*

Nobody ever feels 100% ready when an opportunity arises. Because most great opportunities in life force us to grow beyond our comfort zones, which means we won't feel totally comfortable at first.

13 *Stop getting involved in relationships for the wrong reasons.*

Relationships must be chosen wisely. It's better to be alone than to be in bad company. There's no need to rush. If something is meant to be, it will happen – in the right time, with the right person, and for the best reason. Fall in love when you're ready, not when you're lonely.

14 *Stop rejecting new relationships just because old ones didn't work.*

In life you'll realize that there is a purpose for everyone you meet. Some will test you, some will use you and some will teach you. But most importantly, some will bring out the best in you.

15 *Stop trying to compete against everyone else.*

Don't worry about what others are doing better than you. Concentrate on beating your own records every day. Success is a battle between YOU and YOURSELF only.

16 *Stop being jealous of others.*

Jealousy is the art of counting someone else's blessings instead of your own. Ask yourself this: "What's something I have that everyone wants?"

17 *Stop complaining and feeling sorry for yourself.*

Life's curveballs are thrown for a reason – to shift your path in a direction that is meant for you. You may not see or understand everything the moment it happens, and it may be tough. But reflect back on those negative curveballs thrown at you in the past. You'll often see that eventually they led you to a better place, person, state of mind, or situation. So smile! Let everyone know that today you are a lot stronger than you were yesterday, and you will be.

8   *Stop holding grudges.*

Don't live your life with hate in your heart. You will end up hurting yourself more than the people you hate. Forgiveness is not saying, "What you did to me is okay." It is saying, "I'm not going to let what you did to me ruin my happiness forever." Forgiveness is the answer... let go, find peace, liberate yourself! And remember, forgiveness is not just for other people, it's for you too. If you must, forgive yourself, move on and try to do better next time.

9   *Stop letting others bring you down to their level.*

Refuse to lower your standards to accommodate those who refuse to raise theirs.

20   *Stop wasting time explaining yourself to others.*

Your friends don't need it and your enemies won't believe it anyway. Just do what you know in your heart is right.

21   *Stop doing the same things over and over without taking a break.*

The time to take a deep breath is when you don't have time for it. If you keep doing what you're doing, you'll keep getting what you're getting. Sometimes you need to distance yourself to see things clearly.

22   *Stop overlooking the beauty of small moments.*

Enjoy the little things, because one day you may look back and discover they were the big things. The best portion of your life will be the small, nameless moments you spend smiling with someone who matters to you.

23   *Stop trying to make things perfect.*

The real world doesn't reward perfectionists, it rewards people who get things done.

24   *Stop following the path of least resistance.*

Life is not easy, especially when you plan on achieving something worthwhile. Don't take the easy way out. Do something extraordinary.

Stop acting like everything is fine if it isn't.

It's okay to fall apart for a little while. You don't always have to pretend to be strong, and there is no need to constantly prove that everything is going well. You shouldn't be concerned with what other people are thinking either – cry if you need to – it's healthy to shed your tears. The sooner you do, the sooner you will be able to smile again.

Stop blaming others for your troubles.

The extent to which you can achieve your dreams depends on the extent to which you take responsibility for your life. When you blame others for what you're going through, you deny responsibility – you give others power over that part of your life.

27 Stop trying to be everything to everyone.

Doing so is impossible, and trying will only burn you out. But making one person smile CAN change the world. Maybe not the whole world, but their world. So narrow your focus.

28 Stop worrying so much.

Worry will not strip tomorrow of its burdens, it will strip today of its joy. One way to check if something is worth mulling over is to ask yourself this question: "Will this matter in one year's time? Three years? Five years?" If not, then it's not worth worrying about.

29 Stop focusing on what you don't want to happen.

Focus on what you do want to happen. Positive thinking is at the forefront of every great success story. If you awake every morning with the thought that something wonderful will happen in your life today, and you pay close attention, you'll often find that you're right.

30 Stop being ungrateful.

No matter how good or bad you have it, wake up each day thankful for your life. Someone somewhere else is desperately fighting for theirs. Instead of thinking about what you're missing, try thinking about what you have that everyone else is missing.

30 THINGS to START Doing for *Yourself*

Our previous article, 30 Things to Stop Doing to Yourself, was well received by most of our readers, but several of you suggested that we follow it up with a list of things to start doing. In one reader's words, "I would love to see you revisit each of these 30 principles, but instead of presenting us with a 'to-don't' list, present us with a 'to-do' list that we all can start working on today, together." Some folks, such as readers Danny Head and Satori Agape, actually took it one step further and emailed us their own revised 'to-do' versions of the list.

So I sat down last night with our original article and the two reader's revisions as a guide, and a couple hours later finalized a new list of 30 things; which ended up being, I think, a perfect complement to the original.

Here it is, a positive 'to-do' list for the upcoming year – 30 things to start doing for yourself:

1 *Start spending time with the right people.*

These are the people you enjoy, who love and appreciate you, and who encourage you to improve in healthy and exciting ways. They are the ones who make you feel more alive, and not only embrace who you are now, but also embrace and embody who you want to be, unconditionally.

2 *Start facing your problems head on.*

It isn't your problems that define you, but how you react to them and recover from them. Problems will not disappear unless you take action. Do what you can, when you can, and acknowledge what you've done. It's all about taking baby steps in the right direction, inch by inch. These inches count, they add up to yards and miles in the long run.

> *Remember today, for it is the beginning.*
> *Today marks the start of a brave new future.*

3 Start being honest with yourself about everything.

Be honest about what's right, as well as what needs to be changed. Be honest about what you want to achieve and who you want to become. Be honest with every aspect of your life, always. Because you are the one person you can forever count on. Search your soul, for the truth, so that you truly know who you are. Once you do, you'll have a better understanding of where you are now and how you got here, and you'll be better equipped to identify where you want to go and how to get there.

4 Start making your own happiness a priority.

Your needs matter. If you don't value yourself, look out for yourself, and stick up for yourself, you're sabotaging yourself. Remember, it IS possible to take care of your own needs while simultaneously caring for those around you. And once your needs are met, you will likely be far more capable of helping those who need you most.

5 Start being yourself, genuinely and proudly.

Trying to be anyone else is a waste of the person you are. Be yourself. Embrace that individual inside you that has ideas, strengths and beauty like no one else. Be the person you know yourself to be – the best version of you – on your terms. Above all, be true to YOU, and if you cannot put your heart in it, take yourself out of it.

6 Start noticing and living in the present.

Right now is a miracle. Right now is the only moment guaranteed to you. Right now is life. So stop thinking about how great things will be in the future. Stop dwelling on what did or didn't happen in the past. Learn to be in the 'here and now' and experience life as it's happening. Appreciate the world for the beauty that it holds, right now.

7 Start valuing the lessons your mistakes teach you.

Mistakes are okay; they're the stepping stones of progress. If you're not failing from time to time, you're not trying hard enough and you're not learning. Take risks, stumble, fall, and then get up and try again. Appreciate that you are pushing yourself, learning, growing and improving. Significant achievements are almost invariably realized at the end of a long road of failures. One of the 'mistakes' you fear might just be the link to your greatest achievement yet.

8 *Start being more polite to yourself.*

If you had a friend who spoke to you in the same way that you sometimes speak to yourself, how long would you allow that person to be your friend? The way you treat yourself sets the standard for others. You must love who you are or no one else will.

9 *Start enjoying the things you already have.*

The problem with many of us is that we think we'll be happy when we reach a certain level in life – a level we see others operating at – your boss with her corner office, that friend of a friend who owns a mansion on the beach, etc. Unfortunately, it takes awhile before you get there, and when you get there you'll likely have a new destination in mind. You'll end up spending your whole life working toward something new without ever stopping to enjoy the things you have now. So take a quiet moment every morning when you

first awake to appreciate where you are and what you already have.

10 *Start creating your own happiness.*

If you are waiting for someone else to make you happy, you're missing out. Smile because you can. Choose happiness. Be the change you want to see in the world. Be happy with who you are now, and let your positivity inspire your journey into tomorrow. Happiness is often found when and where you decide to seek it. If you look for happiness within the opportunities you have, you will eventually find it. But if you constantly look for something else, unfortunately, you'll find that too.

11 *Start giving your ideas and dreams a chance.*

In life, it's rarely about getting a chance; it's about taking a chance. You'll never be 100% sure it will work, but you can always be 100% sure doing nothing won't work. Most of the time you just have to go for it! And no matter how it turns out, it always ends up just the way it should be. Either you succeed or you learn something. Win-Win.

12 Start believing that you're ready for the next step.

You are ready! Think about it. You have everything you need right now to take the next small, realistic step forward. So embrace the opportunities that come your way, and accept the challenges – they're gifts that will help you to grow.

13 Start entering new relationships for the right reasons.

Enter new relationships with dependable, honest people who reflect the person you are and the person you want to be. Choose friends you are proud to know, people you admire, who show you love and respect – people who reciprocate your kindness and commitment. And pay attention to what people do, because a person's actions are much more important than their words or how others represent them.

14 Start giving new people you meet a chance.

It sounds harsh, but you cannot keep every friend you've ever made. People and priorities change. As some relationships fade others will grow. Appreciate the possibility of new relationships as you naturally let go of old ones that no longer work. Trust your judgment. Embrace new relationships, knowing that you are

entering into unfamiliar territory. Be ready to learn, be ready for a challenge, and be ready to meet someone that might just change your life forever.

15 Start competing against an earlier version of yourself.

Be inspired by others, appreciate others, learn from others, but know that competing against them is a waste of time. You are in competition with one person and one person only – yourself. You are competing to be the best you can be. Aim to break your own personal records.

16 Start cheering for other people's victories.

Start noticing what you like about others and tell them. Having an appreciation for how amazing the people around you are leads to good places – productive, fulfilling, peaceful places. So be happy for those who are making progress. Cheer for their victories. Be thankful for their blessings, openly. What goes around comes around, and sooner or later the people you're cheering for will start cheering for you.

17 Start looking for the silver lining in tough situations.

When things are hard, and you feel down, take a few deep breaths and look for the silver lining – the small glimmers of hope. Remind yourself that you can and will grow stronger from these hard times. And remain conscious of your blessings and victories – all the things in your life that are right. Focus on what you have, not on what you haven't.

8 Start forgiving yourself and others.

We've all been hurt by our own decisions and by others. And while the pain of these experiences is normal, sometimes it lingers for too long. We relive the pain over and over and have a hard time letting go. Forgiveness is the remedy. It doesn't mean you're erasing the past, or forgetting what happened. It means you're letting go of the resentment and pain, and instead choosing to learn from the incident and move on with your life.

9 Start helping those around you.

Care about people. Guide them if you know a better way. The more you help others, the more they will want to help you. Love and kindness begets love and kindness. And so on and so forth.

20 Start listening to your own inner voice.

If it helps, discuss your ideas with those closest to you, but give yourself enough room to follow your own intuition. Be true to yourself. Say what you need to say. Do what you know in your heart is right.

21 Start being attentive to your stress level and take short breaks.

Slow down. Breathe. Give yourself permission to pause, regroup and move forward with clarity and purpose. When you're at your busiest, a brief recess can rejuvenate your mind and increase your productivity. These short breaks will help you regain your sanity and reflect on your recent actions so you can be sure they're in line with your goals.

22 Start noticing the beauty of small moments.

Instead of waiting for the big things to happen – marriage, kids, big promotion, winning the lottery – find happiness in the small things that happen every day. Little things like having a quiet cup of coffee in the early morning, or the delicious taste and smell of a homemade meal, or the pleasure of sharing something you enjoy with someone else, or holding hands with your partner. Noticing these small pleasures on a daily basis makes a big difference in the quality of your life.

23 Start accepting things when they are less than perfect.

Remember, 'perfect' is the enemy of 'good.' One of the biggest challenges for people who want to improve themselves and improve the world is learning to accept things as they are. Sometimes it's better to accept and appreciate the world as it is, and people as they are, rather than trying to make everything and everyone conform to an impossible ideal. No, you shouldn't accept a life of mediocrity, but learn to love and value things when they are less than perfect.

24 Start working toward your goals every single day.

Remember, the journey of a thousand miles begins with one step. Whatever it is you dream about, start taking small, logical steps every day to make it happen. Get out there and DO something! The harder you work the luckier you will become. While many of us decide at some point during the course of our lives that we want to answer our calling, only an astute few of us actually work on it. By 'working on it,' I mean consistently devoting oneself to the end result.

25 Start being more open about how you feel.

If you're hurting, give yourself the necessary space and time to hurt, but be open about it. Talk to those closest to you. Tell them the truth about how you feel. Let them listen. The simple act of getting things off your chest and into the open is your first step toward feeling good again.

26 Start taking full accountability for your own life.

Own your choices and mistakes, and be willing to take the necessary steps to improve upon them. Either you take accountability for your life or someone else will. And when they do, you'll become a slave to their ideas and dreams instead of a pioneer of your own. You are the only one who can directly control the outcome of your life. And no, it won't always be easy. Every person has a stack of obstacles in front of them. But you must take accountability for your situation and overcome these obstacles. Choosing not to is choosing a lifetime of mere existence.

27 Start actively nurturing your most important relationships.

Bring real, honest joy into your life and the lives of those you love by simply telling them how much they mean to you on a regular basis. You can't be everything to everyone, but you can be everything to a few people. Decide who these people are in your life and treat them like royalty. Remember, you don't need a certain number of friends, just a number of friends you can be certain of.

28 Start concentrating on the things you can control.

You can't change everything, but you can always change something. Wasting your time, talent and emotional energy on things that are beyond your control is a recipe for frustration, misery and stagnation. Invest your energy in the things you can control, and act on them now.

29 Start focusing on the possibility of positive outcomes.

The mind must believe it CAN do something before it is capable of actually doing it. The way to overcome negative thoughts and destructive emotions is to develop opposing, positive emotions that are stronger and more powerful. Listen to your self-talk and replace negative thoughts with positive ones. Regardless of how a situation seems, focus on what you DO WANT to happen, and then take the next positive step forward. No, you can't control everything that happens to you, but you can control how you react to things.

Everyone's life has positive and negative aspects – whether or not you're happy and successful in the long run depends greatly on which aspects you focus on.

30 Start noticing how wealthy you are right now.

tHenry David Thoreau once said, "Wealth is the ability to fully experience life." Even when times are tough, it's always important to keep things in perspective. You didn't go to sleep hungry last night. You didn't go to sleep outside. You had a choice of what clothes to wear this morning. You hardly broke a sweat today. You didn't spend a minute in fear. You have access to clean drinking water. You have access to medical care. You have access to the Internet. You can read. Some might say you are incredibly wealthy, so remember to be grateful for all the things you do have.

HOW TO MAKE ALL THE
DIFFERENCE
IN THE **WORLD**

Every Sunday morning I take a light jog around a park near my home. There's a lake located in one corner of the park. Each time I jog by this lake, I see the same elderly woman sitting at the water's edge with a small metal cage sitting beside her.

This past Sunday my curiosity got the best of me, so I stopped jogging and walked over to her. As I got closer, I realized that the metal cage was in fact a small trap. There were three turtles, unharmed, slowly walking around the base of the trap. She had a fourth turtle in her lap that she was carefully scrubbing with a spongy brush.

"Hello," I said. "I see you here every Sunday morning. If you don't mind my nosiness, I'd love to know what you're doing with these turtles."

She smiled. "I'm cleaning off their shells," she replied. "Anything on a turtle's shell, like algae or scum, reduces the turtle's ability to absorb heat and impedes its ability to swim. It can also corrode and weaken the shell over time."

"Wow! That's really nice of you!" I exclaimed.

She went on: "I spend a couple of hours each Sunday morning, relaxing by this lake and helping these little guys out. It's my own strange way of making a difference."

"But don't most freshwater turtles live their whole lives with algae and scum hanging from their shells?" I asked.

"Yep, sadly, they do," she replied.

I scratched my head. "Well then, don't you think your time could be better spent? I mean, I think your efforts are kind and all, but there are fresh water turtles living in lakes all around the world. And 99% of these turtles don't have kind people like

you to help them clean off their shells.
So, no offense... but how exactly are your
localized efforts here truly making a
difference?"

The woman giggled aloud. She then looked
down at the turtle in her lap, scrubbed off
the last piece of algae from its shell, and
said, "Sweetie, if this little guy could talk,
he'd tell you I just made all the difference
in the world."

30 CHALLENGES

for 30 Days of

Growth

Scientists have suggested that, with a little willpower, it takes roughly 30 days for a person to form a new habit. As with mastering anything new, the act of starting and getting beyond the preliminary stage where everything feels awkward is 80% of the battle. This is precisely why it's important to make small, positive changes every day over the course of at least a 30 day period.

It's like the old saying: "How do you eat an elephant? One bite at a time." The same philosophy holds true for making changes in your life. Trying to bite off more than you can chew will only make you choke. But taking smaller, manageable bites, one at a time – eating a little healthier, exercising a little, creating some simple productive habits, for example – is an amazing way to make positive changes and get excited about life.

And when you start small like this, you won't need a lot of motivation either. The simple act of getting started and doing something will give you the momentum you need, and soon you'll find yourself in a positive spiral of changes – one building on the other. When I started doing this in my life, I was so excited about it that I started this blog to share it with the world.

Below you will find 30 challenges to be accomplished over the course of 30 days. If carried out diligently each of them has the potential to create a new positive habit in your life. Yes, there is some slight overlap between a few of them. And no, you don't have to attempt all at once. Pick 2 to 5 and commit the next 30 days, wholeheartedly, to successfully completing the challenge. Then once you feel comfortable with these habits, challenge yourself with a few more the following month.

1 → Use words that encourage happiness.

Typically, when I ask someone "How are you?" they reply, "I'm fine" or "I'm okay." But one lazy Monday afternoon last month

> *We are what we repeatedly do.*
> *Excellence then, is not an act, but a habit.*
> - Aristotle

a new colleague of mine replied, "Oh, I am fabulous!" It made me smile, so I asked him what was making him feel so fabulous and he said, "I'm healthy, my family is healthy, and we live in a free country. So I don't have any reason not to be happy." The difference was simply his attitude and his choice of words. He wasn't necessarily any better off than anyone else, but he seemed twenty times happier. Spend the next 30 days using words that encourage a smile.

2 Try one new thing every day.

Variety truly is the spice of life. You can see or do something a million times, but you can only see or do it for the first time once. As a result, first time experiences often leave reflective marks in our minds for the rest of our lives. Make an effort to try something new every day for the next 30 days. It can be a whole new activity or just a small experience, such as talking to a stranger. Once you get the ball rolling many of these new experiences will open doors to life changing opportunities.

3 Perform one selfless act every day.

In life, you get what you put in. When you make a positive impact in someone else's life, you also make a positive impact in your own life. Do something that's greater than you, something that helps someone else be happy or suffer less. I promise, it will be an extremely rewarding experience. One you'll likely remember forever. Obviously your options here are limitless, but if you're looking to assist an ordinary person in need without leaving your chair, check out GoFundMe.

4 Learn and practice one new skill every day.

Self-reliance is a vital key to living a healthy, productive life. To be self-reliant one must master a basic set of skills, more or less making them a jack of all trades. Contrary to what you may have learned in school, a jack of all trades is far more equipped to deal with life than a specialized master of only one. And besides, learning new skills is fun.

5 *Teach someone something new every day.*

We all have natural strengths and talents that can dramatically help those around us. What comes easy for you is no doubt challenging for others. We tend to take these gifts for granted, often hardly noticing what we have to offer, and thus we rarely share them with others. Inner happiness and zeal come from using these inherent gifts on a routine basis. What do people thank you for? What do people routinely ask for your help with? Most people's passions and talents help others in one way or another. Perhaps for you it's painting, teaching math, cooking a good meal or leading an exercise class. For the next 30 days devote some time each day to sharing your talents and expertise.

6 *Dedicate an hour a day to something you're passionate about.*

Take part in something you passionately believe in. This could be anything. Some people take an active role in their city council, some find refuge in religious faith, some join social clubs supporting causes they believe in and others find passion in their hobbies. In each case the psychological outcome is the same. They engage themselves in something they strongly believe in. This engagement brings happiness and meaning into their lives.

7 *Treat everyone nicely, even those who are rude to you.*

Being nice to someone you dislike doesn't mean you're fake. It means you're mature enough to control your emotions. Treat everyone with kindness and respect, even those who are rude to you – not because they're nice, but because you are. Do this for 30 days and I guarantee you'll see the rudeness around you dissipate.

8 *Concentrate on being positive at all times.*

The real winners in life cultivate optimism. They have the ability to manufacture their own happiness and drive. No matter what the situation, the successful diva is the chick who will always find a way to put an optimistic spin on it. She knows failure only as an opportunity to grow and learn a new lesson from life. People who think optimistically see the world as a place packed with endless opportunities, especially in trying times. Try to spend the next 30 days looking at the bright side of things.

9 Address and acknowledge the lesson in inconvenient situations.

It's important to remember that everything is a life lesson. Everyone you meet, everything you encounter, etc. They're all part of the learning experience we call 'life.' Never forget to acknowledge the lesson, especially when things don't go your way. If you don't get a job you wanted or a relationship doesn't work, it only means something better is out there waiting. And the lesson you just learned is the first step toward it. Over the next 30 days keep a written log of all the lessons life taught you.

10 Pay attention and enjoy your life as it happens.

When I watched the Academy Awards a few months ago I realized that most of the speeches actors and actresses make when they accept an award go something like this: "This means so much so me. My whole life has been leading up to this moment." But the truth is, our whole lives have been leading up to every moment. Think about that for a second. Every single thing you've gone through in life, every high, every low and everything in between, it has led you to this moment right now. Ask yourself this: How much of life are you actually living? If you're like most people, the answer is likely: "Not

enough." The key is to concentrate on a little less on doing and a little more on being. Remember, right now is the only moment guaranteed to you. Right now is life. Spend the next 30 days living in the now, for real.

11 Get rid of one thing a day for 30 days.

We have so much clutter surrounding us at any given moment (at the office, in our cars, in our homes) and we've become so accustomed to it that we no longer notice how it affects us. If you start cleaning up some of this external clutter, a lot of internal clutter will disappear as well. Choose one needless item each and every day and get rid of it. It's that simple. It might be difficult at first, so expect some resistance. But after some time you will begin to learn to let go of your packrat tendencies, and your mind will thank you for your efforts.

12 Create something brand new in 30 days or less.

Creation is a process like none other. Putting to use your innovative faculties and constructing something with your own two hands will leave you with an indescribable sense of wholeness. There is no substitute for it. The only caveat is that it must be related to something you actually care about. If you are creating financial plans for clients all day and you hate it, that doesn't really count. But if you can find something you love, and create something related to it, it will make all the difference in your life. If you haven't created something in a while just for the sake of creating, do so. Take the next 30 days and let your creativity run wild.

13 Don't tell a single lie for 30 days.

With all the seemingly innocent, white lies that trickle out of us, this is way harder than it sounds. But you can do it. Stop deceiving yourself and others, speak from the heart, speak the whole truth.

14 Wake up 30 minutes early every morning.

Get up 30 minutes earlier than usual so you don't have to rush around like a mad man. That 30 minutes will help you avoid speeding tickets, tardiness and other unnecessary headaches. Give it a legitimate try for 30 days straight and see how it impacts your life.

15 Ditch 3 bad habits for 30 days.

Do you eat too much fast food? Do you play too many video games? Do you argue with your siblings? You know some of your

bad habits. Pick 3 and quit doing them for 30 days. Period.

16 Watch less than 30 minutes of TV every day.

Entertain yourself with real-world experiences. Great memories are the product of interesting life experiences. So turn off the television (or the computer if that's how you watch your TV programs) and get outdoors. Interact with the world, appreciate nature, take notice of the simple pleasures life has to offer, and just watch as life unfolds in front of you.

17 Define one long-term goal and work on it for an hour every day.

Break your goal down into bite-sized pieces and focus on achieving each one piece at a time. It really is all about taking baby steps, and taking the first step is often the hardest. Spend an hour every day for the next 30 days working toward something you've always wanted to accomplish. Take a small dream and make it a reality.

18 Read one chapter of a good book every day.

With the Web's endless stream of informative, easy-to-skim textual snippets and collaborative written works, people are spending more and more time reading online. Nevertheless, the Web cannot replace the authoritative wisdom from certain classic books that have delivered (or will deliver) profound ideas around the globe for generations. Books open doors, in your mind and in your life. Read an online book list and find a good book to grab at the library today. Then spend the next 30 days reading at least one chapter a day until you reach the end.

19 _Every morning, watch or read something that inspires you._

Sometimes all you need is a little pep talk. For the next 30 days, before you eat breakfast, or leave the house, watch a motivational video or read something (quotation, blog post, short story, etc.) that inspires you.

20 _Do something every day after lunch that makes you laugh._

Watch a funny video clip on YouTube, read your favorite comic strip, or find a good joke online. A good chuckle stimulates the mind and can give you a renewed level on energy. The best time for this laugh is during the lull in the mid-afternoon, when you need it most.

21 _Go alcohol and drug free for 30 days._

This challenge depends on your individual circumstance. If you are a heavy user of alcohol or a particular drug it is not recommended that you quit cold turkey. You need to see a physician and ease off of the substance slowly. But if you are a casual user, quit right now for 30 days.

22 _Exercise for 30 minutes every day for 30 days._

Your health is your life. Don't let it go. Eat right, exercise and get an annual physical check-up.

23 _Get uncomfortable and face a fear every day._

With a strategy of continuous small steps into uncomfortable territory we are often able to sidestep the biggest barrier to positive change: Fear. Sometimes we're afraid we'll fail. Sometimes we're subconsciously afraid we'll succeed and then we'd have to deal with all the disruption (growth) and change that follows success. And other times it's our fear of rejection or simply our fear of looking like a fool. The best way to defeat fear is to stare it down. Connect to your fear, feel it in your body, realize it and steadily address it. Greet it by name if you have to: "Welcome, fear." Fear can be a guiding friend if you learn how to swallow it, and listen to it only when it serves its true purpose of warning you when you are in danger. Spend an hour every day for the next 30 day's addressing a fear that is holding you back.

24 Cook one brand new, healthy recipe every day.

Cooking is fun, challenges your mind, and if done correctly, provides vital nutrients to your body. Win-Win-Win. How to Cook Everything by Mark Bittman is great tool for this challenge. Packed with 900 pages of simple instructions on how to cook everything you could ever dream of eating, it's pretty much the greatest cookbook ever written. Prepare one new, healthy recipe every day for the next 30 days.

25 Spend 10 minutes every evening reflecting on what went well.

For the next 30 days spend 10 minutes every evening pondering the small successes that occurred during the course of the day. This process of positive reflection will remind you of all the tiny blessings in your life, and help you to celebrate your personal growth.

26 Have a conversation every day with someone you rarely speak to.

People are interesting creatures, and no two people are exactly alike. Interacting with different people will open your mind to fascinating ideas and perspectives. So for the next 30 days strike up a conversation daily with someone you rarely speak to, or someone you've never met before. Find out what makes them tick.

27 Pay down debt and don't create any new debt for 30 days.

Live well below your means. Don't buy stuff you don't need. Sleep on big purchases. Create a budget and savings plan and stick to them. For the next 30 days pay for things in cash and micro-manage every cent you make and spend.

28 Let go of one relationship that constantly hurts you.

Keep people in your life who truly love you, motivate you, encourage you, enhance you, and make you happy. If you know people who do none of these things, let them go and make room for new positive relationships. Over the next 30 days, if relevant to your situation, gradually let go of one person in your life who has been continuously hurting you and holding you back.

Publicly forgive someone who deserves another chance.

Sometimes good relationships end abruptly because of big egos and arguments based on isolated incidents. If there's someone in your life who truly deserves another chance, give it to them. If you need to apologize too, do it. Over the next 30 days give your story together a new chapter.

Document every day with one photograph and one paragraph.

For 30 days bring a camera with you wherever you go. Do your best to take one photograph that represents a standout experience from each day. Then, before you go to bed each night, write one paragraph in a notebook or journal that highlights your day. If you do it all digitally you can unite your daily photograph and paragraph in one digital space (like a personal blog), which can be easily reviewed in the future. Many moons from now these old photos and journal entries will ignite your recollection of interesting memories you would have otherwise forgotten.

As you progress through these challenges remember, personal growth is a slow, steady process. It can't be rushed. You need to work on it gradually every day. There is ample time for you to be who you want to be in life. Don't settle for less than what you think you deserve, or less than you know you can be. Despite the struggles you'll face along the way, never give up on yourself. You're braver than you believe, stronger than you seem, smarter than you think, and twice as capable as you have ever imagined.

10 THINGS You Must GIVE UP to Be *Successful*

When we think about how to achieve success, we often focus on the skills and habits we should add to our lives. But sometimes the key to success actually lies in our ability to give up certain habits and behaviors. So starting today...

1 Give up the habit of waiting.

The way you spend your time defines who you are. You don't get to choose how you are going to die, or when; you can only decide how you are going to live right now. Trust me, a year from now you will wish you had started today.

2 Give up the excuses.

Sooner or later you will come to realize that it's not what you lose along the way that counts; it's what you do with what you still have. When you let go, forgive, and move on, you in no way change the past, you change the future.

3 Give up trying to be perfect.

Sometimes we try to show the world that we are flawless in hopes that we will be liked and accepted by everyone. But we can't please everyone, and we shouldn't try. The beauty of us lies in our vulnerability, our love, our complex emotions – our authentic imperfections. When we embrace who we are and decide to be authentic, instead of perfect, we open ourselves up to real relationships, real happiness, and real success. There is no need to put on a mask. There is no need to pretend to be someone you're not. You are perfectly imperfect just the way you are.

4 Give up doing things you know are wrong.

Nothing is more damaging to you than doing something that you believe is wrong.

> *"Don't spend time beating on a wall,*
> *hoping to transform it into a door."*
> –Coco Chanel

Your beliefs alone don't help you grow and thrive, your behavior and actions do. So always do what you know in your heart is right, for you.

Give up feelings of entitlement.

Nobody owes you anything. When you approach life with the false sense that you are owed things, you will naturally become less productive and constantly find yourself disappointed by reality. When you are grateful for what you have, and see positive things as bonuses, versus owed entitlements, you will earn great successes gradually as you grow.

Give up relationships that want you to be someone else.

The best kind of relationship is the one that makes you a better person without changing you into someone other than yourself.

7 Give up letting others decide what you can and can't do.

In order to live your own authentic life, you have to follow YOUR inner GPS, not someone else's. When others say, "You can't do it!" or "That's impossible," don't lose hope. Just because they couldn't doesn't mean you can't.

8 Give up being a helpless victim.

Yes, it is unfortunate that sometimes bad things happen to the best of people. Life can be unfair, unkind and unjust. However, being stuck in a victim mentality does not nurture your ability to move onward and upward. You've got to stand back up and take positive steps to heal and grow.

9 Give up worrying about past failures.

Accept your past without regret, handle your presence with confidence, and face your future without fear. You are today where your thoughts and actions have brought you; you will be tomorrow where your thoughts and actions take you.

10 *Give up blaming everyone else.*

Either you own your situation or it will own you. Either you take responsibility for your life, or someone else will. Blame is a scapegoat – it's an easy way out of taking accountability for your own outcome. It's a lot easier to point the finger at someone or something else instead of looking within. Blame is not constructive; it does not help you or anyone else – nobody wins in the blame game. The amount of energy and stress it takes to place blame elsewhere takes away from your ability to move forward and find a real solution.

And remember, the road you are traveling may be the more challenging one, but don't lose faith. Don't listen to the doubters, don't let setbacks keep you down, and most of all, don't give up on yourself.

It's okay if you don't know how much more you can handle. It's fine if you don't know exactly what to do next. Eventually you'll let go of how things 'should be' and start to see all the great possibilities in front of you. This is your life – grab the wheel with both hands and keep steering yourself in the right direction. The best part of your life will start on the day you decide your life

is your own – no one to lean on, rely on, or blame. You are in full control of your future. Believe with all your heart that you will do what you were made to do. It may be tough at times, but refuse to follow some preordained path. Make your own rules and have your own game plan. There is no happiness and success to be found by playing it safe and settling for a life that is less than the one you are capable of living.

10 SUCCESS *Principles* We Often Forget

Sometimes we find ourselves running in place, struggling to get ahead simply because we forget to address some of the basic success principles that govern our potential to make progress. So here's a quick reminder:

1 *You are the only person responsible for your success.*

The best part of your life will start on the day you decide your life is your own – no one to lean on, rely on, or blame. You are in full control of your future. Believe with all your heart that you will do what you were made to do. It may be tough at times, but refuse to follow some preordained path. Make your own rules and have your own game plan. There is no happiness and success to be found by playing it safe and settling for a life that is less than the one you are capable of living.

2 *You don't have to invent the wheel.*

Actually, to be successful you don't have to invent anything at all. Coming up with a new invention or idea is one way to achieve massive success, but it isn't necessary.

And it can be the most challenging road to success there is. You see many people have found lots of success just by taking something that already existed and simply putting their own twist on it (their unique selling proposition). Think about Apple for instance. As Steve Jobs once said, "Good artists copy, great artist steal. Creativity is connecting things." Connecting things means seeking inspiration from great ideas that already exist and adding your own useful twist.

3 *There is no progress without action.*

What is not started today is never finished tomorrow. Some of the greatest ideas never made it. Why? Because the genius behind the idea failed to take action. Just remember, no action always results in a 100% failure rate. So get into action now, and begin to move in the right direction. Once you get started every step

> *Identify your problems but give your power and energy to solutions.*
> -Tony Robbins

afterwards gets easier and easier. Until eventually, what had once been invisible, starts to become visible, and what once felt unattainable, starts to become a reality.

4 *Persistence always wins.*

As Winston Churchill once said, "Success is stumbling from failure to failure with no loss of enthusiasm." It may take more than one swing to compose an efficient hit, so make sure not to give up on strike #1. And remember, a river cuts through rocks not because of its power at a given moment, but because of its persistence over time.

5 *Focus is everything.*

When you are too busy looking behind and around you, people are passing you. If you never focus clearly on something, you will never be 100% efficient at anything. Multi-tasking might seem to make you efficient at getting multiple tasks done at once, but it usually reduces your efficiency in dealing with each individual task.

6 *Failure is necessary.*

Don't wake up at seventy-five years of age sighing over what you should have tried, but didn't because you were afraid to fail. Just do it, and be willing to fail and learn along the way. Very few people get it right the first time. In fact, most people fail to get it right the first 5 times. If what you did today didn't turn out as you hoped, tomorrow is a new opportunity to do it differently. Interpret each failure as a lesson on the road to success.

7 *Positivity fuels productivity.*

Thoughts are like the steering wheel that moves our life in the right direction. Success comes from positive energy. You can choose to get caught up in the negativity surrounding you, or you can decide to do something positive about your situation. You always have a choice. Remember, happiness is an element of success, and the happiest people don't necessarily have the best of everything, they use positive energy to make the best of what they have.

8 *You must believe you can.*

You must find the place inside yourself where anything is possible. It starts with a dream. Add confidence, and it becomes a belief. Add commitment, and it becomes a goal in sight. Add action, and it becomes a part of your life. Add determination and time, and your dream becomes a reality.

9 *Helping others is a big part of being successful.*

Successful people constantly come up with new ideas, new projects, and new and innovative ways of helping others. This means that your aims and objectives just benefit you, but also help benefit others as well. Bottom line: Your long-term success is directly tied to how well you serve your community.

10 *Success is a journey of countless baby steps.*

It's a constant process of growth. If you want to be successful, you must continue to hold yourself to a higher standard than anyone else, and strive to improve. Oftentimes a person or organization will be successful, but then drop off. A person may become lazy, and an organization may succumb to weaknesses or competition. Sustained success means continually improving even if others may not see a need for it. Remember, the great thing in the world is not so much where we stand at any given time, as in what direction we are moving.

20 QUESTIONS

You Should Ask Yourself Every *Sunday*

At the cusp of new beginnings many of us take time to reflect on our lives by looking back over the past and ahead into the future. We ponder the successes, failures and standout events that are slowly scripting our life's story. This process of self reflection helps maintain a conscious awareness of where we've been and where we intend to go. It is pertinent to the organization and preservation of our dreams, goals and desires.

If you would like to maximize the benefits of self reflection, I have 20 questions for you. These questions should be reviewed every Sunday morning or sometime during the weekend when you have some quiet time to think. Remember, reflection is the key to progression.

1 *What did I learn last week?*

If you have trouble answering this question, it's time for a change. It doesn't matter how old you are, you should learn something new every week.

2 *What was my greatest accomplishment over the past week?*

Reflecting on your accomplishments is a healthy way to raise self confidence and contentment. It's also an effective way to track your progress.

3 *Which moment from last week was the most memorable and why?*

It may open up your mind to new passions and goals, or simple pastimes worth revisiting.

4 *What's the #1 thing I need to accomplish this week?*

Everything else is secondary, and should be treated as such. Nevertheless, this question will also shine light on other noteworthy tasks.

5 What can I do right now to make the week less stressful?

Set reminders in your calendar, get your laundry done, fill the car with gas... organize yourself.

6 What have I struggled with in the past that might also affect the upcoming week?

The idea here is to learn from your struggles and better equip yourself for future encounters.

7 What was last week's biggest time sink?

Steer clear of this in the future. Setup physical barriers against distractions if you have to.

8 Am I carrying any excess baggage into the week that can be dropped?

Physical clutter, mental clutter... eliminate the unnecessary so the necessary may shine bright.

9 What have I been avoiding that needs to get done?

Pencil in a time to get these things done. For any 2-minute or less tasks, consider scheduling them first thing Monday morning.

10 What opportunities are still on the table?

If it's still available and you want it, make a concrete plan to go after it this week.

11 Is there anyone I've been meaning to talk to?

Regular communication can solve problems before they fester. Always keep an open line of communication to those around you.

12 Is there anyone that deserves a big 'Thank You'?

Take time each week to thank the people who have helped you. Your kind gesture will not go unnoticed.

13 How can I help someone else this coming week?

The easiest way to get what you want is to help others get what they want. If you help them, they will remember you when you need help.

4 What are my top 3 goals for the next 3 years?

You'll never make any progress in life if you don't setup realistic goals for yourself.

15 Have any of my recent actions moved me closer to my goals?

If the answer is no, something needs to change.

16 What's the next step for each goal?

Knowing the next step is the key to accomplishing the whole.

17 What am I looking forward to during the upcoming week?

The answer can act as a great source of motivation. If nothing exists, schedule something to look forward to.

18 What are my fears?

Consciously address your fears each week and slowly work on resolving them. It's all about taking baby steps.

19 What am I most grateful for?

It's a smart way to keep things in perspective, and something you should never lose sight of.

20 If I knew I only had one week to live, who would I spend my time with?

Another helpful reminder… Life is short. Spend more time with the people you care about.

Take 30 minutes every Sunday and give yourself the gift of self reflection. It has worked wonders for me, and I am confident it will do the same for you.

HOW TO
ACHIEVE
THE IMPOSSIBLE

The **impossible** is what nobody can do until somebody does.

Teleportation is the new air travel. Humans can walk on water. And there is a cure for cancer. These things will happen eventually because, quite simply, the nature of progression dictates that they must happen. And because there are people on this planet who believe they can make them happen.

Are you one of these people?

3 Short Stories on Achieving the Impossible

When I was a high school freshman, a 260 pound freshman girl showed up for track and field try-outs. Her name was Sara, and she was only there because her doctor said her health depended on it. But once she scanned the crowd of students who were trying-out, she turned around and began walking away. Coach O'Leary saw her, jogged over, and turned her back around. "I'm not thin enough for this sport!" Sara declared. "And I'll never be! It's impossible for me to lose enough weight. I've tried." Coach O'Leary nodded, and promised Sara that her body type wasn't suited for her current weight. "It's suited for 220 pounds," he said. Sara looked confused. "Most people tell me I need to lose 130 pounds," she replied. "But you think I only need to lose 40?" Coach O'Leary nodded again. Sara started off as a shot put competitor, but spent every single afternoon running and training with the rest of the track team. She was very competitive, and by the end of our freshman year she was down to

220 pounds. She also won 2nd place in the county-wide shot put tournament that year. Three years later, during our senior year, she won 3rd place in the 10K run. Her competitive weight at the time was 130 pounds.

When Charles Darwin wrote The Origin of Species, which proposed the groundbreaking idea of evolution by natural selection, it launched a worldwide debate. Supporters included scientists, historians, and others whose professions and worldviews required that they carefully analyze new ideas and adopt those that seemed to make sense. Critics included theologians, conservative extremists, and others who were convinced that the current explanation of our ancestry was the only possible explanation. This group of people, the ones who refused to accept the possibility of new ideas, eventually alienated themselves from the debate, and arguably failed to assist in the progression of mankind. The people who didn't blindly reject evolution, who instead questioned it, researched it, and sought to explore its possibilities, were able to achieve previously impossible feats by making important advances in various fields of study from sociology to history to medicine.

When Sergey Brin and Larry Page founded Google, they had absolutely no intention of building the most powerful Internet-based company in the world. In the mid 1990's the Internet was already saturated with hundreds of established search engine companies like Yahoo, Lycos, and Alta Vista. Competing and succeeding in such a competitive environment seemed impossible to them. So instead, they tried to sell their search technology to these companies. And although Google, with its PageRank algorithm and efficient scaling, was clearly more cutting-edge than any search technology currently in place, none of these established companies wanted to get their hands dirty with Google's new technology. So after exhausting their options, Brin and Page decided to release Google to the public and directly compete with the biggest names in the business. As we know, they blew them out of the water.

'Impossible' is Simply a State of Mind

If we can find the patience to see the world for what it is – dynamic, flexible, and loaded with untapped potential – and if we can accept the fact that change is an inevitable and brilliant part of life, then we can partake in the thrill of progression, and help shape a world in which the impossible becomes possible.

To achieve the impossible, we must first understand that the 'state of impossible' is simply a 'state of mind.' Nothing is truly impossible. Impossibility only exists when we lack the proper knowledge and experience to comprehend how something can be possible.

Sara was convinced that it was impossible
to lose weight because, in her past
experience, it had never worked-out
the way she had hoped. 19th-century
theologians laughed at Charles Darwin's
theories because his theories didn't
come from the Bible, which, at the time,
was their sole source of knowledge and
truth. Google's old competitors didn't
recognize the next big thing when it was
offered to them on a silver platter. Why?
Because they didn't want to bother with
a new technology that they didn't fully
understand. This ultimately forced
Google's Brin and Page to achieve their
version of the 'impossible.'

Conclusion

When people say something is impossible,
what they really mean is, "I can't imagine
how it could be possible." But with more
knowledge and experience, they'd begin
to realize that anything is possible, it
just takes a change in mindset. Because
'impossible' is what we get when we haven't
trained our minds and our hearts to see
past the systems that currently exist to
ones that don't yet exist.

So let's start training our minds and our
hearts, today, so we can turn today's
impossibility into tomorrow's possibility.

The acquisition of knowledge doesn't mean you're growing.

Growing happens when what you know changes how you live.

It's not so much about finding opportunities as it is about creating them.

No matter how smart you are, you will make mistakes.

A good idea without action is nothing at all.

What we don't start today won't be finished by tomorrow.

There is a lesson in everything you do, and learning the lesson is how you move forward.

If you keep doing what you're doing, you'll keep getting what you're getting.

INCONVENIENT
Personal Development
Truths

The harder you work, the luckier you will become.

Nobody succeeds all by themselves.

Being busy and being productive are two different things.

Being successful is a journey, not a destination.

Tough times don't last, but tough people do.

Having a plan, even a flawed one at first, is better than no plan at all.

It's uncomfortable to challenge the status quo, but it's worth it.

Lots of successful people have failed as many times as they have succeeded.

Success QUESTIONS to Make You *think*

What's the number one thing you want to **ACHIEVE** in the *next five* years**?**

If you could **LEARN** *anything* what would it be**?**

If we learn from our **MISTAKES**, why are we always so *afraid* to make a mistake**?**

What is something you will **CONTINUE** to do until the day you *die***?**

What's something that used to **SCARE** you, but *no longer* does**?**

What is the best **ADVICE** you have ever *received***?**

What **MISTAKE** do you *make* over and over again**?**

If I were to say to you, **"JUST GO FOR IT"** what would *"it"* be**?**

What **FEAR** of *failure* stopped you from doing**?**

What's something you must **GIVE UP** to *move forward***?**

Part Eight
Simplicity

Life is not complicated.
We are complicated.
When we stop doing the
wrong things and start
doing the right things,
life becomes simple.

WHAT WE **WANT** TO BE WHEN WE **GROW** UP

When I was in elementary school my parents told me it didn't matter what I did when I grew up, so long as it made me happy. "Happiness is the whole point of life", my father said. "Your mother loves to help people, so she became a nurse. I love reading, writing and poetry, so I became an English teacher. We both find happiness in the work we do each day."

A few years later when I was in junior high, my grumpy 6th grade homeroom teacher put me in detention for "being difficult". She went around the classroom and asked each student what they wanted to be when they grew up. When she got to me, I told her I wanted to be happy. She told me I was missing the whole point of the question. I told her she was missing the whole point of life.

What do we all want to be when we grow up? Happy... that is all. Find what makes you happy and do it until you die.

12 THINGS

You Should Be Able to SAY About *Yourself*

You know you're on the right track when you can repeat each of the following headlines to yourself, honestly. (And if you can't, this list gives you something positive to work on.)

1 *I am following my heart and intuition.*

Don't be pushed by your problems. Be led by your dreams. Live the life you want to live. Be the person you want to remember years from now. Make decisions and act on them. Make mistakes, fall and try again. Even if you fall a thousand times, at least you won't have to wonder what could have been. At least you will know in your heart that you gave your dreams your best shot.

Each of us has a fire in our hearts burning for something. It's our responsibility in life to find it and keep it lit. This is your life, and it's a short one. Don't let others extinguish your flame. Try what you want to try. Go where you want to go. Follow your own intuition. Dream with your eyes open until you know exactly what it looks like. Then do at least one thing every day to make it a reality.

2 *I am proud of myself.*

And as you strive to achieve your goals, you can count on there being some fairly substantial disappointments along the way. Don't get discouraged, the road to your dreams may not be an easy one. Think of these disappointments as challenges – tests of persistence and courage. At the end of the road, more often than not, we regret what we didn't do far more than what we did.

You are your own best friend and your own biggest critic. Regardless of the opinions of others, at the end of the day the only reflection staring back at you in the mirror is your own. Accept everything about yourself – EVERYTHING! You are you and that is the beginning and the end – no apologies, no regrets.

People who are proud of themselves tend to have passions in life, feel content and

> ## *You only live once, but if you do it right, once is enough.*
> ### - Mae West

set good examples for others. It requires envisioning the person you would like to become and making your best efforts to grow.

Being proud isn't bragging about how great you are; it's more like quietly knowing that you're worth a lot. It's not about thinking you're perfect – because nobody is – but knowing that you're worthy of being loved and accepted. All you have to do is be yourself and live the story that no one else can live – the story of your own unique life. Be proud, be confident, you never know who has been looking at you wishing they were you.

3 *I am making a difference.*

Act as if what you do makes a difference. It does.

Is it true that we all live to serve? That by helping others we fulfill our own destiny? The answer is a simple 'yes.' When you make a positive impact in someone else's life, you also make a positive impact in your own life. Do something that's greater than you – something that helps someone else to be happy or to suffer less.

You are only one, but you are one. You cannot do everything, but you can do

something. Smile and enjoy the fact that you made a difference – one you'll likely remember forever.

4 *I am happy and grateful.*

Happiness is within you, in your way of thinking. How you view yourself and your world are mindful choices and habits. The lens you choose to view everything through determines how you feel about yourself and everything that happens around you.

Being grateful will always make you happy. If you're finding it hard to be grateful for anything, sit down close your eyes and take a long slow breath and be grateful for oxygen. Every breath you take is in sync with someone's last.

5 *I am growing in to the best version of me.*

Wearing a mask wears you out. Faking it is fatiguing. The most arduous activity is pretending to be what you know you aren't. Trying to fit some idealistic mold of perfection is a fool's game. It's much wiser to just be yourself – faults and all.

Remember, trying to be anyone else is a waste of the person you are. Embrace that individual inside you that has ideas, strengths and beauty like no one else. Be the person you know yourself to be – the best version of you – on your terms. Improve continuously, take care of your body and health, and surround yourself with positivity. Become the best version of you.

6 *I am making my time count.*

Time is the most valuable constituent of life. Make the time for what does matter today. Really being in the moment, finding passion in your life, seeing the world and traveling, or just seeing the world that's around you right now, being with great people, doing amazing things, eating amazing food and savoring life's little pleasures.

Remember, your time is priceless, but it's free. You can't own it, but you can use it. You can spend it, but you can't keep it. Once you've lost it you can never get it back. You really do only have a short period to live. So let your dreams be bigger than your fears and your actions louder than your words. Make your time count!

7 *I am honest with myself.*

Be honest about what's right, as well as what needs to be changed. Be honest about what you want to achieve and who you want to become. Be honest with every

aspect of your life, always. Because you are the one person you can forever count on.

Search your soul, for the truth, so that you truly know who you are. Once you do, you'll have a better understanding of where you are now and how you got here, and you'll be better equipped to identify where you want to go and how to get there.

8 *I am good to those I care about.*

In human relationships distance is not measured in miles, but in affection. Two people can be right next to each other, yet miles apart. So don't ignore someone you care about, because lack of concern hurts more than angry words. Stay in touch with those who matter to you. Not because it's convenient, but because they're worth the extra effort.

When was the last time you told your family and close personal friends that you loved them? Just spending a little time with someone shows that you care, shows that they are important enough that you've chosen — out of all the things to do on your busy schedule — to find the time for them. Talk to them. Listen to them. Understand them.

Many times it's our actions, not just our words that really speak what our heart feels for another.

9 *I know what unconditional love feels like.*

Whether your love is towards a child, a lover, or another family member, know the feeling of giving love and not expecting anything in return – this is what lies at the heart of unconditional love. Life through unconditional love is a wondrous adventure that excites the very core of our being and lights our path with delight. This love is a dynamic and powerful energy that lifts us through the most difficult times.

Love is beautiful and unpredictable. It begins with ourselves, for without self-love, we cannot know what true love can be. In loving ourselves, we allow the feeling to generate within us and then we can share it to everyone and everything around us. When you love unconditionally, it isn't because the person you love is perfect, it's because you learn to see an imperfect person perfectly.

10 *I have forgiven those who once hurt me.*

We've all been hurt by another person at some point or another – we were treated badly, trust was broken, hearts were hurt. And while this pain is normal, sometimes that pain lingers for too long. We relive the pain over and over, letting them live rent-free in our head and we have a hard time letting go.

Grudges are a waste of perfect happiness, it causes us to miss out on the beauty of life as it happens. To forgive is to set a prisoner free and discover the prisoner was you.

11 *I take full accountability for my life.*

Own your choices and mistakes, and be willing to take the necessary steps to improve upon them. Either you take accountability for your life or someone else will. And when they do, you'll become a slave to their ideas and dreams instead of a pioneer of your own.

You are the only one who can directly control the outcome of your life. And no, it won't always be easy. Every person has a stack of obstacles in front of them. But you must take accountability for your situation and overcome these obstacles. Choosing not to is choosing a lifetime of mere existence.

12 *I have no regrets.*

This one is simply a culmination of the previous eleven...

Follow your heart. Be true to yourself. Do what makes you happy. Be with who makes you smile. Laugh as much as you breathe. Love as long as you live. Say what you need to say. Offer a helping hand when you're able. Appreciate all the things you do have. Smile. Celebrate your small victories. Learn from your mistakes. Realize that everything is a lesson in disguise. Forgive. And let go of the things you can't control.

12 AMAZINGLY *Achievable* Things To Do Today

"What can I start doing today to make my life happier and more rewarding?"

This is the most common question readers ask us via email, Facebook and Twitter. So today I dug into our archives and came up with a list of twelve simple, actionable ways to improve your well being on a daily basis. (Each tip links back to its original corresponding article, so you can read more at your leisure.)

Starting today...

1 *Smile.*

A smile is a choice, not a miracle. Don't wait for people to smile. Show them how. A genuine smile makes you and everyone around you feel better. The simple act of smiling sends a message to your brain that you're happy. And when you're happy, your body pumps out all kinds of feel-good endorphins. This reaction has been studied since the 1980's and has been proven a number of times. Bottom line: Smiling actually makes you happier.

2 *Treat everyone with kindness and respect.*

Yes, treat everyone with kindness and respect, even those who are rude to you – not because they are nice, but because you are. There are no boundaries or classes that define a group of people that deserve to be respected. Treat everyone with the same level of respect you would give to your grandfather and the same level of patience you would have with your baby brother. People will notice your kindness.

3 *Perform one selfless act.*

In life, you get what you put in. When you make a positive impact in someone else's life, you also make a positive impact in your own life. Do something that's greater than you, something that helps someone else be happy or suffer less. I promise, it will be an extremely rewarding experience. One you'll likely remember forever.

4 Avoid needless drama and those who create it.

Never create unnecessary drama, and don't surround yourself with those who do. Choose to spend time with people who you are proud to know, people you admire, who love and respect you – people who make your day a little brighter simply by being in it. Don't walk away from negative people, RUN! Life is too short to spend time with folks who suck the happiness out of you.

5 Think of the positives.

Stop being afraid of what could go wrong, and start thinking of what could go right. Better yet, think of everything that already is right. Be thankful for nights that turned into mornings, friends that turned into family, and past dreams and goals that turned into realities. And use this positivity to fuel an even brighter tomorrow.

6 Inject a little love into the world around you.

Love what you are doing, until you can do what you love. Love where you are, until

you can be where you love. Love the people you are with, until you can be with the people you love most. This is the way we find happiness.

7 Take decisive and immediate action on something that needs to get done.

It doesn't matter if you have a genius IQ and a PhD in Quantum Physics, you can't change anything or make any sort of real-world progress without taking action. There's a huge difference between knowing how to do something and actually doing it. Knowledge and intelligence are both useless without action. It's as simple as that.

8 Follow your intuition when making decisions.

Following your intuition means doing what feels right, even if it doesn't look or sound right to others. Only time will tell, but our human instincts are rarely ever wrong. So don't worry about what everyone else thinks, and keep living and speaking your truth. The only people that will get mad at you for doing so are those who are set on living a lie.

9 _Spend time working on something you believe in._

Never put off or give up on a goal that's important to you. Not because you still have tomorrow to start or try again, but because you may not have tomorrow at all. Life is shorter than it sometimes seems. Follow your heart today.

10 _Meet someone new._

Most humans have a habit of stagnating in a small circle of friends; but it doesn't help us grow. Get out there and meet new people. You'll be surprised at the lessons they will teach you and the new opportunities they will inject into your life.

1 _Exercise and eat healthy._

Taking care of your body is crucial to being the happiest person you can be. If you don't have your physical energy in good shape, then your mental energy (your focus), your emotional energy (your feelings), and your spiritual energy (your purpose) will all be negatively affected. Those who exercise have a higher sense of self-accomplishment and self-worth.

2 _Be a student of life._

Experience it, learn from it, and absorb all the knowledge you can. Prepare yourself for greatness by keeping your mind conditioned with fresh knowledge and new challenges. Remember, if you stay ready, you don't have to get ready when great opportunities arise.

10 COMMANDMENTS
For a *Good* Life

A good life is when you assume nothing, do more, need less, smile often and realize how fortunate you are right now. It's about the simple pleasures that make you happy, the compassionate deeds you perform, the personal goals you strive to achieve, the relationships you nurture and the legacy you leave behind.

So starting today, choose to take control. Here are ten commandments to help you live a good life.

1 *I am not perfect and I will not try to be.*

Think of how many things don't get done in this world simply because people are waiting for the perfect time, place and circumstance.

The real world doesn't reward perfectionists. It rewards people who get things done. And the only way to get things done is to be imperfect 99% of the time.

2 *I cannot, and will not try, to please everyone.*

No matter what you do or how you do it, there will always be people that disagree with what you're doing. That's life. So don't try to please everyone. Simply do what you know is right.

And remember, it doesn't matter how many people don't get it, it matters how many people do.

3 *I will take part in something I believe in.*

This could be anything. Some people take an active role in their city council, some find refuge in religious faith, some join social clubs supporting causes they believe in and others find passion in their careers. In each case the psychological outcome is the same. They engage themselves in something they strongly believe in. This engagement brings happiness and meaning into their lives.

> *And in the end, it's not the years in your life that count.*
> *It's the life in your years.*
>
> - Abraham Lincoln

4 *I will prioritize my obligations and do important things first.*

Set priorities for yourself and act accordingly. It's the only way to get things done.

It's the only way to turn a dream into a reality.

5 *I will choose my friends wisely.*

Your friends are family you choose. So make sure you choose friends who are worthy of your time and attention.

Surround yourself with people who reflect the person you want to be. Choose friends who you are proud to know, people you admire, who love and respect you – people who make your day a little brighter simply by being in it.

6 *I will help others when I am able.*

When you make a positive impact in someone else's life, you also make a positive impact in your own life. The more

you help others, the more they will want to help you.

7 *I will focus on the positive.*

Positive thinking is at the forefront of every great success story. The mind must believe it can do something before it is capable of actually doing it.

The way to overcome negative thoughts and destructive emotions is to develop opposing, positive emotions that are stronger and more powerful. Listen to your self-talk and replace negative thoughts with positive ones. Regardless of how a situation seems, focus on the next positive step forward.

8 *I can only be me.*

Judy Garland once said, "Always be a first rate version of yourself instead of a second rate version of somebody else." Live by this statement.

There is no such thing as living in someone else's shoes. The only shoes you can occupy are your own. If you aren't being yourself, you aren't truly living – you're merely existing. And ask yourself this:

If you don't like who you really are, why should I like you?

Trying to be somebody you're not is not sexy. Be you. That's when you're beautiful.

9 *I will be here now.*

Life is happening right now. Instead of dwelling on the past or worrying about the future, practice being and living in the present moment.

Remember, right now is the only moment guaranteed to you. Right now is life. Don't miss it.

10 *Life never gets any better, only my perception of it does.*

The world around you changes when you change.

If you awake every morning with the thought that something wonderful will happen in your life today, and you pay close attention, you'll often find that you're right. The opposite is also true. The choice is yours to make.

12 RULES for Being a *Human Being*

Don't try to be perfect. Just be an excellent example of being human.

Here are a few things to keep in mind:

1 *Growth requires pain.*

Be patient and tough, someday this pain will be useful to you. Those with the strength to succeed in the long run are the ones who lay a firm foundation of growth with the bricks that life has thrown at them. So don't be afraid to fall apart for a little while. Because when it happens, the situation will open an opportunity for you to grow and rebuild yourself into the brilliant person you are capable of being.

2 *You will learn as long as you live.*

There is no stage of life that does not contain new lessons. As long as you live there will be something more to learn. And as long as you follow your heart and never stop learning, you'll turn not older, but newer every day.

3 *There is a positive lesson in every life experience.*

Don't forget to acknowledge the lesson, especially when things don't go your way. If you make a mistake that sets you back a little, or a business deal or a relationship doesn't work, it only means a new opportunity is out there waiting. And the lesson you just learned is the first step towards it.

4 *True beauty lives under the skin.*

When you start to really know someone, most of their physical characteristics vanish in your mind. You begin to dwell in their energy, recognize their scent, and appreciate their wit. You see only the essence of the person, not the shell. That's why you can't fall in love with physical beauty. You can lust after it, be infatuated by it, or want to own it. You can love it with your eyes and your body for a little while, but not your heart in the long-term. And that's why, when you really connect with a person's inner self, most physical imperfections become irrelevant.

5 Only you know what you're capable of.

Unless someone can look into the core of your heart, and see the degree of your passion, or look into the depths of your soul and see the extent of your will, then they have no business telling you what you can or cannot achieve. Because while they may know the odds, they do not know YOU, and what you're capable of. That's something only you know.

6 Your love creates your happiness.

The happiness you feel is in direct proportion to the love you give. When you love, you subconsciously strive to become better than you are. When you strive to become better than you are, everything around you becomes better too. During your youth, love will be your teacher; in your middle age, love will be your foundation; and in your old age, love will be your fondest memories and your greatest delight.

7 You earn respect by being respectful.

Respect isn't something you can demand or manipulate by saying what you think people want to hear. You earn respect by listening, acknowledging feelings and treating others with the same respect you hope to get in return. Treat everyone with kindness and respect, even those who are rude to you – not because they are nice, but because you are.

8 Negativity poisons the soul.

Don't let needless drama and negativity stop you from being the best you can be. Avoid the drama, and focus on what truly matters. Life is insanely short and your time is precious, so don't waste your time on trivial matters. Let go of the things that are weighing you down. As you unclutter your life, you will slowly free yourself to answer the callings of your inner spirit.

9 Your health is your life.

Regardless of the size and shape of your body, it is the greatest tool you will ever own. Without it, you wouldn't be alive. How you take care of it or fail to take care of it can make an enormous difference in the quality of your life. Exercise to be fit, not skinny. Eat to nourish your body. To truly be your best, you must give your body the fuel it needs. Toss the junk and fill your kitchen with fresh, whole foods. Run, swim, bike, walk – sweat! Good health is essential for having the energy, stamina and outlook to tackle your goals and dreams.

10 *Letting go is part of moving on to something better.*

You will not get what you truly deserve if you're too attached to the things you're supposed to let go of. Sometimes you love, and you struggle, and you learn, and you move on. And that's okay. You must be willing to let go of the life you planned for so you can enjoy the life that is waiting for you.

11 *This moment is a gift.*

The truth is, your whole life has been leading up to this moment. Think about that for a second. Every single thing you've gone through in life, every high, every low, and everything in between, has led you to this moment right now. This moment is priceless, and it's the only moment guaranteed to you. This moment is your 'life.' Don't miss it.

12 *Your choices design your life.*

You have a choice each and every single day. Choose to appreciate what you have. Choose to make time for yourself. Choose to do something that makes you smile. Choose to be excited. Choose to laugh at your own silliness. Choose to spend time with positive people. Choose to be persistent with your goals. Choose to try again and again. Within your choices lie all the tools and resources you need to design the life of your dreams, it's just a matter of choosing wisely.

WHAT **PERFECT IS**

Do perfect men have big muscles? Do perfect women have big breasts? Do perfect couples have lots of children? Do perfect husbands earn upwards of $100K a year? Do perfect wives cook delicious meals?

Do perfect people have lots of friends? Do perfect people have loads of life experience? Do perfect people ever fail?

Yeah! You bet they do! All of this and soooooo much more...

Perfect men are scrawny. Perfect men struggle with obesity. Perfect men can barely do one pull-up. Perfect men have bad backs that prevent them from lifting heavy objects. Perfect men were only born with one arm.

Perfect women have tiny breasts. Perfect women have fake breasts. Perfect women have breast reductions. Perfect women haven't finished growing their breasts yet. Perfect women have lost both breasts to cancer.

Perfect couples have one child. Perfect couples have ten children. Perfect couples adopt because, medically, they can't have their own children. Perfect couples adopt even when they can have their own. Perfect couples never have children because they don't want them.

Perfect husbands are stay-at-home dads. Perfect husbands own multi-million dollar businesses. Perfect husbands are migrant farmers. Perfect husbands switch careers in their mid-50's. Perfect husbands have no idea what they want to do for a living.

Perfect wives don't cook because they're too tired when they get home from work. Perfect wives only know how to cook Italian food. Perfect wives hate cooking even though they're good at it. Perfect wives are chefs at fancy restaurants. Perfect wives make Ramen Noodles.

Perfect people are introverts with two close friends. Perfect people are extroverts with five hundred Facebook friends they communicate with regularly. Perfect people hangout with their marching band friends. Perfect people have famous friends. Perfect people have a best friend with four legs.

Perfect people have traveled and lived all over the world. Perfect people have yet to explore beyond their hometown in rural Montana. Perfect people still live at home with their parents. Perfect people are happy where they are. Perfect people haven't figured out how to get to where they want to go.

Perfect people fail a hundred times and lose hope. Perfect people succeed on their very first attempt. Perfect people don't like to admit when they fail. Perfect people see failure as an opportunity for growth. Perfect people never fail because they never stretch themselves beyond their comfort zones.

Perfect people have scars on their faces and perfect complexions. Perfect people have long brown hair at 60 and short grey hair at 35. Perfect people wear wigs. Perfect people have sex with men, women, both or none at all. Perfect people can barely see over the grocery store counter and sometimes bump their heads at the top of doorways. Perfect people have waistlines that are infinite in size and geometry. Perfect people have skin tones as light as vanilla ice-cream and as rich dark chocolate.

Perfect people come from every corner of this beautiful planet and can be seen everywhere – even in the mirror.

Yeah! That's right!

Perfect is the way we are born. Perfect is the way we are now. Perfect is exclusively unique.

We are what perfect is.

10 SIMPLE *Truths* that Smart People Forget

Some of the smartest people I know continuously struggle to get ahead because they forget to address a few simple truths that collectively govern our potential to make progress. So here's a quick reminder:

1 *Education and intelligence accomplish nothing without action.*

It doesn't matter if you have a genius IQ and a PhD in Quantum Physics, you can't change anything or make any sort of real-world progress without taking action. There's a huge difference between knowing how to do something and actually doing it. Knowledge and intelligence are both useless without action. It's as simple as that.

2 *Happiness and success are two different things.*

I know an extremely savvy businesswoman who made almost a million dollars online last year. Every entrepreneur I know considers her to be wildly successful. But guess what? A few days ago, out of the blue, she told me that she's depressed. Why? "I'm burnt out and lonely. I just haven't taken enough time for myself lately," she said. "Wow!" I thought. "One of the most successful people I know isn't happy."

I also know a surfer who surfs almost all day, every day on the beach in front of our condo complex in San Diego. He's one of the most lighthearted, optimistic guys I've ever met – always smiling from ear to ear. But he sleeps in a van he co-owns with another surfer and they both frequently panhandle tourists for money. So while I can't deny that this man seems happy, I wouldn't classify his life as a success story.

"What will make me happy?" and "What will make me successful?" are two of the most important questions you can ask yourself. But they are two different questions.

3 Everyone runs their own business.

No matter how you make a living or who you think you work for, you only work for one person, yourself. The big question is: What are you selling, and to whom? Even when you have a full-time, salaried, 'Corporate America' position, you are still running your own business. You are selling one unit of your existence (an hour of your life) at a set price (the associated fraction of your salary) to a customer (your employer).

So how can you simultaneously save your time and increase your profit? The answer is slightly different for everyone. But it's an answer you should be seeking.

4 Having too many choices interferes with decision making.

Here in the 21st century where information moves at the speed of light and opportunities for innovation seem endless, we have an abundant array of choices when it comes to designing our lives and careers. But sadly, an abundance of choice often leads to indecision, confusion and inaction.

Several business and marketing studies have shown that the more product choices a consumer is faced with, the less products they typically buy. After all, narrowing down the best product from a pool of three choices is certainly a lot easier than

narrowing down the best product from a pool of three hundred choices. If the purchasing decision is tough to make, most people will just give up.

So if you're selling a product line, keep it simple. And if you're trying to make a decision about something in your life, don't waste all your time evaluating every last detail of every possible option. Choose something that you think will work and give it a shot. If it doesn't work out, choose something else and keep pressing forward.

5 All people possess dimensions of success and dimensions of failure.

This point is somewhat related to point #2 on happiness and success, but it stands strong on its own as well…

Trying to be perfect is a waste of time and energy. Perfection is an illusion.

All people, even our idols, are multidimensional. Powerful business men, polished musicians, bestselling authors, and even our own parents all have dimensions of success and dimensions of failure present in their lives.

Our successful dimensions usually encompass the things we spend the most time doing. We are successful in these dimensions because of our prolonged commitment to them. This is the part of our lives we want others to see – the successful part that holds our life's work. It's the notion of putting our best foot forward. It's the public persona we envision as our personal legacy: "The Successful ABC" or "The Award Winning XYZ."

But behind whichever polished storyline we publically promote, there lies a multi-dimensional human being with a long list of unprofessed failures. Sometimes this person is a bad husband or wife. Sometimes this person laughs at the expense of others. And sometimes this person merely takes their eyes off the road and rear-ends the car in front of them.

6 Every mistake you make is progress.

Mistakes teach you important lessons. Every time you make one, you're one step closer to your goal. The only mistake that can truly hurt you is choosing to do nothing simply because you're too scared to make a mistake.

So don't hesitate – don't doubt yourself. In life, it's rarely about getting a chance; it's about taking a chance. You'll never be 100% sure it will work, but you can always be 100% sure doing nothing won't work. Most of the time you just have to go for it!

And no matter how it turns out, it always ends up just the way it should be. Either you succeed or you learn something. Win-

Win. Remember, if you never act, you will never know for sure, and you will be left standing in the same spot forever.

7 People can be great at doing things they don't like to do.

Although I'm not suggesting that you choose a career or trade you dislike, I've heard way too many smart people say something like, "In order to be great at what you do, you have to like what you do." This just isn't true.

A good friend of mine is a public accountant. He has told me on numerous occasions that he dislikes his job – "that it bores him to death." But he frequently gets raises and promotions. At the age of 28, out of nearly a thousand Jr. Accountants in his division, he's one of only two who were promoted to be Sr. Accountants this past year. Why? Because even though he doesn't like doing it, he's good at what he does.

I could come up with dozens of other examples just like this, but I'll spare you the details. Just realize that if someone dedicates enough time and attention to perfecting a skill or trade, they can be insanely good at doing something they don't like to do.

8 The problems we have with others are typically more about us.

Quite often, the problems we have with others – our spouse, parents, siblings, etc. – don't really have much to do with them at all. Because many of the problems we think we have with them we subconsciously created in our own mind. Maybe they did something in the past that touched on one of our fears or insecurities. Or maybe they didn't do something that we expected them to do. In either case, problems like these are not about the other person, they're about us.

9 Emotional decisions are rarely good decisions.

And that's okay. It simply means these little predicaments will be easier to solve. We are, after all, in charge of our own decisions. We get to decide whether we want to keep our head cluttered with events from the past, or instead open our minds to the positive realities unfolding in front of us.

All we need is the willingness to look at things a little differently – letting go of 'what was' and 'what should have been,' and instead focusing our energy on 'what is' and 'what could be possible.'

Decisions driven by heavy emotion are typically misguided reactions rather than educated judgments. These reactions are the byproduct of minimal amounts of conscious thought and primarily based on momentary 'feelings' instead of mindful awareness.

The best advice here is simple: Don't let your emotions trump your intelligence. Slow down and think things through before you make any life-changing decisions.

10 You will never feel 100% ready when an opportunity arises.

The number one thing I persistently see holding smart people back is their own reluctance to accept an opportunity simply because they don't think they're ready. In other words, they believe they require additional knowledge, skill, experience, etc. before they can aptly partake in the opportunity. Sadly, this is the kind of thinking that stifles personal growth.

The truth is nobody ever feels 100% ready when an opportunity arises. Because most great opportunities in life force us to grow emotionally and intellectually. They force us to stretch ourselves and our comfort zones, which means we won't feel totally comfortable at first. And when we don't feel comfortable, we don't feel ready.

Just remember that significant moments of opportunity for personal growth and development will come and go throughout your lifetime. If you are looking to make positive changes in your life you will need to embrace these moments of opportunity even though you will never feel 100% ready for them.

10 THINGS I WISH I KNEW 10 Years Ago

Stay in tune with your spirit. Be calm and think. Listen to your inner voice. Anticipate and plan. Take 100% responsibility for your life. Lean into your struggles. Act with courage. Maintain an open mind. Practice kindness and compassion. Keep your promises. Forgive, let go, and move forward. This is how you get from where you are to where you want to be.

I've learned these concepts gradually over the last decade. Together they have helped me live a life of purpose. Had I understood these things 10 years ago, I could have avoided quite a bit of confusion and grief. So today I figured I'd share a few more things I wish I had known sooner. My hope is that they help you hurdle over some of the barriers I stumbled into on the road of life.

1 Loving someone should not mean losing YOU.

True love empowers you, it doesn't erase you. True love allows human beings to build amazing things, by working together through passion, kindness, and good will. So be strong enough to stand alone, be yourself enough to stand apart, but be wise enough to share your love and stand together when the time comes.

2 Getting even doesn't help you get ahead.

You will never get ahead of anyone as long as you try to get even with them. Sometimes we don't forgive people because they deserve it. We forgive them because they need it, because we need it, and because we cannot move forward without it. To forgive is to rediscover the inner peace and purpose that at first you thought someone took away when they betrayed you.

3 You attract what you show to the world.

So if you want it, reflect it. Happiness, freedom, and peace of mind are always attained by giving them out to others without expectation. The one who blesses others is abundantly blessed; those who help others are eventually helped. You have two hands; one to help yourself, the second to help those around you.

4 Failure is success when you learn from it.

Experience is what you get when you don't get what you want. Obstacles can't stop you. Problems can't stop you. Other people can't stop you. These barriers are temporary – they come and go. Which is why, over the course of a lifetime, the only barrier that can truly stop you, is YOU. So don't give up. Sometimes you have to journey through hell on Earth to find heaven on Earth.

5 You are not what you have done, but what you have overcome.

All the hardships. All the mistakes. All the rejections. All the pain. All the times you questioned why. All of these things have given birth to the wisdom and strength that will help you shine your light on the world, even in the darkest of hours.

6 Your past can only hurt you today if you let it.

Do not pay any attention to what the past whispers if all it's doing is bad-mouthing what today has to offer. There are times when you need to release the bitterness and grab a firm hold of happiness, without permission and without reason. The only way to get over the past is to leave it behind. If you spend your time re-living moments that are gone forever, you might miss the special moments that are yet to come.

7 It's never too late to become the person you are capable of being.

Repeat after me: "I AM FREE." You can fulfill your life purpose by starting here, in this moment. The purpose of life is not to simply be happy, but to matter, to be productive, to be useful, to make some kind of difference that you have lived at all. Remember, life is constant change, but growth is optional. Choose wisely, starting now.

8 Passion is important.

If you are trapped between your dreams and what other people think is right for you, always travel the route that makes you happy – unless you want everybody to be happy, except you. And whatever you do, don't chase the money. Catch up to the

ideas and activities that make you come
alive. Go for the things of greater value –
the things money can't buy – and use them
to create a relevant profession.

9 *The pain is worth it.*

You can't really begin to appreciate life
until it has knocked you down a few times.
You can't really begin to appreciate love
until your heart has been broken. You
can't really begin to appreciate happiness
until you've known sadness. You have to
struggle up the mountainside to appreciate
the breathtaking view at the mountaintop.

10 *Sometimes what you don't want is what you need.*

Sometimes the things you can't change end
up changing you for the better. Master
your responses to external events; don't
always attempt to control them. You will
rarely end up exactly where you wanted
to go, but you will always end up exactly
where you need to be.

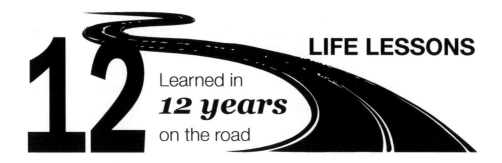

LIFE LESSONS

Learned in
12 years
on the road

For the past twelve years, since I entered college, I've been on the road – traveling (business and pleasure), studying, living in different cities, working for different companies (and myself), and meeting remarkable and unusual people everywhere in between.

Today I want to share twelve life lessons I've learned along the way.

1 *Everyone has the same basic wants and needs.*

When you get to know people with different ethnic backgrounds, from different cities and countries, who live at various socioeconomic levels, you begin to realize that everyone basically wants the same things. They want validation, love, happiness, fulfillment and hopes for a better future. The way they pursue these desires is where things branch off, but the fundamentals are the same. You can relate to almost everyone everywhere if you look past the superficial facades that divide us.

2 *What you do every day is what's most important.*

The difference between who you are and who you want to be, is what you do. You

don't have to be great to get started, but you do have to get started to be great. Every accomplishment starts with the decision to try. Remember, people seldom do things to the best of their ability; they do things to the best of their willingness. Follow your heart, and do something every day that your future self will thank you for.

3 *You can't always be agreeable.*

That's how people take advantage of you. You have to set boundaries. Don't ever change just to impress someone. Change because it makes you a better person and leads you to a better future. Being your true self is the most effective formula for happiness and success there is. Sometimes you need to step outside, get some air, and remind yourself of who you are and what

The journey is the reward.

you want to be. And sometimes you just have to do your own thing your own way, no matter what anyone else thinks or says about you.

4 *You're not perfect, but you're great at being you.*

You might not be the most beautiful, the strongest, or the most talented person in the world, but that's okay. Don't pretend to be someone you're not. You're great at being you. You might not be proud of all the things you've done in the past, but that's okay too. The past is not today. Be proud of who you are, how you've grown, and what you've learned along the way.

5 *You DON'T want perfect people in your life.*

Even though you probably sometimes get confused, you don't really want your friends and lovers to be perfect. What you do want is people you can trust, who treat you right – people you can act silly with, who love being around you as much as you love being around them. It's about finding people who know about your mistakes and weaknesses and stand by your side when others walk away.

6 *Life is change. You must embrace it.*

Everything in life is temporary. So if things are good, enjoy it. It won't last forever. If things are bad, don't worry because it won't last forever either. Just because life isn't easy right now, doesn't mean you can't laugh. Just because something is bothering you, doesn't mean you can't smile. Always focus on the positives in your life. You have a lot to look forward to. Every moment gives you a new beginning and a new ending. You get a second chance, every second. And don't forget, just because something doesn't last forever, doesn't mean it wasn't worth your while.

7 *Your scars are symbols of your growth.*

Don't ever be ashamed of the scars life has left you with. A scar means the hurt is over and the wound is closed. It means you conquered the pain, learned a lesson, grew stronger, and moved on. A scar is the tattoo of a triumph to be proud of.

8 *The truth is always the best choice.*

Respect and trust are two of the easiest things in life to lose and the hardest to get back. Never make a big decision when you're angry, and never make a big promise when you're overjoyed. Never mess with someone's feelings just because you're unsure of yours. Always be open and honest.

9 *It's the small, free things that matter most in life.*

It's nice to have money and the things that money can buy, but it's also important to make sure you haven't lost track of the things that money can't buy. Maturity is not when you start speaking and thinking about the big things, it's when you start understanding and appreciating the small things.

10 *Everyone's story is more complicated than it seems.*

Every passing face on the street represents a story every bit as compelling and complicated as yours. It's not always the tears that measure a person's pain, sometimes it's the smile they fake. Not all scars show. Not all wounds heal by themselves. You usually can't see the pain that someone feels. Don't judge a person negatively for their past or feelings without a full understanding of their situation. Just because you don't agree based on what you see, doesn't mean you're right. And don't be so quick to point out the flaws in other

people's lives when you are not willing to look at the flaws in your own life.

11 *Giving up and moving on are two different things.*

There is a difference between giving up and knowing when you have had enough. It doesn't make sense to hold onto something that's no longer there. Accepting what is, letting go, and moving on are skills that you must learn when facing the realities of life. Some relationships and situations just can't be fixed. If you try to force them back together, things will only get worse. Holding on is being brave, but letting go and moving on is often what makes us stronger.

12 *You are not alone in being alone.*

To lose sleep worrying about a friend. To have trouble picking yourself up after someone lets you down. To feel like less because someone didn't love you enough to stay. To be afraid to try something new for fear you'll fail. None of this means you're dysfunctional or crazy. It just means you're human, and that you need a little time to right yourself. You are not alone. No matter how embarrassed or pathetic you feel about your own situation, there are others out there experiencing the same emotions. When you hear yourself say, "I am all alone," it is your mind trying to sell you a lie. There's always someone who can relate to you. Perhaps you can't talk to them right now, but they're out there.

And remember, sometimes a break from your routine is the very thing you need. Sometimes you need to take a step back to see things clearly. Traveling is one of the best ways I know to remain psychologically grounded. If you've been stuck in an emotional rut for awhile, without any positive change, perhaps it's time to take a short hiatus – get out of town for a few days, experience something new, and stimulate your mind.

28 to STOP COMPLICATING Your Life
WAYS

Life is not complicated. We are complicated. When we stop doing the wrong things and start doing the right things, life is simple.

So starting today...

1 Stop berating yourself for being a work in progress.

Start embracing it! Because being a work in progress doesn't mean you're not good enough today. It means you want a better tomorrow, and you wish to love yourself completely, so you can live your life fully. It means you're determined to heal your heart, expand your mind and cultivate the gifts you know you're meant to share. May we all be works in progress forever, and celebrate the fact that we are!

2 Stop doing immoral things simply because you can.

Start being honest with yourself and everyone else. Don't cheat. Be faithful. Be kind. Do the right thing! It is a less complicated way to live. Integrity is the essence of everything successful. When

you break the rules of integrity you invite serious complications into your life. Keep life simple and enjoyable by doing what you know in your heart is right.

3 Stop meaning what you don't say.

Start communicating clearly. Don't try to read other people's minds, and don't make other people try to read yours. Most problems, big and small, within a family, friendship, or business relationship, start with bad communication. Someone isn't being clear.

4 Stop wasting time and money trying to acquire more of everything.

Start focusing on quality. High quality is worth more than any quantity, in possessions, friends and experiences. Truly 'rich' people need less to be happy. Live a comfortable life, not a wasteful one. Too many people buy things they don't need with money they don't have to impress people they don't know. Do not spend to impress others. Do not live life trying to fool yourself into thinking wealth is measured in material objects. Manage your money wisely so your money does not manage you.

5 Stop spending time with negative people.

Start spending time with nice people who are smart, driven and likeminded. Relationships should help you, not hurt you. Surround yourself with people who reflect the person you want to be. Choose friends who you are proud to know, people you admire, who love and respect you – people who make your day a little brighter simply by being in it. Life is too short to spend time with people who suck the happiness out of you. When you free yourself of negative people, you free yourself to be YOU – and being YOU is the simplest way to live.

6 Stop trying to change people.

Start accepting people just the way they are. In most cases it's impossible to change them anyway, and it's rude to try. So save

yourself from needless stress. Instead of trying to change others, give them your support and lead by example.

7 Stop being lazy and cutting corners.

Start avoiding future headaches by doing things right the first time. Always put your best foot forward. Doing the best at this moment puts you in the best place for the next moment. Why give less than 100%? Life is too short to waste it by living below your full potential. If something is worth doing, then it's worth doing well.

8 Stop procrastinating.

Start taking action and making changes. Action and change are often resisted when they're needed most. Get a hold of yourself and have discipline. Discipline is choosing what you really want over what you want right now. Putting something off makes it instantly harder and scarier. What we don't start today won't be finished by tomorrow. And there's nothing more stressful than the perpetual lingering of an unfinished task.

9 Stop worrying and complaining.

Start focusing on the things you can control and do something about them. Those who complain the most accomplish the least.

And when you spend time worrying, you're simply using your imagination to create things you don't want. It's usually only as good or bad as you think it is.

10 Stop being dramatic.

Start spending less time gossiping about problems and more time helping yourself and others solve them. Stay out of people's needless drama and don't create your own.

1 Stop trying to be everything to everyone.

Helping or pleasing everyone is impossible. But making one person smile can change the world. Maybe not the whole world, but their world. So narrow your focus and be yourself.

12 Stop making promises you can't keep.

Starting under-promising and over-delivering on everything you do. Period.

3 Stop blaming others.

Start accepting responsibility for everything in your life. Blaming others accomplishes nothing and prolongs the complications you're facing. Either you own your problems, or they will own you. Your choice. When you blame others for what you're going through, you deny

responsibility – you give up your power over that part of your life.

14 Stop reacting without a plan.

Start planning and working toward specific goals. Make a list of your top 3 - 5 goals. What's most important to you? What do you value most? What 3 - 5 things do you most want to do in your life? Simplifying your life starts with these priorities, as you are trying to make room in your life so you have more time for these things. Having a plan, even a flawed one at first, is better than no plan at all. There is good reason why you should wake each morning and mindfully consider what and who you will give your day to: Because unlike other things in life – love, money, respect, good health, hope, opportunities, etc. – time is the one thing you can never get back once it's gone.

15 Stop confusing 'being busy' with 'being productive.'

Start tracking and measuring your progress. Being busy and being productive are two very different things. Results are more important than the time it takes to achieve them.

16 Stop over-committing and trying to do too much at once.

Start saying "no" more often. If you never say "no," you will take on too much and get nothing accomplished. In the beginning, you need to say "yes" to a lot of things to discover and establish your goals. Later on, you need to say "no" to a lot of things and concentrate on your goals. Once your goals are established, focus on doing one thing at a time and doing it well. Also, leave space around commitments in your day. Whether you have appointments, or things you need to do, don't stack them back-to-back. Leave a little space between things you need to do, so you will have room for contingencies, and you'll go through your day much more relaxed.

17 Stop being inefficient simply because you've always done it that way.

Start opening your mind to making positive changes. If you keep doing what you're doing, you'll keep getting what you're getting. Many times we live with unplanned, complex systems in our lives simply because we haven't given them much thought. Instead, streamline your life by finding better ways of handling common tasks. Focus on one system at a time (your cleaning system, your errands system, your paperwork system, your email system, etc.) and try to make it simplified, efficient, and logical. Then, once you have it perfected, stick to it.

18 Stop cluttering your space.

Start clearing clutter. Get rid of stuff you don't use and then organize what's left. If you have a cluttered living or working space, it can be distracting and stressful. A clear space is like a blank canvas, available to be used to create something great. Getting truly organized and clutter-free can vastly improve anyone's life.

19 Stop overloading your mind by consuming useless information.

Start unsubscribing from useless e-lists and news feeds, and keep the TV off. Limit your time on Facebook, Twitter, CNN.com and your other favorite websites, etc.

20 Stop obsessing over the past and future.

Paying more attention to the current moment can make a huge difference in simplifying your life. It keeps you aware of life, of what's going on around you and within you. It does wonders for your sanity and stress levels.

21 Stop waiting for things to be perfect.

Start thinking of how many things don't get done in this world simply because people are waiting for the perfect time, place and circumstance. If you're waiting for the perfect conditions, ideas or plans to get started, you'll never achieve anything. A good idea without action is nothing at all. Keep it simple and just start. Focus on the next positive step forward.

22 Stop focusing so much energy on trying to avoid mistakes.

Start learning from your mistakes, then smile and move on. No matter how smart you are, you will make mistakes. Trying to avoid them will only waste time and complicate your life. There is a lesson in every mistake you make, and learning the lesson is how you move forward.

23 Stop making emotional decisions.

Start taking a few steps back so you can think things through. When you're caught up in the moment and your emotions are soaring, you're bound to make poor decisions that will lead to needless complications. The best advice here is simple: Don't let your emotions trump your intelligence. Slow down and think things through before you make any big decisions.

24 Stop being unhealthy.

Start taking care of your body. Start sleeping eight hours every night. A tired, malnourished mind is over-stressed and rarely productive. Your health is your life, don't let it go. Eat right, exercise and get an annual physical check-up.

25 Stop holding on to intimate relationships that make you unhappy.

Start looking out for yourself when it comes to intimate relationships. It's better to WAIT, and give your hand to someone who will never let go, rather than holding on to the outside of a hand that has never fully opened for you. If someone wants you in their life, they'll make room for you. You shouldn't have to fight for a spot. Never, ever insist yourself to someone who continuously overlooks your worth. Remember, anyone can come into your life and say how much they love you. But it takes someone really special to stay in your life and show you how much they love you. So slow it down. True love is worth the wait.

26 Stop holding on to hate.

Start letting hate go! Keep your sights set on the future. Holding on to hate and anger is like grasping hot coals with the intent of throwing them at someone else – you are the one who gets burned. If you want to forget someone, and move on, you must give up hating them. It's hard to forget someone you hate, because hate takes pieces of your heart – thereby keeping this person within your heart. If you want to forget them, let go of the hate, and create peace in your heart instead. Also, remember that whenever you hate something, it usually hates you back: people, situations, and inanimate objects alike; which will only further complicate your life.

27 Stop pretending like you know everything.

Start accepting the fact that there's a lot you don't know. Nobody has it all figured out. Nobody knows more than a minuscule fraction of what's going on in the world. Why? Because the world is simply way too vast for any one person to know everything well. And most of what we see is only what we think about what we see. The sooner you accept this, the sooner you will stop making the same unnecessary mistakes, and the sooner new doors of opportunity will open in your life.

28 Stop giving what you don't want to receive.

Start practicing the golden rule. If you want love, give love. If you want friends, be friendly. If you want money, provide value. It works. It really is this simple.

HOW **LOVE** BEGINS

*The greatest thing you'll ever learn
is to **love** and be **loved** in return.*

- Natalie Cole

O n a chilly October night nine years ago...

I would have preferred not to write to you. In fact, about a week ago, I put a post-it note on my computer monitor that said, "What would Skyman do?" (Skyman is my cat). It was supposed to remind me not to do things that Skyman wouldn't do.

Skyman would just wag his tail or wiggle his little nose, and hope that whoever he's wagging or wiggling to understands that he's hungry, or lonely, or in love, or whatever. But he certainly wouldn't write a silly love letter to the coolest girl he knows. Because he can't form complex thoughts. And because he's smart enough not to be so stupid.

This evening, the post-it note fell off of my computer monitor and landed on the floor. And although post-it notes usually lose their stick after a few days, this one was different. It was still really sticky and shouldn't have come unstuck. And it was light green, which is the color of your eyes. These were obvious signs I couldn't ignore.

So I decided to write to you... To tell you that Hanging by a Moment is a totally awesome song. That Diet Coke tastes better when you smile. And that the world seems easier to understand today than it did yesterday.

But still not as easy to understand as two days ago, when a friend and I shared a three scoop 5 & Diner ice cream sundae at midnight. And decided that some people are like hot fudge and others are like hard candy. And I don't remember why we decided that.

But it had something to do with friendship. And ice cream with two spoons instead of one. And later that night, after I dropped you off, I wanted to call you to ask whether you preferred hard candy or hot fudge, just to find out whether you'd sigh and giggle simultaneously when I'd ask. Because that's what I think you'd do.

I didn't call you because Skyman wouldn't do that. He wouldn't even know how to dial your phone number. Because a cat's paws are not nearly as dexterous as human hands. Which must be nice for Skyman, because love is a lot simpler when you have paws.

Anyway, it's midnight again. And I'm sitting up in bed with my laptop thinking about how our lives begin and end in the time it takes the universe to blink. Which isn't too long. But long enough for letters that aren't too long. Letters that ramble instead of saying what they want to say. Which is...

I wish you were here. Just breathing beside me.

Don't try to read other people's minds. Don't make other
people try to read yours. Communicate.

Your health is your life, keep up with it. Get an annual physical
check-up.

Get enough sleep every night. An exhausted mind is rarely productive.

Get up 30 minutes earlier so you don't have to rush around like
a mad man. That 30 minutes will help you avoid speeding tickets,
tardiness, and other unnecessary headaches.
Don't waste your time on jealously. The only person you're competing against is yourself.

Organize your
living space and
working space.
Get rid of stuff
you don't use.

==================
WAYS
To Make
Life
Simple Again
==================

Handle
important
two-minute
tasks
immediately.

Don't try to please everyone. Just do what you know is right.

Make mistakes, learn from them, laugh about them, and move along.

Don't try to please everyone. Just do what you know is right.

Say "I love you" to your loved ones as often as possible.

Realize that the harder you work, the luckier you will become.

Spend time with nice people who are smart, driven, and likeminded.

Simplicity QUESTIONS
to Make You *think*

What do you need to **SPEND** less *time* doing**?**

The **BEST** part of *waking up* is _____**?**

What makes you **FEEL** *comfortable***?**

What's one thing you **LOVE** about your *life***?**

What's something **SIMPLE** that makes you *smile***?**

What would the **CHILD** you once were think of the *adult* you have become**?**

What would you **REGRET** not *fully* doing, being, or having in your life**?**

What's something you look **FORWARD** to almost *every day***?**

When you're 90 years old, what will **MATTER** to you *most***?**

What's something that makes you **INSTANTLY** feel *better***?**

Part Nine
Finance

Too many people buy things
they don't need with money
they don't have to impress
people they don't know.

HOW TO
RETIRE BEFORE **40**
WITHOUT **WINNING** THE **LOTTERY**

A Different Question

"How much do I need to retire?" is a common question people ask themselves. But the key to retiring before 40, or just early in general, requires most people to ask themselves a different question: "How little do I need to live?"

Think about the drastic difference in perspective required to answer these two questions. The first motivates you to think about acquiring more money, while the latter suggests you cut back on expenses. In a society driven by consumerism and needless accumulation, most people don't get it. They think retiring before 40 is impossible, when in fact it's only impossible for them because of the way they choose to live.

It's also common to hear people say they need between $40,000 and $50,000 of retirement income – meaning they have to acquire roughly $1,000,000 before they can retire. But that's like saying I need a

Corvette in order to drive to the grocery store. People don't need either of these two things, they want them. And since the average person makes less than $50,000 a year, they'll be working from 8 to 5 well into their 60's to get what they want.

Living a Not-So-Normal Lifestyle

Making more money isn't necessarily the key to retiring early. I know of numerous professional athletes and pop stars who made millions of dollars, but went broke trying to afford the maintenance on 25,000 square foot mansions lined with gold. I also personally know an electrician who made $55,000 a year most of his working life and retired at 40 by living frugally, downsizing his house, going car-free, and cutting expenses (he also paid off all his debt over a decade before he retired).

This tells me that it is possible for an average person with an average salary to retire before 40 without winning the lottery. It just depends on how much they are willing to give up. One's ability to retire early is simply a combination of low expense levels and high savings rates. e.g. $55,000 a year income and a 75% savings rate as opposed to a $75,000 a year income and a 5% savings rate.

A 75% savings rate? It sounds impossible, right? It's not though. It can be done. But not if you want to live a normal consumerist lifestyle like everyone else. It requires you to be creative and think and live differently. And different doesn't have to mean a downgraded lifestyle either. Instead of mowing the yard yourself, rent an affordable apartment without a yard in a walkable neighborhood (and get some roommates or live with family to bring down the cost of rent). Instead of driving an old clunker, go car-free. Instead of eating at your favorite Italian restaurant, learn to recreate the meals in your own kitchen. Instead of vacationing at hotels, visit and stay with relatives.

These ideas may not seem normal to you, because they're not. Normal in this society is working nine hours a day five days a week until you're in your sixties. Retiring early means living a 'not-so-normal' lifestyle. If you can't be creative and you feel you must be normal by living in a big house, driving a new car, shopping for things you don't need to impress people

you don't know, and paying the bills for all of it, then early retirement is not for you.

When can I retire? The Basic Math

When you can retire is based on two things:

1. Determining how little you need to live.

2. Having enough money invested/saved so that your annual expenses are less than 3% of your invested savings.

Why 3%? Because we're assuming that you're going to invest your savings somewhat conservatively in an investment portfolio consisting of stocks, bonds and equities and then live off this investment portfolio for 40+ years. In the finance world there's something called the Safe Withdrawal Rate (SWR) which is usually set at 4% for a 30 year retirement duration. But since we're talking about retiring early (longer retirement duration) we need to be more conservative and withdraw less every year to guarantee that we won't run out of money.

So the equation is:

$$\textbf{your annual expenses} < \textbf{3\% of your invested savings}$$

Now, you can solve that equation either by reducing your expenses or by working longer to save more money. The most common problem in solving this equation is that most people tend to spend money based on their income. For example, if Johnny gets a 25% raise, he spends roughly 25% more. As discussed above, the only real way to make this equation and early retirement work is to live on much less than you earn.

So let's assume you're 28 years old, you make $55,000 a year after taxes and, as discussed above, you have learned to live frugally with a 75% savings rate.

Therefore:

1. You're saving $41,250 a year.

2. You've learned to live off of $13,750 a year.

3. $13,750 is 3% of $458,333

4. $458,333 / $41,250 = ~11

So you need $458,333 to retire. Which means you'll have to save $41,250 every year for roughly 11 years – until you're 39 years old.

And yes, I realize that living off of $13,750 a year is extremely hard to imagine for most people. But it's not impossible. It simply requires a significant lifestyle adjustment.

The Importance of Self Education

Money compensates for lack of skill. Therefore, self education is another primary component of early retirement. It's all about learning life skills that most people pay others to know. For instance, if your kitchen sink clogs, you could spend a few hundred dollars on a professional plumber's services or you could learn to fix it yourself for pennies. The end result is the same: A kitchen sink that drains properly.

Yes, it takes time to learn such life skills. But remember, if you're not trading nine hours of your life away every day for a paycheck, you'll have a lot more time to learn these skills over the long-term.

Unclogging a kitchen sink, fixing a computer, patching drywall, re-paving a driveway, and similar projects are not rocket science. They simply require a person to acquire basic skills that almost anyone is capable of learning. And the vast majority of these skills can be learned online for free with a few simple Google searches.

Most people can't imagine doing things like this for themselves in lieu of paying others – which is also why most people can't imagine living on the $13,750 a year as we discussed above. It's a different way of thinking. To illustrate the impact of self education, consider this: $2000 will buy you a decent laptop computer. But, $2000 will also buy you enough computer parts to build two (or even three) equivalent laptop computers. Most can't imagine doing that – "Don't you need a degree in computer science to do that?" No. And in the same regard, $100 carefully spent could feed a family for a month, while a $100 spent in a restaurant will feed a family for one night.

Using Time Instead of Money

When you spend less money, you lose the ability to do certain things. But when you have more free time (early retirement), you gain things that would be impossible with a day job. For instance, if you retire early, you won't be able to afford week-long vacations in Key West at fancy hotels, but you could find affordable housing in Key West and move there permanently. If you want to get in shape, you won't be able to afford a personal trainer, but you could commit several hours a day to fitness and slowly figure it out on your own. You won't be able to afford private tutoring for your kids, but you could tutor them yourself every afternoon as soon as they get home from school.

You get the idea. Time and effort can easily compensate and, in many ways, surpass the buying power of money.

Conclusion

People who are willing to make sacrifices by spending less, saving more and

educating themselves can retire before 40. But they have to be willing to live an unconventional lifestyle outside the boundaries most people live in.

My goal here isn't to convince you to retire before 40, but instead point out that doing so, although extreme in many ways, is possible. If nothing else, I hope the information covered in this article has been an eye-opener for you – perhaps one that has you reevaluating the way you currently manage your money.

6 TRUTHS
You Should Know About Making
Money

Just a few simple truths I frequently see people overlook when it comes to earning a living, and dreaming of making more money.

1 *Everyone is the CEO of their own corporation.*

No matter how you make a living or who you think you work for, you only work for one person, yourself. The only question is: What are you selling, and to whom? Even when you have a full time, salaried, 'Corporate America' position, you are still running your own business. You are selling one unit of your existence *(an hour of your life)* at a set price *(the associated fraction of your salary)* to a customer *(your employer)*.

2 *We only have two products: Time and Knowledge.*

No matter what your profession is, you only have two products to sell, your time and your knowledge. Here are a few example scenarios:

Migrant farmer – Sells hours of his/her life to pick fruit or vegetables for a farmer in exchange for money. A perfect example of trading hours for dollars.

Doctor – Sells hours of his/her life to perform medical treatments based on the knowledge stored in his/her brain. A perfect example of trading hours and knowledge for dollars.

Best-selling author – Spends time crafting a book based on his/her knowledge or intellectual capacity and then sells the book (knowledge) many times over. A perfect example of trading knowledge for dollars. The key benefit here is residual, passive income.

In almost all cases of real world business, the business owner is taking information out of his or her brain, or out of the brains of his or her employees, and spending the necessary time to convert it into a product of value.

This concept confuses some people, and to others it seems obvious. The bottom line is that the only way to make money is to have customers *(your employer can be your customer)*; and the only two things your customers pay you for is your time and knowledge. Financial success is often achieved by properly crafting the two into one convenient bundle that can be sold many times over *(think of products vs. services)*.

What knowledge do you have in your brain that provides value to others? How can you extract this information and sell it?

3 The implementation of knowledge is what's valuable.

Knowledge alone is not power! The implementation of knowledge is power. Knowledge is simply a commodity; it's a product like any other that has the potential to be sold. How knowledge is organized, packaged, presented, shared, and received by others is what makes knowledge so powerful.

Knowledge is useless unless it's effectively shared with others. Your ability to educate or assist others in a way that allows them to be more effective is what makes knowledge an asset – something worth buying.

4 Time is more valuable than money.

One of the most important points to understand is the fact that there are two basic forms of currency, money and time. Of the two, time is the most valuable, for it cannot be replenished. A surplus of time, and the unfettered liberty to do with it as you choose, is priceless.

Your time must be gradually extracted from the formula of making money. No matter how skilled you are at transferring your knowledge to others, if you are endlessly paid on an 'hours for dollars' basis, your ability to expand your income will eventually plateau. You will run out of time.

Many independently wealthy people have made this realization and concentrate the majority of their time and effort on productizing their knowledge to generate passive income. Passive income is achieved by applying what you know into a package that can be designed and built once, and then repeatedly sold over and over again. Finding a unique way to promote and sell this knowledge is the key.

Passive income examples: Useful books and guides, instructional videos, time saving computer and smartphone applications, etc.

5 Selling hours for dollars is a flawed business plan.

Let's take a quick look at the components of a good business plan vs. that of the standard hours for dollars routine.

A good business plan:

Multiple products – Providing multiple options to your customers.

Product development growth – Innovating and expanding the core capabilities of your product.

Multiple customers – Your total income revenue is acquired from several sources. The loss of a single customer will not jeopardize your sustainability.

Scalable – Your business can grow naturally without disproportionately increasing costs. Also, it cannot be shutdown by the absence of a single worker.

Inventory expansion – Inventory can be expanded to meet increasing customer demands.

The business of strictly selling hours for dollars:

One product – A single hour of your life.

Static product growth – You can change your level of productivity within an hour, but you can't change the dynamics of the hour itself (which is the metric you are being paid by).

One customer – Your employer. If you lose your one customer, you lose your business.

Single point of failure – If something happens to you (injured, ill, etc.), your business suffers.

Ever declining inventory – Life has a limited inventory of hours. They cannot be reproduced.

6 Working on something that interests you is essential.

There is, however, a silver lining even in an 'hours for dollars' work environment. When you are interested in the subject matter of your work, you open the floodgates to a world of accelerated personal growth and contentment. Suddenly, you are working to learn, mindfully indulging in the task at hand. This passion is the byproduct of interest. You have to be genuinely interested in the subject matter of your profession. In other words, dollars cannot be the primary source of motivation. Once you find work that resonates with you, here are six ideas for maximizing your career growth potential:

Learn as much as you can. This becomes a natural process when you are truly passionate about your work. Obviously, the more you know the more valuable your time will be to others.

Pursue unpaid growth opportunities. Get out of the "hours for dollars" mindset. See if you can barter your skill set with others in your industry. You educate them as they educate you. Knowledge and relationships are worth far more than money.

Provide value from within a black box. This is how you increase your level of impressiveness. Your efforts must make someone think, "Wow! How does he/she do that?" They can easily see your inputs and your results, but aren't 100% sure how you got from point A to point B.

Innovate. If you think there might be a better way, try it. The worst case scenario is you'll have to revert back to the way things are now.

Help other people. The best way to get what you want is to help others get what they want. This will also aid you in establishing strong professional relationships.

Market your visibility. Don't be bashful. Take credit where credit is due.

Bottom line: Even when working in an 'hours for dollars' environment, you can avoid the 'hours for dollars' mentality.

Find something you're passionate about, or at least genuinely interested in, and take it to the next level. Become a guru. This should help you to strategically position yourself as a 'go to guy/gal,' someone your superiors (and industry insiders) see as a vital asset.

Doing so will ultimately free you from the bounds of an arbitrary hourly rate, because you (your business) will become entwined with the future objectives of your employer (and maybe even the industry as a whole). This typically translates into big raises, bonuses, etc. You'll start getting paid based on the tangible value you provide. Eventually, this position of power could be leveraged into starting a venture of your own.

18 You Are WASTING *Money* On
THINGS

Money can buy freedom – freedom from trading hours for dollars. Money can buy options – the option to do what you want to do instead of what you have to do. Money is great to have as long as you manage and spend it wisely. But most of us never do – we waste it and we don't even realize it.

How? Why?

Because many of the items and services we buy aren't worth what we pay for them.

Here are 18 common money wasters to beware of:

1 *Bottled Water*

Water is one of the most abundant, freely available resources on planet Earth. So is air. If I bottled some air, would you pay 2 to 3 dollars a bottle for it? I doubt it. Bottom line: Buy a water filter for your tap and stop wasting your money.

2 *Magazine and Newspaper Subscriptions*

The same exact articles are online for free. I can read them right now and I didn't pay a dime. Why are you?

3 *Printer Ink Cartridges*

If you're buying brand new ink cartridges every time you need new ink for your printer you're paying about $8000 a gallon for ink. Yep, that's right! Computer printer ink is one of the most overpriced consumer goods. For home users, instead of buying new ink cartridges, take your old ones to a store that will refill them for half the price. For businesses that do lots of printing, consider outsourcing the bulk of your printing.

4 More House Than You Need

When you buy or rent a house that's bigger than you need, you end up wasting lots of money on larger monthly payments, higher upkeep costs, higher utility bills, and lots of random 'stuff' to fill up the extra empty space.

5 Insurance

Car insurance, homeowner's insurance, title insurance, etc. Insurance companies love to rip us off. And while you can't totally avoid them from a legal standpoint, you can shop around and save yourself a boat-load of cash. Don't get comfortable paying what you're paying simply because you're used to it. Make sure you're getting the best deal.

6 Premium Cable or Satellite Television

Hulu.com offers thousands of television shows and full-length movies – all for free. And Netflix charges $9 a month for access to hundreds of thousands of television episodes and movies on DVD, or you can stream them live to your computer. So if you're paying more than $9 a month, you're wasting your money.

7 Retail Furniture

Most people don't realize that home furniture has a 200% to 400% markup on it. A typical retail furniture store must maintain warehouse inventory, a showroom, commission salesmen, etc. which all equates to a fairly high overhead. For this reason it is normal for furniture retailers to maintain extremely high markups. A typical piece of furniture that has a 'suggested retail price' of $500 will usually cost the retailer less than $200, so even when they put it 'on sale' for $400, they're still making over 100% profit. The best way to save big money on furniture is to buy from an online furniture store with low overhead, buy wholesale, or buy slightly used on eBay or craigslist.

8 Restaurants and Prepared Foods

I don't need to tell you this. Eating out is ridiculously expensive. So is buying prepared foods at the grocery store. Buy both every once in awhile as a treat, but learn to cook and prepare your own food on a regular basis. It's not just cheaper, it's healthier too.

9 Nutritional Supplements

Protein powders, vitamins, sports drinks, etc. – all of them are overpriced and have been proven by doctors to be mediocre sources of nourishment. The answer to good health rests not in a once or twice a day supplement solution, but in an integrated approach to good baseline nutrition though healthy eating habits that give us the energy we need to enjoy our lives and the best chance of warding off illnesses.

10 *Luxury Name Brand Products*

A car gets you from point 'A' to point 'B.' A purse holds your personal belongings. A pair of sunglasses shades your eyes from the sun. A shirt keeps you warm. If you're paying premium prices just to get a fashionable brand name labeled on each these products without any regard for how efficiently the products actually serve their practical purpose, you're wasting your money.

11 *New Cars*

See my previous point. A car is a means of transportation to get you from one place to another. If you're buying a new car every few years even when your old car works perfectly fine, you're likely trying too hard to impress the wrong people... and you're going broke in the process.

12 *Electronics Warranties*

When you buy new electronics a warranty might seem like a decent thing to invest in. After all, a warranty covers everything from technical problems to spilling soda on the circuits. But don't be fooled. Most of the time the numbers just don't make sense. For instance, a two-year extended warranty on a $400 laptop at Best Buy will cost you upwards of $280 – that's about 70% of the original price. You're better off saving your money and taking your chances.

13 *Retail Computer Software*

Most retail computer software is marked way up. You can easily find OEM copies of the exact same software online (on eBay and similar sites) for 25% - 50% less. Also, look into free open source software alternatives. For instance, Microsoft Office Professional 2010 costs $300 at Best Buy, but you can download OpenOffice.org's professional office suite which has all the same word processing, spreadsheet, etc. capabilities for free. And OpenOffice.org is 100% compatible with Microsoft Office files.

14 *Medical Issues that Can Be Avoided*

Eat right and exercise regularly! Keep your body and mind healthy! Major medical problems drain back accounts, increase insurance rates, keep you from working and earning money, and generally guarantee that you will have long-term financial problems.

15 *Prescription Medication*

The previous bullet leads directly into this one. Prescription medicine has one of the highest markups of any consumer good. The sky high cost of prescription medications is crippling parts of the US economy and keeping necessary medicines out of the hands of those who need it most – people living on fixed incomes with acute or chronic health issues. Unlike other countries, there are no price controls on prescription medications here in the US. So we end up paying 200% - 5000% markups on essential medicines and drugs such as Prozac and Xanax. The solution is to buy wholesale at wholesale resellers such as Costco. Costco's prices are typically half the cost of the local retail pharmacy on many popular prescription medications.

16 *Jewelry and Precious Gems*

All jewelry is subject to volatile changes in price and high markups. The industry average markup varies widely – 100% to up to over 1000%. And jewelers thrive on the uneducated buyer, so do your research. Also, jewelry is almost always an emotional purchase, so you need to think logically about what you're getting, how much you're paying for it, and what your other options are. And even then, you probably won't get a great deal. Buying and wearing less jewelry is always the smartest choice.

17 *Second-rate Entertainment*

The best things in life are free. Stop wasting your money on movies, games, and other second-rate entertainment and take a good look around you. Mother Nature offers lots of entertainment free of charge. Go hiking, go skinny dipping, play in the rain, build a bonfire with your friends, watch the sunset with your lover, etc.

18 *Nasty Money-sucking (and life-sucking) Habits.*

Smoking, drinking and gambling are all perfect examples of bad habits in which you choose to trade short term pleasure for long term debt and discomfort. So light one up, shoot one down, and toss another chip across the table. It's only your life and livelihood.

11 PRACTICAL Ways to Spend Your *Money*

I know, I know. Saving and investing your money for the future is one of the most practical things you can do. This is solid advice, but when you do decide to spend your hard earned money it should be spent on something practical, useful, and meaningful to the wellbeing of your existence. So many people save their money only to blow it on worthless crap. Here are 11 practical ways to spend your money on something useful:

1 *Travel to See the Significant People in Your Life*

There may be no better way to spend your money than to use it to nurture and rekindle personal relationships with the most significant people in your life. As time quickly passes, we sometimes forget how essential strong personal relationships are to our mental wellbeing. The older we get the more we need true friends and family to be regular parts of our lives.

2 *Hire a Personal Trainer*

Your health is your life. Without it, all the success and affluence in the world is meaningless. Committing yourself to a regular exercise routine is one of the best ways to maintain the health of your body and mind. Sometimes it's hard to tackle this endeavor on your own. Spending money on a knowledgeable personal trainer who can set you on the right course creates priceless results. Make sure you stick with the trainer until you are committed to exercising on your own.

3 *Fix What Is Broken*

Have you been ignoring your screeching brakes? What about the excessively loud hum from your AC compressor? Or the scratching noise coming from your computer system? Sooner or later these small annoyances will wear down the reliability of the product and you will be left with a completely broken product instead of just a halfway broken one. Use your money wisely to fix and maintain your belongings.

4 *Educate Yourself*

Use your money to purchase educational courses or books pertaining to your career, or to a miscellaneous topic that interests and intrigues you. Remember, knowledge is power and your brain is the container of that knowledge. There are few options for spending money on something more practical than the development and facility of your brain.

5 *Add Value to Your Home*

Your home should be your sanctuary, the place on this planet where you feel the most comfortable. Adding value to your home, be it personal value or increased monetary value, is always a practical choice for spending your money. If the additions you make increase your level of comfort for years to come, you win. If they increase the value of the home to a third party someday when you sell, you win. If both occur, you win big.

6 *Take a Healthy, Relaxing Vacation*

A vacation revitalizes your mind by pulling you away from the daily stress factors in your life. It can spark creative thought by stimulating your brain with new material. And finally, a vacation allows you to be yourself without the external influences present in your typical surroundings. Does

that sound like something worth spending money on? It should.

7 *Upgrade Something You Use Regularly*

There is nothing wrong with splurging on a practical item that you actually use on a regular basis. If you are a hardcore movie buff that loves to watch movies on Saturday nights with your family and friends, having a 65 inch HDTV and a Blue-ray player makes sense. If you love computer games, purchasing a powerhouse laptop gaming rig makes sense. The idea is to never waste money on stuff you don't use. Spending money on upgrading your hobbies is one of the reasons you work so hard in the first place.

8 *Buy Meaningful Gifts for Key People in Your Life*

One of the most rewarding acts in life is the act of giving; especially to those key people you truly care about the most. Spend a little money every now and then on a sensible gift for some of the key people in your life. Surprise them. It doesn't have to be their birthday or a holiday. Remember, there is no better gift than an unexpected gift. You will make them feel special. For instance, my buddy Donny brought me back a cool souvenir from Amsterdam a few months back and it just made me feel good.

9 *Update Your Wardrobe*

You don't have to waste money on the latest overpriced fashion line to look good. However, if you are still wearing the same ratty shirts, slacks and shoes from 5 years ago, it might be time to go shopping. While appearance isn't everything, it can make you look older, smarter and more emotionally mature. First impressions for job interviews, dates, and the like are heavily weighted on the way you look. Sometimes it is practical to dress to impress.

10 *Buy Healthier Food*

"You are what you eat." There is a great deal of truth in that statement. It is impossible to maintain a healthy body and mind if you pump your body full of junk food. Fresh, healthy food is usually more expensive, but this is an expense with priceless benefits to the longevity and wellbeing of your future. Eating healthygoes right along with bullet number 2 about hiring a personal trainer. Your health is your life.

11 *Pay Down Debt*

This one is a no brainer, so I just couldn't bring myself to leave it off the list. If you have a great deal of high interest debt it would be foolish not to pay it down before you go off and splurge on additional

purchases. There is nothing less practical than being a slave to your debts.

The only way to get out of debt is to understand why you're in debt in the first place.

And the harsh truth is...

You will not save money when you get your next raise. You will not save money when your car is paid off. You will not save money when your kids are supporting themselves someday. And you wouldn't even save a dime if I handed you $100,000 in cash right now.

How do I know this?

Because saving money has very little to do with the amount of money you have. In fact, you will only start to save money when saving becomes an emotional habit – when you start treating the money you handle everyday differently.

So this is why you are in debt:

1 *You buy miscellaneous crap you don't need or use.*

Stop buying 'stuff' on impulse! Avoid the mall! The mall is not a source for entertainment. It's a source for personal debt. There's no reason to tease yourself by staring at a bunch of brand new crap you don't need. And as you know, the novelty of a new purchase wears thin long before the credit card bill arrives.

2 *You use credit to purchase things you can't afford to buy in cash.*

If you can't pay for it in cash today, don't buy it today! It's as simple as that.

3 *You buy things you could have borrowed from a friend or rented.*

After you bought that DVD, how many times did you actually watch it? Do you really want a 20 inch chainsaw collecting dust in your garage? So you own a pressure washer you only use once every three years? You get the point... borrow and rent when it makes sense.

4 *You pay retail prices on everything you buy.*

If you're paying retail prices, you're getting screwed. You can easily save well over $1000 a year on general purchases by waiting for sales and shopping at discount outlets.

5 *You don't follow any sort of formal budgeting plan.*

Do you assume that if you wait around and make more money your finances and credit debt will magically resolve themselves? I'm sorry to say, you're dead wrong! It takes a lot of planning and proactive budgeting to erase a pile of debt and build a nest egg of wealth. So start now!

6 *You don't automate 401K or savings deposits.*

We're ten years into the new millennium. If you aren't using simple technology to automate savings deposits, you pretty much deserve to be broke.

7 *You don't leverage the small investments you do have.*

You have to give your money the opportunity to make money. Any capital you do have, no matter how small, should be invested using a basic, long-term investment strategy. If your capital isn't invested, it's just losing value as inflation rises.

8 *You're married to (or dating) a spend-thrift.*

You'll never get out of debt if you're married to a person who spends every dime you make. So help your soul mate become financially responsible, or except life in the poorhouse.

9 *You've never educated yourself on basic money management.*

Responsible money management is not an innate human instinct. You have to properly educate yourself. If you don't, you'll stay exactly where you are now, in debt.

10 *You have a 'get rich quick' mentality.*

For 99.99% of us, wealth doesn't come instantly. You're far more likely to be struck by lightning twice than win the lottery once. If you're spending your time and money on a 'get rich quick' scheme, the debt will just keep piling up.

1 You waste too much of your own time.

They say "time is money," but I think time is way more valuable than money. It's the single greatest constituent of life. If you fail to properly manage your time, you'll absolutely fail to properly manage your money... and you'll likely fail in every other aspect of your life as well. So focus your time and energy on the important stuff and forget the rest.

2 You aren't taking care of your health.

Keep your body and mind healthy! Major medical problems drain back accounts, increase insurance rates, keep you from working and earning money, and generally guarantee that you will have long-term financial problems.

13 You went through an unfortunate divorce.

This final point might seem cruel, but it's impossible to discuss the major reasons why people accumulate financial debt without mentioning divorce. Divorce absolutely destroys the finances of both

parties involved. So the best advice I can give you is: Don't get married until you're certain you want to spend the rest of your life with your significant other. And don't get a divorce until you've truly exhausted all of your other possible options (marriage therapy, etc.).

Please remember, financial debt can be avoided and erased. It just takes a little effort, education, and determination on your end to make it possible. So as I've said before, live a comfortable life, not a wasteful one. Do not spend to impress others. Do not live life trying to fool yourself into thinking wealth is measured in material objects. Manage your money wisely so your money does not manage you. And always live well below your means.

18 For Living BELOW Your Means MEANS

Live a comfortable life, not a wasteful one. Do not spend to impress others. Do not live life trying to fool yourself into thinking wealth is measured in material objects. Manage your money wisely so your money does not manage you. Always live well below your means.

1 *Redefine your definition of "rich".*

"I remember sitting in a cubicle at my first professional job staring at a picture of an SUV I wanted to buy (and eventually did). Now, I sit in my office and look at the pictures of my kids, and just outside my window I can see the beater I drive sitting in the company parking lot. What a difference a decade makes! To sum things up, my definition of being rich is having enough money to meet my family's basic needs, a few of our wants, and to be able to give some away to others." – via Frugal Dad

2 *Borrow and share. Everyone wins!*

"We borrowed a DVD from a friend instead of renting or buying and had a little snack from our own fridge! Way cheaper than using gas to drive to the theater/rental place, paying for a movie, and paying for a snack." – via My Dollar Plan

3 *Avoid the mall.*

"Going to the mall is not entertainment! We used to go when we were bored. Of course, we usually ended up spending money while we were there. If you need clothes, then shop sales or go to stores that offer name-brands at a discount. You can save a ton on these items if you are a smart shopper. Dave Ramsey says, "Never pay retail!" We probably save $15 to $30 per month by staying away from the mall." – via My Super-Charged Life

> ## *A penny saved is a penny earned.*
> – Benjamin Franklin

4 *Limit your intake of advertisements.*

"Advertising sucks. That's the cold, hard truth. It's engineered to make you feel like you're incomplete, that you have an unfulfilled need, that you're not good enough." – via On Simplicity

5 *Buy with cash.*

"You can't spend money you don't have. Many bank accounts provide overdraft protection, so even with a debit card, it's easier to go over your account balance than you think." – via Simple Mom

6 *Find a better deal and actually SAVE the difference.*

"Regardless of what they sell, if you've switched companies for price reasons, save the difference. Think of phone companies, internet access, cell phones, credit cards, and others." – via The Wisdom Journal

7 *Adhere to a long-term investment strategy.*

"I'm a long-term investor. The stock portion of my portfolio is spread over several mutual funds, a few ETFs and a few individual stocks. Each and every one of these holdings was carefully chosen, after thorough research. I believe in these stocks and funds. I consider them as my best bet in growing my money - LONG TERM." – via MomGrind

8 *Curb your consumerism!*

"Have you ever watched how a child can play with a cardboard box for hours, and leave the toy that came in it by the wayside? How is it that children can enjoy themselves without a lot of "stuff", but we as adults feel the need to reward ourselves by buying more stuff?" – via Billionaire Woman

9 *Stay Healthy! Medical problems drain bank accounts.*

James M. Rippe, M.D is a best-selling author, world-renowned cardiologist, and founder of the Rippe Lifestyle Institute. He explains that if you look at all the risk factors for dying, the one that is most predictive is fitness level. In addition, an older person with high cardiovascular fitness is healthier than a younger person who is physically inactive. By increasing your fitness level, you can actually roll back your biological clock." – via Abundance Blog

10 *Stay in and relax.*

"So, think about it the next time you go out. Are you going for with a purpose? Maybe the solution is to not go out at all. Stay home and save! Save up for something you really want or need." – via The Jungle of Life

1 *Gradually prepare yourself for a rainy day.*

"Even when things are going great, and you feel on top of the world, you must always be prepared for a change. If you take the time and patience to set yourself up properly, then when things to take a turn for the worse, you will be prepared to handle it. If you live above your means, then when the slightest change occurs, you will not be prepared to adapt. Financial flexibility is more important then keeping up with the Jones'." – via Yin vs. Yang

2 *Stop competing. Forget about the Jones' altogether.*

"If getting rich makes us happy, then why don't countries as a whole get happier as they grow wealthier? They discovered that as a country gets wealthier there's no overall increase in happiness. Why? We continually compare our wealth against

that of others. We are competitive and envious. Add to that the fact that Western countries encourage people to strive for more and more, and you have a formula that spins many into depression." – via Color Your Life Happy

13 *Get out of the "easy street" mentality.*

"I think there is too much emphasis on the quick fix or the easy option in today's society. For example taking diet pills to lose weight instead of the "hard option" - exercising and eating well.... money is sometimes being used as a substitute for hard work. Do you think there is an increasing expectation that you can get want you want by throwing money around instead of working hard and "earning" it? – via Forever Change

14 *Avoid impulse buying. Buy things you truly need.*

"Don't you just love the excitement you feel after coming home with a new TV? Driving home in a new car? Opening the box on a new pair of shoes? I sure do. But, from watching the behavior of myself and my friends I've found that the new quickly becomes just another item. The excitement of novelty passes quickly." – via Think Simple Now

15 *Time is money. Properly manage your time.*

Properly manage your time. – "The fewer tasks you have, the less you have to do to organize them. Focus only on those tasks that give you the absolute most return on your time investment, and you will become more productive and have less to do. You will need only the simplest tools and system, and you will be much less stressed. I think that's a winning combination. Focus always on simplifying, reducing, eliminating. And keep your focus on what's important. Everything else is easy." – via LifeDev

16 *Find ways to give without spending.*

"Want a quick, easy and (almost) free way to be guaranteed that you'll make someone's day special? Send them a letter. Why not set aside some time this weekend to sit down and write to a few people? If you don't enjoy writing, try buying some nice postcards of your home town. If you've got an artistic streak, why not design your own note cards? You don't have to write a long letter for it to be effective. It's the thought that counts and the personal touch that makes it special." –via Dumb Little Man

17 *Don't let greed and deceit get the best of you.*

"According to Stephen R. Covey, if you reach an admirable end through the wrong means it will ultimately turn to dust in your hands. This is due to unintended consequences that are not seen or evident at first. The example he gives in The 8th Habit is: The parent who yells at their kids to clean their rooms will accomplish the end of having a clean room. But this very means has the potential to negatively affect relationships, and it is unlikely the room will stay clean when the parent leaves town for a few days. Now, to return to the topic of wealth, I think it is possible to see much of the world's current financial problems as stemming from people who wrongly believe the ends justify the means. My advice? It is fine to aspire to wealth, but don't lose sight of the means to accomplishing it." – via The Change Blog

18 *Never ever pay retail.*

"You can easily save hundreds of dollars a year on clothing purchases by waiting for sales or shopping at discount retailers like Marshalls. Better yet, avoid name brand clothing all together."

10 REASONS You Are RICH

Even in times of financial uncertainty, it's always important to keep things in perspective.

> *Wealth is the ability to fully experience life.*
> - Henry David Thoreau

1. *You didn't go to sleep hungry last night.*

2. *You didn't go to sleep outside.*

3. *You had a choice of what clothes to wear this morning.*

4. *You hardly broke a sweat today.*

5. *You didn't spend a minute in fear.*

6. *You have access to clean drinking water.*

7. *You have access to medical care.*

8. *You have access to the Internet.*

9. *You can read.*

10. *You have the right to vote.*

Some might say you are rich, so remember to be grateful for all the things you do have.

What **MONEY** Can't *Buy*

> ## *You aren't wealthy until you have something money can't buy.*
>
> - Garth Brooks

1 *A First Kiss from Someone Special*

The sweet rush of butterflies in your tummy when you kiss someone special for the very first time.

2 *The Realization of True Love*

The warm feeling you get many years after your first kiss when you realize you married the right person.

3 *Beauty*

Because beauty is in the eye of the beholder.

4 *True Friendship*

Through thick and thin, they stood by your side. They were there when you had nothing but them.

5 *Peace of Mind*

It can only be acquired with an honest heart.

6 *Beginner's Eyes*

You'll never see it again for the very first time.

7 The Joy of Telling an Interesting True Story

One of the most enticing roles we lead in life is that of a storyteller. There are few things more satisfying than telling a true story that others enjoy listening to.

8 Happiness

True happiness is achieved by doing what you love and being involved in something you believe in.

9 Success

Success is simply excelling at doing what you love.

10 A Single Moment of Time

Once it's gone, it's gone. Don't miss it.

11 A Baby's Laughter

Babies don't care about money. They care about kindness, love, and living in the moment.

12 Surprise Encounters with Long-Lost Friends

You haven't seen them in years, and you figured you'd probably never see them again. Then suddenly, there they are standing right in front of you.

13 The Feeling of Self-Accomplishment

You set your sights on a specific goal and followed through until you achieved it. Now that's something to celebrate.

14 The Sound of Raindrops Outside

...as you snuggle up on the couch. Few sounds are more soothing.

15 A Good, Genuine Conversation

Those moments of verbal bonding when the topic of conversation flows seamlessly and all parties involved gain as much as they put in.

16 An Unexpected Compliment

It seems like just another dreary Monday afternoon, but then she walks into your office and says, "I love your shirt. That color looks great on you."

17 The Feeling You Get When Your Idea Works

You've been struggling to resolve a complex problem all day, but you just can't seem to get it right. Filled with frustration, you decide to try one last idea before calling it a night. You've had many ideas before that failed miserably... but this time it works.

18 Randomly Hearing Your Favorite Song

You're stuck in bumper to bumper rush hour traffic, so you crank on a radio station for a little distraction. The opening notes to your favorite song instantly chime in.

9 Watching a Live Blooper Unfold in Front of You

As you walk alongside a friend, she trips over her own feet, wobbles erratically, regains her balance, and then tries to play it off like nothing happened. Hilarious!

20 A Sunny Sunday Afternoon

The birds are chirping, a light breeze is blowing through your hair, and the sun's rays are warming your cheeks.

21 The Rush of Adolescent Love

Those magical moments of adolescent lust and affection that only you and one other person rightly remember.

22 Being In The Right Place at The Right Time

You're sitting in the nosebleed seats at a professional baseball game. The home team batter cranks a monstrous, game-winning home run. The ball bounces off another fan's glove two seats in front of you and lands right in your lap.

23 The Recollection of Great Childhood Memories

Do you remember the first time you learned to ride a bike? What about wrestling with your dad? Or climbing trees with your friends?

24 Reminiscing About Old Times with Your Best Friend

Those crazy life experiences only the two of you lived through together. Like that wild 24 hour road trip to Atlanta, or that drunken night on the 3rd floor balcony of your college apartment.

25 Passion

True wealth comes naturally to those who follow their hearts. You can't pay someone to be emotionally passionate about something. Nor can you pay them to psychologically give-up on their passions.

26 Objects of Sentimental Value

Old family photos, your great grandmother's music box, that painting your baby brother made for you... some things are priceless.

27 The Comfort of an Old Familiar Smell

You just pulled into your parent's driveway after being away for a long while. You smell familiarity in the air, the scent of the pine tree in the neighbor's yard. As you head through the front door, more familiar smells consume your senses. Gosh, it feels good to be home.

28 The Hilarity of an Inside Joke

You'll never get it unless you were there at its inception.

29 Amazing Talents You Are Born With

Like the mind of a genius or the voice of an angel.

30 The Excitement of Making Someone Else Smile

Because her smile makes you smile back.

31 Exercising Your 5 Senses

Sight, hearing, smell, taste and touch. Each provides a gateway to rewarding personal experiences.

32 Sharing a Good Laugh with Friends and Family

Some of the most memorable moments in your life will be moments spent in laughter.

33 The Warm Coziness of Your Own Bed

No bed is more comfortable than your own.

34 Watching Wild Animals in Nature

Like a hawk gracefully soaring above the tree line, or a deer prancing across a grassy field.

35 A Home

Money can buy a house, but not a home. Because home is where the heart is.

35 Waking Up to the Smell of a Home Cooked Meal

You were still asleep, but someone special knew you'd be hungry soon.

37 The Peaceful Sound of Absolute Silence

Shhhhh...

38 Streams of Consciousness and Clarity

You're 'in the zone!' Act while your mind is hot.

39 The Sound of a Light Breeze Through the Trees

It's the sound of Mother Nature all around you.

40 The Captivating Experience of People Watching

The interesting (and sometimes foolish) things people do never ceases to please. You can't buy this quality of entertainment.

41 Watching the Sunrise and Sunset with Your Beloved

Make time for this. It's worth it.

42 The Sound and Sight of Ocean Waves

Another phenomenal act of Mother Nature.

43 The 'Pump' After a Great Workout

You feel like you can conquer the world.

44 The Blissful Act of Daydreaming

Just being... and thinking... and dreaming.

45 When She Says "I Love You"

...and you know she means it because you can read the sincerity in her eyes.

46 When an Unlikely Someone Remembers Your Birthday

A friend you haven't seen in over a month calls you at 9AM on your birthday just to say "happy birthday."

47 Finding Something You Thought You'd Lost Forever

You searched for it for days and finally gave up. Now, six months later, it basically appears right in front of you.

48 The Inspiration Behind Creative Works of Art

Every piece of art is priceless in the eyes of someone who can relate to it. The creative inspiration behind these works of art is no different.

When Your Pet Snuggles Up Next to You

It's just soooo cute.

50 A Moment of Eye Contact with an Attractive Stranger

You've never seen them before, and you may never see them again. But a moment was shared.

A Long Hug from a Loved One

Those deep, warm hugs you wish you could nestle in forever.

52 Happily Singing at The Top of Your Lungs

Well... You know you make me wanna shout! Kick my heels up and shout! Throw my hands up and shout! Throw my head back and shout! Come on now... Shout!

53 Seeing Your Breath on a Chilly Night

A simple phenomenon that has entertained children since the beginning of mankind.

54 The Feeling of Acceptance

You're now a part of something greater... and it feels good.

55 Watching the Clouds Form Cool Shapes

Never the same show twice.

56 Cuddling a Newborn Baby

Precious... simply precious.

57 When You Know You Can Trust Someone

You can see it in their eyes and you can feel it in your heart. They have no ulterior motive.

58 Sitting Around a Bonfire with Your Friends

One of the greatest settings for reminiscing and storytelling with those your care about.

59 Seeing Two Elderly Folks Who are Madly in Love

It's a sight of love that has surpassed the tests of time.

The Beauty of a Moonlit Sky

Few simple pleasures are more satisfying than gazing up into a starry, moonlit sky.

The Awesomeness of Skipping Rocks Across Water

It doesn't matter how old you get, this one never gets old.

The Awesomeness of Skipping Rocks Across Water

Peaceful and powerful at the same time.

Slow Dancing in Your Living Room

Dancing is like dreaming with your feet.
-Constanze

64 Knowing She'll Be There When You Get Back

Yes. There is stability in your life. And she's a big part of it.

65 Watching Her Sleep

Just being with her and breathing with her.

66 The Colors of Fall

It's Mother Nature's artwork.

67 People Who Make You Smile Just by Thinking of Them

Wherever I am, no matter what I'm doing, just thinking of her makes me smile.

68 The Warm Touch of Your Beloved

It's the touch no one else has.

69 When You Realize People Are Reading What You Write

Words can't explain it. Thank you.

70 The Excitement of a New Comment on Your Blog

We love these.

Spend less than you earn, go without until you have the money in hand.

If you want to feel rich, just count all the great things you have that money can't buy.

Normal is getting dressed in clothes that you buy for work and driving through traffic in a car that you financed – in order to get to the job you need to pay for the clothes and the car, and the house you leave vacant all day so you can afford to live in it.

Don't think of cost. Think of value.

Too many people buy things they don't need with money they don't have to impress people they don't know.

Money makes life easier only when the money is yours free and clear.

If it were easy everyone would do it. This is why get rich quick schemes will never be true. If it was so quick and easy then everyone would be millionaires. Making money and accomplishing tasks is hard work, but well worth it.

Keep money on your mind but out of your heart.

It's easier to find wealth by needing less, instead of making more.

Keep six months of your salary in an emergency savings account just in case you lose your job or have an emergency that prevents you from working for a prolonged period of time.

Finance QUOTES

Finance
QUESTIONS
to Make You *think*

What's the **MOST** *valuable* thing you own**?**

What could you **SELL** to raise *extra* cash if needed**?**

TIME or *Money***?**

What are you teaching (or will you teach) your **KIDS** about *money***?**

What's more statisfying to you: saving **TIME** or saving *Money***?**

What steps can you take today to **IMPROVE** your *financial* situation**?**

What **MAKES** a person truly *rich***?**

Are you being **SMART** about *debt***?**

What do you **DESIRE** more than *money***?**

How much are you **SPENDING** (and *saving*) each month**?**

Part Ten
Inspiration

Have an unrelenting belief
that things will work out,
that the long road has a
purpose, that the things that
you desire may not happen
today, but they are coming
up over the horizon.

THE SMARTEST
CHOICE WE CAN MAKE

The Only Way

My cell phone rang just after midnight. I didn't answer. Then it rang again a minute later. I rolled over, grabbed the phone off the night stand, and squinted at the bright, glowing caller ID screen. "Claire," it read. Claire is a close friend – a friend who tragically lost her husband to a car accident six months ago. And I figured since she rarely calls me in the middle of the night, it was probably important.

"Hey, Claire. Is everything okay?" I asked.

"No!" she declared as she burst into tears. "I need to talk… I need help…"

"I'm listening," I reassured her. "What's on your mind?"

"I lost my job this evening, and I'm tired, and I just don't know anymore…"

"A job is just a job. They come and go. Remember, Angel lost her job last year and it was a blessing in disguise. She found something better."

"I know, I know," she sighed over her tears. "I just felt like the world was going to end after the accident… Ya know? And then my friends and family helped me get back on my feet…"

"And you're still on your feet right now," I added.

"Well, sometimes I feel like I am, and sometimes I feel like I'm barely maintaining my balance, and sometimes I feel like I'm falling again. And this series of feelings just keeps cycling over and over again in a loop – good days followed by bad days and vice versa. It's just one long struggle. And I'm exhausted!"

"But you keep moving forward…"

"Actually," she continued over more tears. "The only way I've found to keep myself moving forward from moment to moment through the hard times is by repeating a short saying my grandfather taught me when I was a kid. And I don't know how or why it helps now, but it does."

"What's the saying?" I asked.

"Do your best with what's in front of you and leave the rest to the powers above you," she replied.

I smiled. Because I love pieces of inspirational prose that help people progress through even the hardest of times. And because it suddenly reminded me of a short story my grandfather told me when I was a kid – one that's also applicable to Claire's circumstance.

"Your grandfather was a wise man," I said. "And it's funny, because your grandfather's saying reminds me of a short story my grandfather once told me. Would you like to hear it?"

"Yeah," she replied.

My Grandfather's Story

Once upon a time, in a small Indian village, the village fisherman accidentally dropped his favorite fishing pole into the river and was unable to retrieve it. When his neighbors caught word of his loss, they came over and said, "That's just bad luck!" The fisherman replied, "Perhaps."

The following day, the fisherman hiked a mile down the bank of the river to see if he could find his fishing pole. He came upon a small, calm alcove in the river bank that was loaded to the brim with salmon. He used a back-up fishing pole to catch nearly 100 salmon, loaded them into his wagon, and brought them back to the village to barter with other villagers. Everyone in the village was ecstatic to receive the fresh salmon. When his neighbors caught word of his success, they came over and said, "Wow! What great luck you have!" The fisherman replied, "Perhaps."

Two days later, the fisherman began hiking back towards the alcove so he could catch more salmon. But a tenth of a mile into the hike, he tripped on a tree stump and severely sprained his ankle. He slowly and painfully hopped back to the village to nurse his health. When his neighbors caught word of his injury, they came over and said, "That's just bad luck!" The fisherman replied, "Perhaps."

Four days went by, and although the fisherman's ankle was slowly healing, he could not yet walk, and the village was completely out of fish to eat. Three other villagers volunteered to go to the river to fish while the fisherman recovered. That evening, when the three men did not return, the village sent a search party out for them only to discover that the men had been attacked and killed by a pack of wolves. When the fisherman's neighbors caught word of this, they came over and said, "You're so lucky you weren't out there fishing. What great luck you have!" The fisherman replied, "Perhaps."

"A few days later... well, you can guess how the story continues," I said.

The Moral of the Story

Claire chuckled and said, "Thank you." Because the moral of the story was immediately clear to her. We just don't know – we never do. Life is an unpredictable phenomenon. No matter how good or bad things seem right now, we can never be 100% certain what will happen next.

And this actually lifts a huge weight off of our shoulders. Because it means that regardless of what's happening to us right now – good, bad or indifferent, it's all just part of the phenomenon we call 'life' – which flows like the river in my grandfather's story, unpredictably from one occurrence to the next. And the smartest choice we can make is to swim with the flow of the river.

Which means, quite simply, not panicking in the face of unforeseen misfortunes or losing our poise in limelight of our triumphs, but instead "doing our best with what's in front of us and leaving the rest to the powers above us."

11 THINGS You Should LEAVE in the Past

You might not be proud of all the things you've done in the past, but that's okay. The past is not today.

Here are 11 things to leave behind and grow beyond:

1 Letting other people write your life's story.

You could spend your whole life worrying about what other people think of you, or what they want for you, but it won't get you very far. If you don't take charge and design your own life plan, chances are you'll fall into someone else's plan. And guess what they have planned for you? NOT MUCH!

2 The fear of making mistakes.

Past mistakes should teach you to create a wonderful future; not cause you to be afraid of it. Be less afraid of making a mess out of your life. For oftentimes, our greatest achievements and our most beautiful creations ascend from the emotions we live, the lessons we learn, and the messes we make along the way. Just ask a poet, an artist, a songwriter, a lover, or a parent; in the long-run things rarely turn out as planned, just better than you ever imagined.

3 The belief that 'perfect' means the same thing to everyone.

Perfect people have scars on their faces and perfect complexions. Perfect people have long brown hair at 60 and short grey hair at 35. Perfect people wear wigs. Perfect people have sex with men, women, both, or no one at all. Perfect people can barely see over the grocery store counter, and sometimes bump their heads at the top of doorways. Perfect people have waistlines that are infinite in size and geometry. Perfect people have skin tones as light as vanilla ice-cream and as rich dark chocolate. Perfect people come from every corner of this beautiful planet and can be seen everywhere – even in the mirror. Yeah! That's right! Perfect is the way we are born. Perfect is the way we are now. Perfect is exclusively unique. We are all perfect just the way we are.

! *Negative thinking.*

If there is one thing I am certain of, it's that our thinking can get in the way of our happiness. It is our thoughts that really dictate the way we feel, so why not choose thoughts that make you feel amazing? The more you praise and celebrate your life, the more there is in life to celebrate. You can choose to make the rest of your life the best of your life.

! *Doing something just because others are.*

Give yourself permission to immediately walk away from anything that gives you bad vibes. There is no need to explain or make sense of it. Just trust what you feel. Don't make a decision based solely on popularity. Just because other people are doing it doesn't mean it's the best choice for you.

! *Not following your intuition.*

One day your life will flash before your eyes; make sure it's worth watching. Stop and think about it. Really think about it. What is it that you really want to do with your life? Forget what you think you should do. What excites you? What feels impossible? Be honest with yourself. Your answers don't need to make an impression on anyone but you.

7 *Procrastinating on your goals and passions.*

The difference between who you are and who you want to be, is what you do. Yes, it will hurt. It will take time. It will require dedication. It will require willpower. You will need to make healthy decisions. It will require sacrifice. You will need to push your mind and body to its max. There will be temptation. But, I promise you, when you reach your goal, it will be worth it. And remember, nothing you have passion for is ever a waste of time, no matter how it turns out.

8 *The belief that failure is the opposite of success.*

Failure is not the opposite of success, it is part of success. Failure becomes success when we learn from it. If you change the way you look at things, the things you look at change. Instead of looking at what's missing, and how far you still have to go, focus on what's present, and how far you have come.

9 *Showing a lack of respect.*

Sometimes you have to respect another person's feelings even if they don't mean anything to you, because your gesture could mean everything to them. And remember, what goes around comes around in the world. You get respect when you give respect. So treat everyone with kindness and respect, even those who are rude to you – not because they are nice, but because you are.

0 *People who want you to be someone else.*

Sometimes we grow strong when someone sets us free, and sometimes we grow even stronger when we let someone go. Remember, you are too fabulous to fit in. It is better to be hated for what you are than loved for what you are not. Never change who you are. Be yourself. People will love you for it, and if they don't, let them go.

1 *People who are already gone.*

There are no failed relationships, because every person in your life has a lesson to teach. Sometimes you simply outgrow people. Don't try to fix the unfixable, just accept it and move on. When someone leaves you, it's important to emotionally release them. And know it's not an ending – it's a new beginning. It just means that their part in your story is over. Your story will go on.

28 DIGNIFIED Ways to *Impress* Everyone Around You

Far more often than any of us like to admit, our actions are driven by an inner desire to impress other people. This desire is often reflected in the brand name products we use, the bars and restaurants we frequent, the houses and cars we buy and the careers we choose.

But are name brand products, fancy bars, houses and cars really that impressive? What about a person who holds an elite position in a career field they dislike? Some of these things might capture our attention for a minute or two, but they won't hold it for long.

Why? Because tangible possessions are not as impressive as intangible qualities.

Consider the following questions:

He drives a Porsche, but can he truly afford the car payment?

He owns a big house, but is it a loving household?

He makes a lot of money, but does he enjoy what he does for a living?

You get the idea. Whenever the answer to questions like these is 'no,' the subject who initially appeared to be impressive no longer does.

Now take a moment and imagine a person who loves what he does for a living, smiles frequently and bleeds passion in every breath he takes. Would he impress you? Would it matter that he wasn't a millionaire?

Here are 28 dignified ways to impress everyone around you. If you practice these tips on a regular basis, they won't just impress others, they'll help you become a better person too.

> *We make a living by what we get.*
> *We make a life by what we give.*
>
> - Winston Churchill

1 Be authentic. Be true to yourself.

If the face you always show the world is just a mask, someday there will be nothing beneath it. Because when you spend too much time concentrating on everyone else's perception of you, or who everyone else wants you to be, you eventually forget who you really are. So don't fear the judgments of others; you know in your heart who you are and what's true to you. You don't have to be perfect to impress and inspire people. Let them be impressed and inspired by how you deal with your imperfections.

2 Care about people.

If you don't genuinely care about people, they won't care about you. The more you help others, the more they will want to help you. Love and kindness begets love and kindness. And so on and so forth.

3 Make others feel good.

People will rarely remember what you did, but they will always remember how you made them feel.

4 Be honest and take ownership of your actions.

Nobody likes a liar. In the long-run, the truth always reveals itself anyway. Either you own up to your actions or your actions will ultimately own you.

5 Smile often.

Everyone likes the sight of a genuine smile. Think about how you feel when a complete stranger looks into your eyes and smiles. Suddenly they don't seem like a stranger anymore, do they?

6 Respect elders. Respect minors. Respect everyone.

There are no boundaries or classes that define a group of people that deserve to be respected. Treat everyone with the same level of respect you would give to your grandfather and the same level of patience you would have with your baby brother. People will notice your kindness.

7 Address people by their name.

People love the sight and sound of their own name. So make sure you learn to remember names. Use them courteously in both oral and written communication.

8 Say "Please" and "Thank you."

These two simple phrases make demands sound like requests, and they inject a friendly tone into serious conversations. Using them can mean the difference between sounding rude and sounding genuinely grateful.

9 Excel at what you do.

I am impressed by great guitarists, writers, bloggers, painters, motivational speakers, internet entrepreneurs, computer engineers, mothers, fathers, athletes, etc. There is only one thing they all have in common: They excel at what they do. There's no point in doing something if you aren't going to do it right. Excel at your work and excel at your hobbies. Develop a reputation for yourself, a reputation for consistent excellence.

10 Help others when you're able.

In life, you get what you put in. When you make a positive impact in someone else's life, you also make a positive impact in your own life. Do something that's greater than you – something that helps someone else to be happy or to suffer less. Everyone values the gift of unexpected assistance and those who supply it.

11 Put a small personal touch on everything you do.

Think of it as branding your work. If you're funny, add a little humor into it. If you're an artist, decorate it with illustrations. Whatever you do, customize it with a little personal touch of 'you.'

12 Over-deliver on all of your promises.

Some people habitually make promises they are just barely able to fulfill. They promise perfection and deliver mediocrity. If you want to boost your personal value in the eyes of others, do the exact opposite. Slightly under-sell your capabilities so that you're always able to over-deliver. It will seem to others like you're habitually going above and beyond the call of duty.

13 Get organized.

How can you get anything accomplished if you aren't organized? You can't. Make a regular habit of organizing your living space and working space.

14 Do your research and ask clarifying questions.

Don't be that clueless dude in the room who just nods like he knows what's going on. Prepare yourself by doing research ahead of time. And if something still doesn't make sense to you, ask questions. The people involved will respect your desire to understand the material.

15 Share knowledge and information with others.

When you can, be a resource to those around you. If you have access to essential information, don't hoard it. Share it openly.

Be positive and focus on what's right.

Everything that happens in life is neither good nor bad. It just depends on your perspective. And no matter how it turns out, it always ends up just the way it should. Either you succeed or you learn something. So stay positive, appreciate the pleasant outcomes, and learn from the rest. Your positivity will rub off on everyone around you.

Listen intently to what others have to say.

Eyes focused, ears tuned, mobile phone off. In a world that can't move fast enough, someone who can find time to listen to others is always appreciated.

18 Be faithful to your significant other.

Tiger Woods was everyone's hero until recently, wasn't he? Sustained fidelity in a long-term intimate relationship is not only impressive, it creates a healthy foundation for everything else you do.

19 Learn to appreciate and love Mother Nature.

Those who truly appreciate and love the natural world surrounding us typically exhibit the same high regard for all humanity. It's a positive way to live, and it's something people notice.

20 Invest time, energy and money in yourself every day.

When you invest in yourself, you can never lose, and over time you will change the trajectory of your life. You are simply the product of what you know. The more time, energy and money you spend acquiring pertinent knowledge, the more control you have over your life and the more valuable you will be to everyone around you.

21 Perform random acts of kindness on a regular basis.

Pay for a stranger's coffee in line at Starbucks. Buy the office receptionist flowers just to say, "Thank you." Help an elderly lady with her groceries. There's nothing more rewarding than putting smiles on the faces around you.

22 Compliment people who deserve it.

Go out of your way to personally acknowledge and complement the people who have gone out of their way to shine. Everybody likes to hear that their efforts are appreciated.

23 Speak clearly and make eye contact.

Most people have a very low tolerance for dealing with people they can't understand. Mystery does not fuel strong relationships and impressiveness. Also, there's little doubt that eye contact is one of the most captivating forms of personal communication. When executed properly, eye contact injects closeness into human interaction.

24 Make yourself available and approachable.

If people cannot get a hold of you, or have trouble approaching you, they will forget about you. Your general availability and accessibility to others is extremely important to them. Always maintain a positive, tolerant attitude and keep an open line of communication to those around you.

25 Be self-sufficient.

Freedom is the greatest gift. Self-sufficiency is the greatest freedom. And self-sufficiency is quite impressive too. In the business world, it's one of the primary dreams that inspire people to give-up their day jobs to pursue entrepreneurship.

26 Focus on the resources you do have access to.

It all begins and ends in your mind. What you give power to has power over you, if you allow it. Too many of us are hung up on what we don't have, can't have, or won't ever have. We spend too much energy being down, when we could use that same energy – if not less of it – doing, or at least trying to do, some of the things we really want to do. So focus on the opportunities you DO have, and exploit the resources you DO have access to.

27 Be a part of something you believe in.

This could be anything. Some people take an active role in their local city council, some find refuge in religious faith, some join social clubs supporting causes they believe in, and others find passion in their careers. In each case the psychological outcome is the same. They engage themselves in something they strongly believe in. This engagement brings happiness and meaning into their lives. It's hard not to be impressed by someone who's passionate about what they're doing.

28 Stand up for your beliefs without flaunting them.

Yes, it is possible to stand up for your beliefs without foisting them down someone else's throat. Discuss your personal beliefs when someone asks about them, but don't spawn offensive attacks of propaganda on unsuspecting victims. Stand firm by your values and always keep an open mind to new information.

Of course, the coolest thing about this list is that everything you need to impress everyone around you is already contained within you. So stop trying to impress people with the possessions you own and start inspiring them with who you are and how you live your life.

18 THINGS

I Wish SOMEONE Told Me When I Was *18*

This morning I was reading a book at my favorite beach-side coffee shop when an 18-year-old kid sat down next to me and said, "That's a great read, ain't it?" So we started chatting.

He told me he was getting ready to graduate from high school in a couple of weeks and then immediately starting his college career in the fall. "But I have no clue what I want to do with my life," he said. "Right now I'm just going with the flow."

And then, with eager, honest eyes, he began asking me one question after the next:

"What do you do for a living?"

"When and how did you decide what you wanted to do?"

"Why did you do this? Why didn't you do that?"

"Is there anything you wish you had done differently?"

Etc, etc, etc...

I answered his questions as best as I could, and tried to give decent advice with the time I had. And after a half-hour conversation, he thanked me and we parted ways.

But on the walk home I realized the conversation I had with him was actually quite nostalgic for me. He reminded me of me ten years ago. So I started thinking about his questions again, and I began imagining all of the things I wish someone had told me when I was 18.

Then I took it a step further and thought about all the things I would love to tell myself if I could travel back in time to give my 18-year-old self some advice about life.

So after a few cups of coffee and a couple hours of deliberation, here are 18 things I wish someone told me when I was 18:

1 *Commit yourself to making lots of mistakes.*

Mistakes teach you important lessons. The biggest mistake you can make is doing nothing because you're too scared to make a mistake. So don't hesitate – don't doubt yourself. In life, it's rarely about getting a chance; it's about taking a chance. You'll never be 100% sure it will work, but you can always be 100% sure doing nothing won't work. Most of the time you just have to go for it! And no matter how it turns out, it always ends up just the way it should be. Either you succeed or you learn something. Win-Win. Remember, if you never act, you will never know for sure, and you will be left standing in the same spot forever.

2 *Find hard work you love doing.*

If I could offer my 18-year-old self some real career advice, I'd tell myself not to base my career choice on other people's ideas, goals and recommendations. I'd tell myself not to pick a major because it's popular, or statistically creates graduates who make the most money. I'd tell myself that the right career choice is based on one key point: Finding hard work you love doing. As long as you remain true to yourself, and follow your own interests and values, you can find success through passion. Perhaps more importantly, you won't wake up several years later working in a career field you despise, wondering "How the heck am I going to do this for the next 30 years?" So if you catch yourself working hard and loving every minute of it, don't stop. You're on to something big. Because hard work ain't hard when you concentrate on your passions.

3 *Invest time, energy and money in yourself every day.*

When you invest in yourself, you can never lose, and over time you will change the trajectory of your life. You are simply the product of what you know. The more time, energy and money you spend acquiring pertinent knowledge, the more control you have over your life.

4 *Explore new ideas and opportunities often.*

Your natural human fears of failure and embarrassment will sometimes stop you from trying new things. But you must rise above these fears, for your life's story is simply the culmination of many small, unique experiences. And the more unique experiences you have, the more interesting your story gets. So seek as many new life experiences as possible and be sure to share them with the people you care about. Not doing so is not living.

5 When sharpening your career skills, focus more on less.

Think in terms of Karate: A black belt seems far more impressive than a brown belt. But does a brown belt really seem any more impressive than a red belt? Probably not to most people. Remember that society elevates experts high onto a pedestal. Hard work matters, but not if it's scattered in diverse directions. So narrow your focus on learning fewer career related skills and master them all.

6 People are not mind readers. Tell them what you're thinking.

People will never know how you feel unless you tell them. Your boss? Yeah, he doesn't know you're hoping for a promotion because you haven't told him yet. That cute girl you haven't talked to because you're too shy? Yeah, you guessed it; she hasn't given you the time of day simply because you haven't given her the time of day either. In life, you have to communicate with others. And often, you have to open your vocal cords and speak the first

words. You have to tell people what you're thinking. It's as simple as that.

7 Make swift decisions and take immediate action.

Either you're going to take action and seize new opportunities, or someone else will first. You can't change anything or make any sort of progress by sitting back and thinking about it. Remember, there's a huge difference between knowing how to do something and actually doing it. Knowledge is basically useless without action.

8 Accept and embrace change.

However good or bad a situation is now, it will change. That's the one thing you can count on. So embrace change, and realize that change happens for a reason. It won't always be easy or obvious at first, but in the end it will be worth it.

9 Don't worry too much about what other people think about you.

For the most part, what other people think and say about you doesn't matter. When I was 18, I let the opinions of my high school and early college peers influence my decisions. And, at times, they steered me away from ideas and goals I strongly believed in. I realize now, ten years later, that this was a foolish way to live, especially when I consider that nearly all of these people whose opinions I cared so much about are no longer a part of my life. Unless you're trying to make a great first impression (job interview, first date, etc.), don't let the opinions of others stand in your way. What they think and say about you isn't important. What is important is how you feel about yourself.

10 *Always be honest with yourself and others.*

Living a life of honesty creates peace of mind, and peace of mind is priceless. Period.

11 *Talk to lots of people in college and early on in your career.*

Bosses. Colleagues. Professors. Classmates. Social club members. Other students outside of your major or social circle. Teaching assistants. Career advisors. College deans. Friends of friends. Everyone! Why? Professional networking. I have worked for three employers since I graduated from college (I left my first two employers by choice on good terms), but I only interviewed with the first employer. The other two employers offered me a job before I even had a formal interview, based strictly on

the recommendation of a hiring manager (someone I had networked with over the years). When employers look to fill a position, the first thing they do is ask the people they know and trust if they know someone who would do well in the position. If you start building your professional network early, you'll be set. Over time, you'll continue talking to new people you meet through your current network and your network's reach and the associated opportunities will continue to snowball for the duration of your career.

12 *Sit alone in silence for at least ten minutes every day.*

Use this time to think, plan, reflect, and dream. Creative and productive thinking flourish in solitude and silence. With quiet, you can hear your thoughts, you can reach deep within yourself, and you can focus on mapping out the next logical, productive step in your life.

13 *Ask lots of questions.*

The greatest 'adventure' is the ability to inquire, to ask questions. Sometimes in the process of inquiry, the search is more significant than the answers. Answers come from other people, from the universe of knowledge and history, and from the intuition and deep wisdom inside yourself. These answers will never surface if you never ask the right questions. Thus, the simple act of asking the right questions is the answer.

Exploit the resources you do have access to.

The average person is usually astonished when they see a physically handicap person show intense signs of emotional happiness. How could someone in such a restricted physical state be so happy? The answer rests in how they use the resources they do have. Stevie Wonder couldn't see, so he exploited his sense of hearing into a passion for music, and he now has 25 Grammy Awards to prove it.

Live below your means.

Live a comfortable life, not a wasteful one. Do not spend to impress others. Do not live life trying to fool yourself into thinking wealth is measured in material objects. Manage your money wisely so your money does not manage you. Always live well below your means.

16 Be respectful of others and make them feel good.

In life and business, it's not so much what you say that counts, it' how you make people feel. So respect your elders, minors, and everyone in between. There are no boundaries or classes that define a group of people that deserve to be respected. Treat everyone with the same level of respect you would give to your grandfather and the same level of patience you would have with your baby brother. Supporting, guiding, and making contributions to other people is one of life's greatest rewards. In order to get, you have to give.

17 Excel at what you do.

There's no point in doing something if you aren't going to do it right. Excel at your work and excel at your hobbies. Develop a reputation for yourself, a reputation for consistent excellence.

18 Be who you were born to be.

You must follow your heart, and be who you were born to be. Some of us were born to be musicians – to communicate intricate thoughts and rousing feelings with the strings of a guitar. Some of us were born to be poets – to touch people's hearts with exquisite prose. Some of us were born to be entrepreneurs – to create growth and opportunity where others saw rubbish. And still, some of us were born to be or do whatever it is, specifically, that moves you. Regardless of what you decide to do in your lifetime, you better feel it in every fiber of your being. You better be born to do it! Don't waste your life fulfilling someone else's dreams and desires.

But above all, laugh when you can,
apologize when you should, and let go of
what you can't change. Life is short, yet
amazing. Enjoy the ride.

12 THINGS

My GRANDMOTHER *Told* Me Before She Died

When my grandmother, Zelda, passed away a few years ago at the age of 90, she left me with a box of miscellaneous items from her house that she knew I had grown to appreciate over the years. Among these items is an old leather-bound journal that she aptly named her 'Inspiration Journal.'

Throughout the second half of her life, she used this journal to jot down ideas, thoughts, quotes, song lyrics, and anything else that moved her. She would read excerpts from her journal to me when I was growing up, and I would listen and ask questions. I honestly credit a part of who I am now to the wisdom she bestowed on me when I was young.

Today I want to share some of these inspiring excerpts with you. I've done my best to sort, copyedit, and reorganize the content into twelve inspiring bullet points. Enjoy.

1 *Breathe in the future, breathe out the past.*

No matter where you are or what you're going through, always believe that there is a light at the end of the tunnel. Never expect, assume, or demand. Just do your best, control the elements you can control, and then let it be. Because once you have done what you can, if it is meant to be, it will happen, or it will show you the next step that needs to be taken.

2 *Life CAN be simple again.*

Just choose to focus on one thing at a time. You don't have to do it all, and you don't have to do it all right now. Breathe, be present, and do your best with what's in front of you. What you put into life, life will eventually give you back many times over.

3 | Let others take you as you are, or not at all.

Speak your truth even if your voice shakes. By being yourself, you put something beautiful into the world that was not there before. So walk your path confidently and don't expect anyone else to understand your journey, especially if they have not been exactly where you are going.

4 | You are not who you used to be, and that's OK.

You've been hurt; you've gone through numerous ups and downs that have made you who you are today. Over the years, so many things have happened – things that have changed your perspective, taught you lessons, and forced your spirit to grow. As time passes, nobody stays the same, but some people will still tell you that you have changed. Respond to them by saying, "Of course I've changed. That's what life is all about. But I'm still the same person, just a little stronger now than I ever was before."

5 | Everything that happens helps you grow, even if it's hard to see right now.

Circumstances will direct you, correct you, and perfect you over time. So whatever you do, hold on to hope. The tiniest thread will twist into an unbreakable cord. Let hope anchor you in the possibility that this is not the end of your story – that the change in the tides will eventually bring you to peaceful shores.

6 | Do not educate yourself to be rich, educate yourself to be happy.

That way when you get older you'll know the value of things, not the price. In the end, you will come to realize that the best days are the days when you don't need anything extreme or special to happen to make you smile. You simply appreciate the moments and feel gratitude, seeking nothing else, nothing more. That is what true happiness is all about.

7 | Be determined to be positive.

Understand that the greater part of your misery or unhappiness is determined not by your circumstances, but by your attitude. So smile at those who often try to begrudge or hurt you, show them what's missing in their life and what they can't take away from you.

8 | Pay close attention to those you care about.

Sometimes when a loved one says, "I'm okay," they need you to look them in the eyes, hug them tight, and reply, "I know you're not." And don't be too upset if some people only seem to remember you when they need you. Feel privileged that you are like a beacon of light that comes to their minds when there is darkness in their lives.

9 Sometimes you have to let a person go so they can grow.

Because, over the course of their lives, it is not what you do for them, but what you have taught them to do for themselves that will make them a successful human being.

10 Sometimes getting the results you crave means stripping yourself of people that don't serve your best interests.

This allows you to make space for those who support you in being the absolute best version of yourself. It happens gradually as you grow. You find out who you are and what you want, and then you realize that people you've known forever don't see things the way you do. So you keep the wonderful memories, but find yourself moving on.

11 It's better to look back on life and say, "I can't believe I did that," than to look back and say, "I wish I did that."

In the end, people will judge you in some way anyway. So don't live your life trying to impress others. Instead live your life impressing yourself. Love yourself enough to never lower your standards for anyone.

12 If you're looking for a happy ending and can't seem to find one, maybe it's time to start looking for a new beginning.

Brush yourself off and accept that you have to fail from time to time. That's how you learn. The strongest people out there – the ones who laugh the hardest with a genuine smile – are the same people who have fought the toughest battles. They're smiling because they've decided that they're not going to let anything hold them down, they're moving on to a new beginning.

WHY I **LIVE** EVERY DAY LIKE IT'S MY **LAST**

Laugh with every breath.
Love as long as you live.

A Good Girl

Alyssa was my best friend. She was a talented musician, a graceful gymnast, a brilliant writer, and a deeply passionate individual. She cared so much about people. Love bled from every facet of her being. When she spoke, her eyes were as sincere as her words. And she always wanted to understand what was wrong so she could strive to make it better.

But Alyssa woke up one day during her senior year in college with a strange pain in her chest. The on-campus doctors didn't understand why, so they referred her to a specialist. After several MRIs and blood tests, they determined that she had a rare, escalated case of Hodgkin's lymphoma – a form of cancer. She spent the next three years suffering through varying degrees of pain and sickness as multiple doctors treated her with radiation and chemotherapy. And although these doctors were initially hopeful, Alyssa's condition worsened, and she eventually passed away on her 25th birthday.

A Bad Guy

Ethan was also my friend. Though not as multi-talented as Alyssa, he was insanely smart – particularly when it came to money and business tactics. But he didn't care about people. I eventually learned, just before ending our eight year friendship, that he ripped people off for a living. He primarily targeted elderly folks who had a relatively small life savings. "They're all suckers," he told me. And he felt no remorse because, he continued, "they'll be dead soon anyway."

Today, at the age of 28, Ethan is a multi-millionaire. And although we haven't spoken in years, I've heard from others that he still hasn't gotten into any legal trouble – largely, I think, because of the calculated threats that I've heard he makes to anyone he suspects might have a good conscience. I hear, also, that he doesn't suffer from any major health problems, and that he, his trophy wife, and his two healthy sons live in a mansion somewhere in Southern California.

The Reason

These are old stories – familiar stories. The people and the circumstances differ slightly for everyone who tells them, but the core lessons remain the same. Life isn't fair. Bad things do happen to good people. And good things do happen to bad people.

Yet, these are the excuses many of us use when we choose not to follow our hearts. And they are the excuses many of us use when we choose to treat ourselves and each other without dignity and respect. "Why care?" we argue, "When the Alyssa's of the world suffer and die young while the Ethan's of the world sip wine at a five-star resort well into their 80's."

But for some of us, Alyssa and Ethan are the reason we do follow our hearts. His story is the reason we live to make the world a little brighter, to make people a little happier. And her story is the reason

we use all of the strength we have right now. Because we know we may not have the same strength tomorrow.

Because a world with no guarantees requires us to live every day...

As if it were our last.

9 THINGS

No One Wants to **REGRET** When They're *Older*

The things you didn't do when you had the chance. That priceless relationship you neglected. Those important words you left unspoken...

Every one of us has experienced feelings of regret. But it's not too late to set things straight. We're still here breathing. Right now we have an opportunity to change our future. Right now we can choose to erase regret from our later years.

Here are nine things no one wants to regret when they're older, and some thoughts on avoiding these regrets:

1 *Not spending enough time smiling with the people you love.*

You've heard the saying, 'The best things in life are free.' Well spending quality time with family and friends, enjoying the antics of a pet, seeing your child smile, experiencing intimate and heart-felt moments with your significant other – these times are precious and free.

Don't get so caught up in the rat race, working 50+ hours a week, to the point where you are too stressed and exhausted to enjoy your closest relationships. By simplifying your lifestyle and making conscious choices along the way, it is possible to live on less money, and thus work fewer hours and enjoy more of what matters most.

As we get older, fun is often underrated. With all of our responsibilities, fun seems like an indulgence. It shouldn't be. It should be a requirement. When your work life is busy, and all your energy is focused in that arena, it's all too easy to find yourself off balance. While drive and focus is important, if you intend to maintain happiness and peace in your life you still need to balance in the soccer games, the family dinners, the intimate dates with your significant other, etc.

> *In the end, we only regret the chances we didn't take,*
> *relationships we were afraid to have,*
> *and the decisions we waited too long to make.*

2 Holding a grudge and never forgiving someone you care about.

We've all been hurt by another person at some point – we were treated poorly, trust was broken, hearts were hurt. And while this pain is normal, sometimes it lingers for too long. We relive the pain over and over and have a hard time letting go.

This creates problems. It not only causes us to be unhappy, but it can strain or ruin our relationships, distract us from work and family and other important things, and make us reluctant to open up to new things and people. We get trapped in a cycle of anger and hurt, and miss out on the beauty of life as it happens.

Grudges are a waste of perfect happiness. If there's someone in your life who deserves another chance, give it to them. If you need to apologize, do it. Give your story together a happy new beginning.

3 Fulfilling everyone else's dreams, instead of your own.

Unfortunately, just before you take your first step on the righteous journey to pursue your dreams, people around you, even the ones who deeply care for you, will give you awful advice. It's not because they have evil intentions. It's because they don't understand the big picture – what your dreams, passions, and life goals mean to you.

Have the courage to live a life true to YOU, not the life others expect of you. Make time to pursue your passion, no matter how busy you are or what anyone else says.

As our friend Steve Jobs once said:

"Your time is limited, so don't waste it living someone else's life. Don't be trapped by dogma, which is living with the results of other people's thinking. Don't let the noise of others' opinions drown out your own inner voice, heart and intuition. They somehow already know what you truly want to become. Everything else is secondary."

4 Not being honest about how you feel.

Say what you need to say, and never apologize for showing your feelings. Many people suppress their feelings in order to keep peace with others. As a result, they settle for carrying the weight of their own silence. Give yourself permission to feel a full range of emotions. When you're in touch with what you're feeling, you're more likely to understand the situation at hand and resolve it instead of avoiding it.

Also, if you want to connect with others, you need to accept and love yourself first, even when your truth feels heavy. In the end, expressing your feelings will boost your relationships, including your relationship with yourself, to a new healthier level. And your open honesty will also help you to realize and release unhealthy relationships from your life.

5 Being foolish and irresponsible with your finances.

When you spend less than you make you buy lifestyle flexibility and freedom. You are buying the ability to say yes to the things that matter, because you're saving on the things that don't. Money can bring comfort, and there is absolutely nothing wrong with enjoying that comfort. But it's important to spend money on the things that truly matter to you, and let go of spending that does not add value to your life.

Live a comfortable life, not a wasteful one. Stop buying stuff you do not need. Do not spend to impress others. Do not live life trying to fool yourself into thinking wealth is measured in material objects. Manage your money wisely so your money does not manage you.

6 Getting caught up in needless drama and negativity.

Don't expect to achieve long-term happiness if you surround yourself with negative people. Don't give part-time people a full-time position in your life. Know your value and what you have to offer, stay positive, and never settle for anything less than what you deserve.

There comes a time in life when you have to let go of all the pointless drama and the people who create it. Staying out of other people's drama is an incredibly effective way to simplify your life and reduce stress. Surround yourself with positive people who make you laugh so hard that you forget the bad, so you can focus on the good. Life really is too short to be anything but positive and happy.

7 Spending time with people who make you unhappy.

For the average person happiness is a choice, yet numerous people are unhappy. There are many reasons, but it all boils down to one simple principle: They choose something else over happiness. Because it often takes less effort to be unhappy.

To find true happiness in life you have to follow your heart and intuition. You have to be who you are, and design a lifestyle and career that fulfills you – no matter what that entails or what people say about it. And it is never too late to do so.

So be happy; be yourself. If others don't like it, then let them be. Life isn't about pleasing everybody. Begin today by taking responsibility for your own happiness. You are the only one who can create it. The choice is yours.

8 Never making a difference in the lives of others.

Every person can make a difference, and every person should try.

In life, you get what you put in. When you make a positive impact in someone else's life, you also make a positive impact in your own life. Do something that's greater than you – something that helps someone else to be happy or to suffer less.

Remember, making a positive difference in one person's life can change the world. Maybe not the whole world, but their world.

9 Failing because you were scared to fail.

If your fear of failure, or of not being perfect, has driven you to take the safe road of doing nothing, you have already failed. Accept the fact that everyone fails, but don't accept the act of not trying as your form of failure.

If you find yourself at a point of intense decision making where you're caught in a spiral of over-analysis and hesitation, and you're making no progress, take a deep breath, break the spiral, make an educated guess on the next logical step, and take it. Even if you get it wrong, you will learn something that will help you get it right next time.

Your failures along the road to your goals are simply opportunities to learn and grow. You might not be there yet, but if you keep moving forward, you'll get there eventually.

30 TRUTHS I've Learned In 30 YEARS

Since today is my 30th birthday I thought it fitting to share 30 things I understand now that were complete mysteries to me just a few short years ago. These are simple lessons about life in general that I picked up while traveling, living in different cities, working for different companies (and myself), and meeting remarkable and unusual people everywhere in between.

1 There comes a point in life when you get tired of chasing everyone and trying to fix everything, but it's not giving up. It's realizing you don't need certain people and things and the drama they bring.

2 If a person wants to be a part of your life they will make an obvious effort to do so. Don't bother reserving a space in your heart for people who do not make an effort to stay.

3 If you want to fly, you have to give up the things that weigh you down – which is not always as obvious and easy as it sounds.

4 Doing something and getting it wrong is at least ten times more productive than doing nothing.

5 Every success has a trail of failures behind it, and every failure is leading towards success. You don't fail by falling down. You fail by never getting back up. Sometimes you just have to forget how you feel, remember what you deserve, and keep pushing forward.

6 When you get to know people with different ethnic backgrounds, from different cities and countries, who live at various socioeconomic levels, you begin to realize that everyone basically wants the same things. They want validation, love, happiness, fulfillment and hopes for a better future. The way they pursue these desires is where things branch off, but the fundamentals are the same. You can relate to almost everyone everywhere if you look past the superficial facades that divide us.

1 The more things you own, the more your things own you. Less truly gives you more freedom.

While you're busy looking for the perfect person, you'll probably miss the imperfect person who could make you perfectly happy. This is as true for friendships as it is for intimate relationships. Finding a companion or a friend isn't about trying to transform yourself into the perfect image of what you think they want. It's about being exactly who you are and then finding someone who appreciates that.

Relationships must be chosen wisely. It's better to be alone than to be in bad company. There's no need to rush. If something is meant to be, it will happen — in the right time, with the right person, and for the best reason.

0 Making a thousand friends is not a miracle. A miracle is making one friend who will stand by your side when thousands are against you.

Someone will always be better looking. Someone will always be smarter. Someone will always be more charismatic. But they will never be you — with your exact ideas, knowledge and skills.

2 Making progress involves risk. Period. You can't make it to second base with your foot on first.

13 Every morning you are faced with two choices: You can aimlessly stumble through the day not knowing what's going to happen and simply react to events at a moment's notice, or you can go through the day directing your own life and making your own decisions and destiny.

14 Everyone makes mistakes. If you can't forgive others, don't expect others to forgive you. To forgive is to set a prisoner free and discover the prisoner was you.

15 It's okay to fall apart for a little while. You don't always have to pretend to be strong, and there is no need to constantly prove that everything is going well. You shouldn't be concerned with what other people are thinking either — cry if you need to — it's healthy to shed your tears. The sooner you do, the sooner you will be able to smile again.

16 We sometimes do things that are permanently foolish just because we are temporarily upset. A lot of heartache can be avoided if you learn to control your emotions.

17 Someone else doesn't have to be wrong for you to be right. There are many roads to what's right. You cannot judge others by your own past. They are living a different life than you. What might be good for one person may not be good for another. What might be bad for one person might change another person's life for the better. You have to allow people to make their own mistakes and their own decisions.

8 Nobody is perfect, and nobody deserves to be perfect. Nobody has it easy. You never know what people are going through. Every one of us has issues. So don't belittle yourself or anyone else. Everybody is fighting their own unique war.

9 A smile doesn't always mean a person is happy. Sometimes it simply means they are strong enough to face their problems.

20 The happiest people I know keep an open mind to new ideas and ventures, use their leisure time as a means of mental development, and love good music, good books, good pictures, good company and good conversation. And oftentimes they are also the cause of happiness in others – me in particular.

21 You can't take things too personally. Rarely do people do things because of you. They do things because of them.

22 Feelings change, people change, and time keeps rolling. You can hold on to past mistakes or you can create your own happiness. A smile is a choice, not a miracle. True happiness comes from within. Don't make the mistake of waiting on someone or something to come along and make you happy.

23 It's much harder to change the length of your life than it is to change the depth of it.

24 You end up regretting the things you did NOT do far more than the things you did.

25 When you stop chasing the wrong things you give the right things a chance to catch you.

26 One of the greatest challenges in life is being yourself in a world that's trying to make you like everyone else.

27 Enjoy the little things, because one day you may look back and discover they were the big things.

28 Anyone can make a difference. Making one person smile can change the world. Maybe not the whole world, but their world.

29 Everything is a life lesson. Everyone you meet, everything you encounter, etc. They're all part of the learning experience we call 'life.' Never forget to acknowledge the lesson, especially when things don't go your way. If you don't get a job that you wanted or a relationship doesn't work, it only means something better is out there waiting. And the lesson you just learned is the first step towards it.

30 Regardless of how filthy your past has been, your future is still spotless. Don't start your day with the broken

pieces of yesterday. Every day is a fresh
start. Each day is a new beginning. Every
morning you wake up is the first day of the
rest of your life.

15 WAYS To Be IRRESISTIBLY *Attractive*

Be true to your values. Be honest. Do your best. Do things that bring you closer to your dreams. Take care of yourself, your family, and your friends. Treat people with respect. Be the person that makes others feel special. Be known for your kindness and honesty.

In other words, invest love into your life. Because when you love life, life will love you back. And there's no attraction greater than love. People will notice the goodness surrounding you, and they will be naturally attracted to you.

1 *Do the right thing.*

Never be afraid to do what you know in your heart is right, especially if the well being of another person's feelings is at stake. There is no punishment in the world more severe than the wounds we inflict on our soul when we do what we know is wrong.

2 *Stop the gossip and superficial judgments.*

Great minds discuss ideas, average minds discuss events, and small minds gossip about people. Life is much too short to be lived talking about people, gossiping, and stirring up trouble that has no substance. If you don't understand someone, ask questions. If you don't agree with them, tell them. But don't judge them behind their back to everyone else.

3 *Lift others up.*

If you want to lift yourself up, lift someone else up. To be happy and free is not merely to cast off one's chains, but to live in a way that respects and enhances the happiness and freedom of others. When you put faith, hope, and love together, you can nurture positive ideas, relationships, and dreams in a negative world.

4 Give words of encouragement to those in need.

A word of encouragement during a failure is worth more than an hour of praise after success. We all hit a time when we lose hope and need someone to put their arms around us and say, "I've got you right now. You are not facing this alone." Be that person when you can.

5 Be positive.

Think positively; speak properly; apologize rapidly; forgive quickly. Evolve your being and inspire yourself and others. Say it out loud, "I am sorry negativity, I have no time for you. I have far too many positive things to do."

6 Embrace your uniqueness.

If you don't embrace your uniqueness, you will spend your entire life striving to conform to the impossibility of being someone else. By celebrating what makes you different, rather than wasting time trying to be the same, you will discover your unique gifts that nobody else in the world has.

7 Do things for fun and passion.

When you stop doing things for fun and passion, you stop living and you start merely existing. If you truly want to change your life, you must first change your mind and your actions. Once you are ready to truly devote your time and energy to what calls to your soul, you will find your life unimaginably enriched.

8 Be gentle.

When you least expect it, something great will come along – something better than you ever planned for. Mother Nature opens millions of flowers every day without forcing the buds. Let this be a reminder not to force anything, but to simply give beautiful things enough love and an opportunity to grow naturally.

9 Drop the need to always be right.

Someone else doesn't have to be wrong for you to be right. There are many roads to what's right. You cannot judge others by your own past. They are living a different life than you. Express your opinions freely and politely, remembering that if your purpose is to ridicule or prove others are wrong, it will only bring bitterness into the world. Respecting the opinion of others, without judging, always carries more weight than simply being right.

10 *Be loyal. Be honest.*

You can't promise to love someone for the rest of their life, but you can sincerely love them for the rest of yours. When it comes to relationships, remaining faithful is never an option, but a priority. Loyalty and honest affection mean everything.

11 *Be flexible and keep an open mind.*

What looks like an obstacle or road block is oftentimes just life steering you in a better direction. Be flexible and keep an open mind to all the changes that are forcing you to grow, and helping you better align yourself with your vibration and purpose.

12 *Believe in yourself and all that you are.*

Know in your heart that there is strength inside you that is greater than the challenges you face. No one can do it for you – you have to choose to use your wings.

13 *Believe in your dreams.*

Who you hope to be someday is already a big part of who you are now. Your dreams are real. They do not exist in the past; they live in the present, and when you stay committed to doing what needs to be done, you carry them closer to reality as you walk through the gates of tomorrow.

14 *Walk the talk.*

You can make whatever you want out of your life, but first you have to not be afraid to try. We all have to start with ourselves. It is time to walk the talk. Take the journey of making the difficult decisions and taking action. Start removing things from your life that are taking away your happiness, and start adding things that bring joy in to your life.

15 *Embrace the possibilities of tomorrow.*

Don't let your past dictate who you are, but let it be part of who you will become. No regrets. No looking back. Just hold onto life and move forward. We have no way of knowing what lies ahead, but that's what makes the journey even more exciting – that's what makes life worth living.

10 TIMELESS *Lessons* from a Life Well Lived

About a year ago we published an article entitled, 18 Things My Dad Was Right About. The article contained a list of life lessons my dad had shared with me when I was a kid. Today, as promised, my dad emailed me an addendum to his original list. It contains ten additional life lessons from the smartest 69-year-old I know. Enjoy.

1 *Happiness cannot be traveled to, owned, earned, worn or consumed.*

Happiness is the sacred experience of living every moment with love and gratitude. There is always, always, always something to be thankful for and some reason to love. So be sure to appreciate what you've got. Be thankful for the little things in life that mean a lot.

2 *Be a student of life every day.*

Experience it, learn from it, and absorb all the knowledge you can. Prepare yourself for greatness by keeping your mind conditioned with fresh knowledge and new challenges. Remember, if you stay ready, you don't have to get ready when great opportunities arise.

3 *Experience is the best teacher.*

Don't try too hard to memorize the things others are teaching. Learn the best practices and then do your thing. Life itself will teach you over the course of time, and often at the right time and place, so that you will remember forever what is truly important.

4 *Your choices, your actions, your life.*

Live it your way with no regrets. Never let the odds keep you from doing what you know in your heart you were meant to do. Continue to work hard at what you love no matter what the challenges are. Be persistent. Life eventually rewards those who do.

5 *No one is 'too busy' in this world. It's all about priorities.*

It's all about priorities. What you focus on grows. Don't say you don't have enough time. You have exactly the same number of hours per day that were given to Helen Keller, Michaelangelo, Mother Teresea, Leonardo da Vinci, Thomas Jefferson, Albert Einstein, etc...

6 *Be patient and tough. Someday this pain will be useful to you.*

Someday this pain will be useful to you. You will never realize your true strength until being strong is your only option left. Until you are broken, you won't know what you're truly made of. Pain doesn't just show up in your life for no reason. It's a sign that something needs to change – it's a wake-up call that guides you toward a better future. So keep your heart open to dreams, and make that change. For as long as there is a dream and positive action, there is hope; and as long as there is hope, there is joy in living.

7 *Oftentimes it is better to be kind than to be right.*

We do not always need an intelligent mind that speaks, just a patient heart that listens. Be kind whenever possible. And realize that it is always possible. It takes a great deal of strength to be gentle and kind. And when you practice kindness and bring sunshine to the lives of others, you cannot keep it from yourself.

8 *You can become a magnet for good things by wishing everyone well.*

Judge less and love more. If you want inner peace, resist the temptation to gossip about others, or portray them in a poor light. Instead of judging someone for what they do or where they are in their life, figure out why they do what they do and how they got to where they are.

9 *Only you are in charge of your attitude.*

The truth is, unless you let go, unless you forgive yourself, unless you forgive the situation, unless you realize that that situation is over, you cannot move forward. You are responsible for how you feel, no matter what anyone else says or does. You are always 100% in control of your thoughts right now, so choose to feel confident and adequate rather than angry and insecure. Choose to look forward, not backward.

10   *Satisfaction is not always the fulfillment of what you want.*

It is the realization of how blessed you are for what you have. It's not that everything will be easy or exactly as you had expected, but you must choose to be grateful for all that you have, and happy that you got a chance to live this life, no matter how it turns out.

SOME **THINGS** YOU NEED TO **KNOW**

I know you're reading this. And I want you to know I'm writing this for you. Others will be confused. They will think I'm writing this for them. But I'm not.

This one's for you.

I want you to know that life is not easy. Every day is an unpredictable challenge. Some days it can be difficult to simply get out of bed in the morning. To face reality and put on that smile. But I want you to know, your smile has kept me going on more days than I can count. Never forget that, even through the toughest times, you are incredible. You really are.

So smile more often. You have so many reasons to. Time and again, my reason is you.

You won't always be perfect. Neither will I. Because nobody is perfect, and nobody deserves to be perfect. Nobody has it easy, everybody has issues. You will never know exactly what I'm going through. And I will never know exactly what you're going through. We are all fighting our own unique war.

But we are fighting through it simultaneously, together.

Whenever somebody discredits you, and tells you that you can't do something, keep in mind that they are speaking from within the boundaries of their own limitations. Ignore them. Don't give in. In this crazy world that's trying to make you like everyone else, find the courage to keep being your awesome self. And when they laugh at you for being different, laugh back at them for being the same.

Remember, our courage doesn't always roar aloud. Sometimes it's the quiet voice at the end of the day whispering, "I will try again tomorrow." So stand strong. Things turn out best for people who make the best out of the way things turn out.

And I am committed to making the best of it along with you.

Timeless Lessons Life Teaches

Take everything you've ever learned – all the crazy experiences and lessons – and place it all in a box labeled "Thank you."

In life, you usually get what you ask for, but it rarely comes in the package you think it's supposed to come in.

The past can't hurt you anymore – not unless you let it.

Maturity is not when we start speaking about big things, it's when we start understanding the small things.

Life is like a rainbow, you need both the sun and the rain to make its colors appear.

Never let one bad day make you feel like you have a bad life.

When you find yourself cocooned in isolation and despair and cannot find your way out of the darkness, remember that this is similar to the place where caterpillars go to grow their wings.

Live in such a way that if someone decided to speak badly of you, no one would believe it.

It's your road, and yours alone. Others may walk it with you, but no one can walk it for you.

The only time you should look back is to see how far you've come.

Things change, but the sun always rises the next day. The bad news: nothing is permanent. The good news: nothing is permanent.

The best way to gain self-confidence is to do what you are afraid to do.

The mind is like a parachute. It doesn't work unless it's open.

Inspirational
QUESTIONS
to Make You *think*

What does the **CHILD** inside you *long* for?

What have you been **COUNTING** or *keeping track* of recently?

What is one thing right **NOW** that you are totally *sure* of?

What's the difference between being **ALIVE** and truly *living*?

What's the **BEST** *decision* you've ever made?

If you had the **OPPORTUNITY** to get a message across to a large group of people, what would your *message* be?

What is the **BIGGEST** *motivator* in your life right now?

Have you **DONE** anything lately worth *remembering*?

What are you **MOST** *grateful* for?

When is the **LAST** time you tried something *new*?

ABOUT

Passionate writers, admirers of the human spirit, and full time students of life, Marc and Angel Chernoff enjoy sharing inspirational advice and practical tips for life on their popular personal development blog 'Marc and Angel Hack Life'. Currently the site contains about 600 articles on productivity, happiness, love, work, and general self improvement, and has attracted 70 million page views since its inception in the summer of 2006.

Marc and Angel both share a great passion for inspiring others to live to their fullest potential, and they honestly feel best when they are inspiring others to be their best. They started their blog with the goal of inspiring as many people as possible. And they work passionately every day to fulfill this goal through the thoughts and ideas they share online.

Please catch up with them at www.marcandangel.com.

Or you can email them angel@marcandangel.com and marc@marcandangel.com.

AFTERWORD

Subscribe for Free

The series in this book is just the icing on the cake. If you have enjoyed this book and found it useful, you will love all the other articles at Marc and Angel Hack Life. Readers continually leave feedback on how they have benefited tremendously from the site's material and how it's a staple for their personal growth.

By subscribing, you will receive free practical tips and inspirational advice geared for productive living, served fresh 3 times a week directly to your inbox.

Let's Connect

We would love to hear from you and to know what you think. Feel free to get in touch with us via the following channels:

Twitter: @marcandangel
Facebook page: Marc and Angel Hack Life – Practical Tips for Productive Living

Amazing Design Work by Catherina Chia

If you need help with design, please contact our designer, Catherina Chia (Hi@ CatherinaChia.com). Our success is directly related to the time, talent, and energy she gives to make us look good.

Beautiful Book Production by Jonathan Wondrusch

Our book designer/producer Jonathan Wondrusch of www.WinningEdits.com really impressed us with his attention to detail and high standards. If you need a book prepared for publishing, you can trust him to do a beautiful job.

Guest Posts

Some articles are guest posts, as credited to the authors below.

11 Ways Successful People Start Their Mornings by **Sam** of Financial Upside

12 Things Happy People Do Differently by **Jacob Sokol** of Sensophy

5 Character Traits that Make You Happy by **Ken Wert** of Meant to be Happy

74003667R00231

Made in the USA
Lexington, KY
13 December 2017